Cisco® Router Performance
Field Guide

Field Guide

Cisco®Router Performance Field Guide

Gil Held

McGraw-Hill
New York   San Francisco   Washington, D.C.   Auckland   Bogotá
Caracas   Lisbon   London   Madrid   Mexico City   Milan
Montreal   New Delhi   San Juan   Singapore
Sydney   Tokyo   Toronto

McGraw-Hill

A Division of The McGraw-Hill Companies

1 2 3 4 5 6 7 8 9 0   AGM/AGM   0 5 4 3 2 1 0

0-07-212513-6

The executive editor for this book was Steven Elliot, the editing supervisor was Ruth W. Mannino, and the production manager was Claire Stanley. It was set in Stone Serif by Priscilla Beer of McGraw-Hill's desktop composition unit, in cooperation with Spring Point Publishing Services.

Printed and bound by Quebecor/Martinsburg

Contents

Preface

Because the vast majority of routers that operate the Internet and private intranets were manufactured by Cisco Systems, numerous books have been written about Cisco routers, with topics ranging in scope from router configuration to the use of routing protocols and the configuration of access lists. While each topic is important, one topic is conspicuous by its lack of coverage. That topic is router performance.

Router performance is very important to address because of the role of this communications device in modern networks. If your organization's routers are underpowered for the activities they perform, both users and administrators may incorrectly attribute delays to bandwidth constraints, underpowered servers, and other problems, without realizing the actual problem. Conversely, upon occasion you may be enticed into a hardware replacement or upgrade that is unnecessary. For either situation, the ability to understand different router performance metrics as well the ways to retrieve statistical information is important for the LAN or router administrator or network manager.

In this book we will focus our attention upon different aspects of router performance as well as the use of a router as a tool to understand the connected communications environment. Concerning the latter, a router can provide valuable information concerning the activity of connected LANs and serial communications channels to include their general level of utilization and error conditions. Thus, router-provided metrics provide us with the ability to understand traffic as well as a mechanism to note error conditions and arrange for their expedient solution.

One often-overlooked feature of routers is their ability to provide service level agreement (SLA) verification. Because most SLA agreements involve the payment of monthly fees to obtain an enhanced level of network performance, being able to verify that your organization receives what it is paying for is an important use of routers. As we will note in this book, Cisco routers include TCP/IP applications that enable verification of end-to-end latency, which represents a commonly used SLA metric.

As a professional author, I highly value reader feedback. I would appreciate your comments concerning any information presented in this book or information you feel should be included in a subsequent edition. You can contact me through my publisher whose address is located on the jacket of this book, or you can send me an email at *gil_held@yahoo.com*.

Gilbert Held
Macon, Georgia

Acknowledgments

The name of an author on a book is equivalent to the tip of an iceberg when considering the effort involved in converting a manuscript into a printed work. Similar to many sports, the preparation of a book is a team effort with many persons contributing to its success. This book was no exception and the efforts of many persons deserve recognition.

First, I would be remiss if I did not once again thank Steve Elliot of McGraw-Hill for backing this writing project. As an old-fashioned author who likes to use pen and paper because I travel to places where my electrical plug set seems to rarely mate with hotel receptacles, I long ago decided to depend upon an excellent assistant. Thus, once again I am indebted to the efforts of Mrs. Linda Hayes for converting my handwritten notes and diagrams into a professional manuscript. Last, but not least, the preparation of a book is a time-consuming affair which limits evenings and weekends normally devoted for family activities. Thus, once again, I appreciate the understanding of my wife, Beverly, as I hibernated in my office to check certain aspects of router performance on the networks I operate in my home.

CHAPTER 1

Introduction

This chapter focuses on (1) the rationale for obtaining router performance measurements, (2) the use of various router performance measurements achieved through various components that can be monitored, and (3) a preview of the subsequent chapters. The chapter preview can be used by itself or in conjunction with the index to locate specific information that may be of interest.

While the previous three items is the primary focus of this chapter, before we turn our attention to those topics, a few words are in order about the relationship of this book to the series of Cisco field guides published by McGraw-Hill. This book is the third in the series of Cisco field guides to be published. Each field guide focuses on a specific topic: router access lists, IOS IP commands, and now Cisco router performance.

Since Cisco routers have evolved into very complex hardware and software products, it is very difficult and probably not desirable from both the authors' and readers' perspective to attempt to provide a comprehensive book that covers all router features and functions. Not many authors would be willing or have the experience to write a book that covers every router topic and more than likely consist of thousands of pages. Similarly, very few readers need to have in-depth knowledge of all aspects of Cisco routers. As a result, the authors felt that development of the field guide series, with each book focused on a key series of related functions or features on Cisco routers, would be more useful. Thus, this book focuses upon router performance, a narrow but most important topic that LAN administrators and network managers must understand to make the best possible use of Cisco routers and attached networks.

Rationale for Performance Measurements

The preface to this book briefly noted several reasons for periodically extracting router performance measurements. While the verification of *service level agreements* (SLAs) and observation of network errors are important, they are not the only reasons for examining different router metrics. Other reasons include considering when to replace or upgrade a router or individual router components as well as how to decide if additional interfaces are required to support network segmentation. Another reason for examining router performance metrics is to determine if the resources of one or more routers might be employed more efficiently in a different router or if the router is leased or returned to the leasing company. This is because not all routers in a network are used at the same level. Thus, if your organization purchased a number of routers for use in a network, there is a high probability that routers at the periphery of a network do not require the same amount of memory or processor capability as routers at the core of a network.

Occasionally, router performance measurements can provide your organization with information on how to rearrange the use of routers, replace one type of router with a more cost-effective router, or purchase a more suitable router to satisfy organizational communications requirements. Although a router is no substitute for diagnostic testing equipment, it is important to note a router acts as an interface to both *local area networks* (LANs) and *wide area networks* (WANs). As such, a router is a network's focal point, and you can use its display capability to examine the state of different interfaces. This, in turn, provides information on the performance level of both LANs and WANs connected to the router, which indirectly affects router performance. For example, a high level of collisions on an Ethernet LAN connected to a router interface directly affects the ability of the router to transmit frames onto the LAN or receive frames transmitted to the device over that network.

Components to Monitor

From a hardware perspective, a router is a sophisticated computer that operates specialized software. The router's hardware is similar to a computer in that a router has a *central processing unit* (CPU), supports several types of memory, and can support different types of interfaces that provide connectivity to peripherals. However, unlike a computer, where peripherals are commonly printers, scanners, and similar devices, router peripherals are local and wide area networks that are connected to the router via different types of router interfaces.

We can learn about the performance of a router by monitoring its hardware components, including its CPU, memory, and the state of its various interfaces. In addition, as we will note later in this book, various router software settings can be used to expedite the flow of information through a router, which, in effect, can be used to enhance the performance of a router. Thus, an examination of the router hardware and software can be used to determine the current and potential level of router performance.

Chapter Preview

In concluding this brief introductory chapter, let's look at the focus of suc-ceeding chapters in this book. The information in this section is a roadmap to show how we approach the subject of this book—router per-formance. In addition, you can use the information presented in this sec-tion together with the index and table of contents to locate information of specific concern. Although it is suggested that you read this book in the sequence in which the information is presented, different readers may have different levels of information requirements. Thus, this preview sec-tion may help you to locate a specific chapter of immediate interest as well as note the flow of topics covered.

Router Hardware and Software Overview

Since basic knowledge of router hardware and software is essential for understanding performance issues, we review the basic information on this topic in Chapter 2 by examining the basic components of a Cisco router, including how interfaces are specified. We also discuss router switching modes and its initialization process prior to discussing its soft-ware components. In terms of software components, we discuss the basic components of Cisco's *Internetwork Operating System* (IOS), how a router is configured, and the use of the command interpreter.

Since the command interpreter is essential for observing different router performance metrics, we examine the use of router commands and how those commands can be abbreviated for those who need to display information quickly. From the information presented in this chapter, readers with a diverse background will learn the fundamentals of router hardware and software that is used in later chapters in this book.

LAN and WAN Metrics

The ability to observe LAN and WAN metrics through the use of router commands may result in meaningless information unless we are familiar with such metrics. Chapter 3 examines a variety of LAN and WAN metrics. First, we focus on local area networks, examining both Ethernet and token-ring LANs as they account for, by far, the vast majority of LAN inter-faces used with Cisco routers. In our examination of LAN metrics, we review the general frame formats for each type of network. Then we look at the fields in each frame and the type of errors that can occur. The information presented during our discussion of a LAN's operation facilitates our ability to better understand LAN metrics displayed by Cisco routers, a topic covered in considerable detail later in this book.

The second portion of Chapter 3 examines the wide area network, including the serial interface that provides the ability to transmit and receive data via a WAN connection. Since some readers may not be familiar with the fact that the operating rates of the commonly used T1 line facilities differs from its data transfer rate, we will examine this important topic in Chapter 3. For some readers this information explains why their initial computations on the potential upgrade of an existing WAN connection to a higher operating rate may not provide the expected benefit.

Accessing External Performance Measurements

After the basics of router hardware and software in Chapter 2 and LAN and WAN metrics in Chapter 3, we are now ready to begin our examination of router performance measurements. Chapter 4 looks at the use of router commands to display a variety of external performance measurement information. In doing so, we assume that router interfaces provide an external view of factors that affect the overall level of performance of a router. We also use various versions of the `show interfaces` command to learn about information displayed when we examine Ethernet, Fast Ethernet, token-ring, and serial interfaces.

Accessing Internal Performance Measurements

In our preview of Chapter 4 we mentioned that we would examine external performance measurements. In Chapter 5 we refocus our attention on internal performance measurements. After first reviewing the function of four types of router memory, we look at the use of the `show` command to display the state of router memory and router processes. Once this is done, we then examine the use of other commands that can be used to enable various router functions that affect the overall level of a router's performance. Some of the functions we examine include setting permanent entries into a router's *address resolution protocol* (ARP) table, enabling TCP header data compression, and setting various router switching modes. While an argument can be made as to whether some of these functions are internal or external functions because they occur prior to the placement of data onto an interface, the authors decided to include a discussion of these features in this chapter.

Testing, Troubleshooting, and Design Principles

While it is probably fairly easy to visualize the relationship between test-ing and troubleshooting, it may be a bit more difficult to denote their rela-tionship to design principles. However, if we carefully think about the three we can see a considerable degree of relationship between each. This is because years of testing and troubleshooting different types of network problems resulted in certain design principles that provide the basis for the expedient routing of traffic within and between networks.

While this book focuses on router performance, it is important to rec-ognize that, without testing and troubleshooting, you may not be able to enhance router performance. In addition, the information provided through testing and troubleshooting can be of considerable value for con-structing a new network or modifying an existing network. Thus, in this chapter we examine these three topics as an entity, including their rela-tionship to the primary focus of this book—router performance.

As we discuss testing and troubleshooting, we review several built-in testing tools available from the router's command line or from another device. In doing so, we also examine how we can use such tools to verify certain types of SLAs as well as to isolate possible network bottlenecks that warrant attention. Once this is done, we conclude this chapter by looking at router-based network design principles. Information presented in this chapter, as well as in previous chapters, is used as a foundation for under-standing how to construct networks that provide the level of performance our employees both deserve and expect.

Observing Metrics over Time

The last chapter, Chapter 7, focuses on overcoming the inability of Cisco routers to provide most performance-related metrics for more than a 5-min period. It is highly doubtful that LAN administrators and network managers would be willing to make important decisions affecting the state of their network based on the value of a counter that provides a 5-min observation of a metric; we would normally prefer a wider window. Thus, this chapter focuses on learning how to observe various router-related performance metrics over a period of user-defined time.

CHAPTER 2

Router Hardware and Software Overview

This chapter provides an overview of Cisco router hardware and software. First, the basic hardware components of a Cisco router are reviewed, followed by an examination of basic router software modules. Once these topics have been covered, router operational modes are examined and different router functions are described, discussed, and illustrated.

The overall purpose of this chapter is to acquaint you with the general operation of Cisco routers and how they are configured. This information provides users with different backgrounds with a common base of knowledge about Cisco router hardware and software that is useful in understanding performance-related information presented in subsequent chapters. To provide readers with a common base of knowledge, examples of the use of EXEC commands are included. These examples are also included as a review for readers who are familiar with Cisco products and to provide the necessary information about the general configuration of the vendor's routers for persons who may lack prior Cisco experience. In addition, when appropriate, certain guidelines and hints are included in this chapter based on the authors' experience in configuring and operating Cisco routers. Hopefully, these hints and guidelines may save you hours of puzzlement and make your router experience more pleasurable by being able to take advantage of lessons learned by the authors.

Basic Hardware Components

Cisco Systems manufactures a wide range of router products. Although those products differ considerably with respect to their processing power

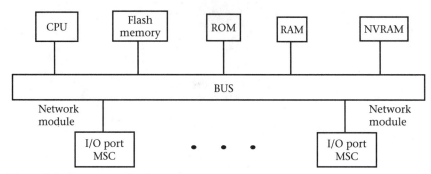

Figure 2-1   Basic router hardware components.

and the number of interfaces they support, they use a core set of hardware components. Figure 2-1 is a generic schematic of the key components of a Cisco Systems' router. While the CPU, or microprocessor; amount of ROM and RAM; and the number and manner by which I/O ports and media converters are used can differ from one product to another, each router has the components indicated in Figure 2-1. An examination of the function of each hardware component will show how the sum of the parts of a router come together to provide its functionality.

Central Processing Unit (CPU)

The CPU, or microprocessor, is responsible for executing instructions that make up the router's operating system as well as user commands entered via the console or via a telnet connection. Thus, the processing power of the CPU is directly related to the processing capability of the router.

Flash Memory

Flash memory is an erasable, reprogrammable type of ROM memory. On many routers flash memory is an option that can be used to hold an image of the operating system and the router's microcode. Since flash memory can be updated without removing and replacing chips, this option can easily pay for itself by saving on chip upgrades over a period of time. It is possible to hold more than one operating system image in flash memory, provided enough space is available. Flash memory is useful for testing new images. The flash memory of a router can also be used to *trivial file transfer protocol* (tftp) an *operating system* (OS) image to another router. Flash memory can also be used to store copies of the router's configuration file, which can be useful in situations where a tftp server is unavailable or in emergency recovery procedures.

Read-Only Memory (ROM)

ROM contains code that performs power-on diagnostics similar to the *power-on self-test* (POST) many PCs perform. In addition, a bootstrap program in ROM is used to load operating system software. Although many routers require software upgrades to be performed by removing and replacing ROM chips on the router's system board, other routers may use different types of storage to hold the operating system.

Random Access Memory (RAM)

RAM is used to hold routing tables, perform packet buffering, furnish an area for the queuing of packets when they cannot be directly output due to too much traffic routed to a common interface, and provide memory for the router's configuration file when the device is operational. In addition, RAM provides space for caching *address resolution protocol* (ARP) information that reduces ARP traffic and enhances the transmission capability of LANs connected to the router. When the router is powered off, the contents of RAM are cleared.

Nonvolatile RAM (NVRAM)

Nonvolatile RAM retains its contents when a router is powered off. By storing a copy of its configuration file in NVRAM, the router can quickly recover from a power failure. The use of NVRAM eliminates the need for the router to maintain a hard disk or floppy disk copy of its configuration file. As a result, there are no moving parts on a Cisco router, which means components last much longer. Most hardware failures in computer systems are due to the wear and tear on moving components such as hard drives.

Since Cisco routers do not have hard or floppy disks, a common practice is to store configuration files on a PC where they can be easily modified by using a text editor. Through the use of tftp you can then load a configuration directly into NVRAM via the network.

When using the network for entering a router configuration, the router functions as a client and the PC where the file resides must function as the server. This means you must obtain tftp server software to operate on your PC to support the movement of files to and from your computer. Later in this chapter, when we discuss software, we also discuss tftp server software.

Input/Output (I/O) Ports and Media-Specific Converters (MSC)

The *input/output* (I/O) port is the connection through which packets enter and exit a router. Each I/O port is connected to a *media-specific con-*

verter (MSC) which provides the physical interface to a specific type of media such as an Ethernet or token-ring LAN or an RS-232 or V.35 WAN interface.

Under Cisco terminology various router functions, such as routing protocol updates and access lists, are applied to, or associated with, an interface. However, an interface, in effect, is an I/O port configured through an `interfaces` subcommand, such as `show interfaces`, which would display information about all interfaces in the router. Since the fabrication of I/O ports can vary within a router, as well as between routers, it is important to understand how ports are referenced.

Port Fabrication and Command Reference

If a port is built into a router, it is referenced directly by its number. For example, serial port 0 is referenced in an `interface` command as follows:

```
interface serial0
```

If a group of ports is fabricated on a common adapter card for insertion into a slot in a router, the reference to a port requires both the slot and port number. Thus, on Cisco 7200 or Cisco 7500 series routers, you would use the following format to specify a particular serial port:

```
interface serial slot#/port#
```

In addition to serial ports, other ports, including Ethernet, Fast Ethernet, and Token Ring, are specified in a similar manner. For example, Figure 2-2 illustrates the use of the `show interfaces` command with the parameter `FastEthernet1/0` to display information concerning the operation of the `FastEthernet` interface on port 0 on a adapter card installed in slot 1 on the router. At first, we purposely entered the slot/port relationship in error to indicate the importance of knowing and entering the correct parameters for an interface. By using the `show interfaces` command by itself, it becomes possible to record the configuration of interface modules used in the router to include those presently not operating, since information about nonactive interfaces will also be displayed.

One variation of the preceding format occurs on Cisco 7x00 series equipment, where multiple ports can be fabricated on a port adapter card and multiple port adapters can reside in a slot. In this situation the following command format would be used to reference a specific serial port:

```
interface serial slot#/port-adapter/port#
```

Similar to our previous notation, this command format is applicable to different types of interfaces. An example of this type of equipment config-

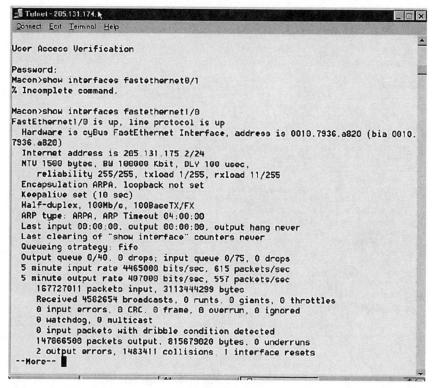

Figure 2-2 Using the show interfaces command to display information about Fast Ethernet port 0 on the adapter card installed in slot 1 in the router.

uration is shown in Figure 2-3. In this example it was assumed that our router had multiple serial ports fabricated on a port adapter and multiple port adapters can be installed into a common slot. In Figure 2-3 we used the show interface serial command to display specific information about serial port 3 fabricated on port adapter 1 installed in slot 0 in the router.

Switching Modes

In terms of the flow of data within a router, as packets are received from a LAN, the layer 2 headers are removed as the packet is moved into RAM. When this action occurs, the CPU examines its routing table to determine the port to which the packet should be output and the manner in which the packet should be encapsulated.

The process just described is called *process switching* mode because each packet must be processed by the CPU to consult the routing table and

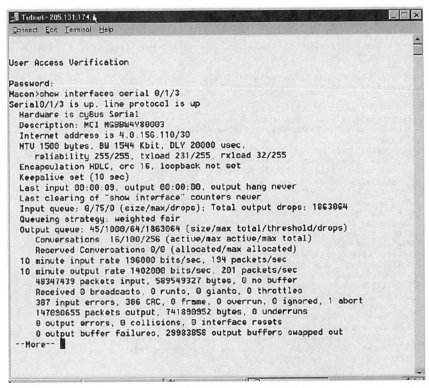

```
User Access Verification

Password:
Macon>show interfaces serial 0/1/3
Serial0/1/3 is up, line protocol is up
  Hardware is cyBus Serial
  Description: MCI MGBBW4Y80003
  Internet address is 4.0.156.110/30
  MTU 1500 bytes, BW 1544 Kbit, DLY 20000 usec,
    reliability 255/255, txload 231/255, rxload 32/255
  Encapsulation HDLC, crc 16, loopback not set
  Keepalive set (10 sec)
  Last input 00:00:09, output 00:00:00, output hang never
  Last clearing of "show interface" counters never
  Input queue: 0/75/0 (size/max/drops); Total output drops: 1863064
  Queueing strategy: weighted fair
  Output queue: 45/1000/64/1863064 (size/max total/threshold/drops)
    Conversations  16/100/256 (active/max active/max total)
    Reserved Conversations 0/0 (allocated/max allocated)
  10 minute input rate 196000 bits/sec, 194 packets/sec
  10 minute output rate 1402000 bits/sec, 201 packets/sec
    48347439 packets input, 589549327 bytes, 0 no buffer
    Received 0 broadcasts, 0 runts, 0 giants, 0 throttles
    387 input errors, 386 CRC, 0 frame, 0 overrun, 0 ignored, 1 abort
    147090655 packets output, 741890952 bytes, 0 underruns
    0 output errors, 0 collisions, 0 interface resets
    0 output buffer failures, 29983858 output buffers swapped out
--More--
```

Figure 2-3   Using the `show interface serial` command to display information about the operation of serial port 3 fabricated on port adapter 1 installed in slot 0 in the router.

determine where to send the packet. Cisco routers also have a switching mode called *fast switching.* In fast switching mode the router maintains a memory cache containing information about destination IP addresses and next hop interfaces.

The router builds this cache by saving information previously obtained from the routing table. The first packet to a particular destination causes the CPU to consult the routing table. However, once the information is obtained about the next hop interface for that particular destination, this information is inserted into the router's fast switching cache and the routing table is not consulted for new packets sent to this destination. This results in the router being able to switch packets at a much faster rate and is a substantial reduction in the load on the router's CPU.

There are variations on fast switching that make use of special hardware architectures included in some higher-end models such as the 7200 and 7500 series. However, the principle is essentially the same for all switching modes: a cache that contains the destination address to the interface mappings. The one exception to this is a switching mode called *netflow switching* which caches not only the destination IP address but also the source IP address and the upper-layer *transfer control protocol* (TCP) or *user diagram protocol* (UDP) ports. In the past, this switching mode was available only on higher-end router platforms. Lower-end routers, such as the 1600, 2500, 2600, 3600, and 4000 series, were only capable of normal fast switching. However, in the latest version of Cisco IOS, version 12.0, it is supported on lower-end platforms, such as the 2600 and 3600 series routers; this is described in considerable detail in Chapter 5.

A few specific points should be noted about fast switching. First, any change to the routing table or the ARP cache forces a purge of the fast switching cache. This is so that during a topology change, the fast switching cache is rebuilt. Additionally, the entries in the fast switching cache vary depending on the contents of the routing table. The entry in the fast switching cache matches the corresponding entry in the routing table. For example, if the router has a route to the 10.1.1.0/24 network, it caches the destination 10.1.1.0/24. If the router has only a route to the 10.1.0.0/16 network, it caches the destination 10.1.0.0/16. If there is no entry in the routing table for the network or subnet, the router uses the default route and uses the default major network mask, so it would cache the destination 10.0.0.0/8.

This pattern holds true if there is only one route to a particular destination. If there are multiple, equal-cost, nondefault paths, the router caches the entire 32-bit destination. For example, if the destination IP address were 10.1.1.1 and the router had two routes to the 10.1.1.0/24 network, the router would cache the value 10.1.1.1/32 and match it to the first hop. The next destination on the 10.1.1.0/24 network, say 10.1.1.2/32, would be cached and matched with the second next hop. If there were a third equal-cost path, the next destination on the 10.1.1.0/24 network would be cached with the third next hop, and so on. Notice the caveat that this is true *only* for nondefault routes. If the router must use the default route to send a packet, it caches only the major network number and not the full 32-bit address as described here.

Essentially, the router uses a round-robin method to cache individual destinations to each successive hop. This means that the router load-shares on a per destination basis. That is, since the fast cache contains a mapping between an end destination and an interface, once the cache has been populated with an entry, all future packets for that destination use the interface in the cache. The router does not place multiple interfaces in the fast switching cache for the same destination.

In process switching mode, the router load-shares on a per packet basis. Since there is no fast switching cache, each packet is sent in a round-robin fashion to each successive interface. While this leads to a more evenly distributed network load if there are multiple paths, it also increases the load on the router CPU and slows down the rate at which the router can move packets. In most cases, it is better to leave fast switching turned on and live with the unequal distribution across multiple network paths.

The Router Initialization Process

When you power-on a router, it performs a sequence of predefined operations. Additional operations performed by the router depend on whether or not you previously configured the device. To learn about the router initialization process, let's examine the major events that occur when you power-on the device.

Figure 2-4 is a flowchart of the major functions performed during the router initialization process. When you apply power to the route, it initially performs a series of diagnostic tests that verify the operation of its processor, memory, and interface circuitry. Since these tests are performed on power-up, it is commonly referred to as a *power-on self-test* (POST).

Once POST is completed, the bootstrap loader executes. The primary function of the loader is to initialize or place a copy of the operating sys-

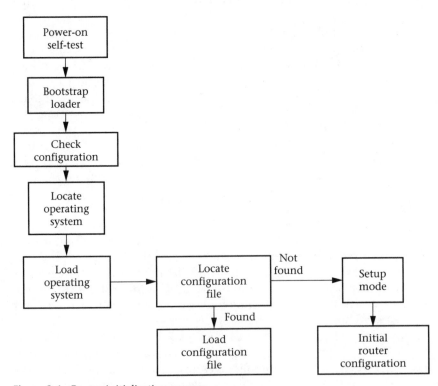

Figure 2-4   Router initialization process.

tem image into main memory. However, to do so, it must first determine where the image of the operating system is located since the image could be located on flash memory, ROM, or even on the network.

To determine the location of the image of the operating system, the bootstrap loader checks the router's configuration register. The configuration register's values can be set either by hardware jumpers or via software, depending upon the router model. The settings of the register indicate the location of the operating system as well as define other device functions such as how the router reacts to the entry of a break key on the console keyboard and whether or not diagnostic messages are displayed on the console terminal.

The configuration register in most current model routers is a 16-bit value stored in NVRAM. It is not a physical entity. In older model routers, such as the MGS and AGS+, the configuration register was a physical jumper with 16 pins. This is the origination of the term *register*. On both the software and the hardware configuration registers, the last 4 bits (pins in the case of the hardware register) indicate the boot field. The boot field tells the router where to locate its configuration file. The software register is displayed as a four-digit hexadecimal number like this: 0x2102. You can display the configuration register with the command show version. Each hexadecimal number represents 4 bits, so the first number, reading from right to left, is the boot field. The boot field can range in value from 0 to 15. In this example, the boot field is 2. Table 2-1 indicates how the router interprets the number in the boot field.

In most cases, the boot register will be set to 2, meaning the router looks in the configuration file for boot commands. If none is found, the router loads the first image found in flash memory. If there is no valid IOS image in flash memory or if flash memory cannot be found, the router

Table 2-1   The Meaning of the Boot Field Settings

Boot Field Value	Router Interpretation
0	RXBOOT mode. The router must be manually booted using the b command.
1	Automatically boots from ROM.
2-F	Examines the contents of the configuration file in NVRAM for boot system **commands.**

attempts to load an image from a tftp server by sending a tftp request to the broadcast address requesting an IOS image.

Once the configuration register is checked, the bootstrap loader knows the location from which to load the operating system image into the router's RAM and it proceeds to do so. After the operating system is loaded, it looks for a previously created and saved configuration file in NVRAM. If the file is found, it is loaded into memory and executed on a line-by-line basis, resulting in the router becoming operational and working according to a predefined networking environment. If a previously created NVRAM file does not exist, the operating system executes a predefined sequence of question-driven configuration displays referred to as a *Setup dialog*. Once the operator completes the Setup dialog, the configuration information is stored in NVRAM and is loaded as the default at the next initialization process. The router can be instructed to ignore the contents of NVRAM by setting the configuration register. If the second hexadecimal value from the right is set to 4, 0x2142, the router ignores the contents of NVRAM. This feature is used during password recovery on the router so that an administrator can bypass the contents of the configuration file.

Figure 2-5 illustrates the initial display generated by a Cisco 4500 router as power is applied, the bootstrap is invoked, and a previously defined configuration is loaded into memory. Note the prompt at the end of the display which can easily scroll off a screen and which occasionally results in a novice waiting a considerable period of time for something to happen without realizing they need to press the RETURN key to access the system.

Now that we understand about the basic hardware components of a router and its initialization process, let's look at router software by reviewing the two key software components of a router and the relationship of router commands to the software components.

Basic Software Components

There are two key router software components: the operating system image and the configuration file. In this section we will review both; however, because the configuration file provides us with the ability to customize the operation of a router, we focus on the configuration file.

Operating System Image

The operating system image is located by the bootstrap loader based on the setting of the configuration register. Once the image is located, it is loaded into the low-addressed portion of memory. The operating system image consists of a series of routines that support the transfer of data through the device, manage buffer space, support different network functions, update routing tables, and execute user commands.

Figure 2-5   Initial display generated by a Cisco 4500 router as power is applied.

```
System Bootstrap, Version 5.2(7b) [mkamson 7b], RELEASE SOFTWARE
(fc1)
Copyright (c) 1995 by cisco Systems, Inc.
C4500 processor with 8192 Kbytes of main memory

program load complete, entrypt: 0x80008000, size: 0x231afc
Self decompressing the image :
#################################################
####################################################################
#######
########################################################### [OK]

                 Restricted Rights Legend

Use, duplication, or disclosure by the Government is
subject to restrictions as set forth in subparagraph
(c) of the Commercial Computer Software - Restricted
Rights clause at FAR sec. 52.227-19 and subparagraph
(c) (1) (ii) of the Rights in Technical Data and Computer
Software clause at DFARS sec. 252.227-7013.

        cisco Systems, Inc.
        170 West Tasman Drive
        San Jose, California 95134-1706

Cisco Internetwork Operating System Software
IOS (tm) 4500 Software (C4500-INR-M), Version 10.3(8), RELEASE
SOFTWARE (fc2)
Copyright (c) 1986-1995 by cisco Systems, Inc.
Compiled Thu 14-Dec-95 22:10 by mkamson
Image text-base: 0x600087E0, data-base: 0x6043C000

cisco 4500 (R4K) processor (revision B) with 8192K/4096K bytes of memory.
Processor board serial number 73160394
R4600 processor, Implementation 32, Revision 2.0
G.703/E1 software, Version 1.0.
Bridging software.
X.25 software, Version 2.0, NET2, BFE and GOSIP compliant.
2 Ethernet/IEEE 802.3 interfaces.
1 Token Ring/IEEE 802.5 interface.
2 Serial network interfaces.
128K bytes of non-volatile configuration memory.
4096K bytes of processor board System flash (Read/Write)
4096K bytes of processor board Boot flash (Read/Write)
Press RETURN to get started!
```

Configuration File

The second major router software component is the configuration file. This file is created by the router administrator and contains statements that are interpreted by the operating system and that tell it how to perform different functions built into the OS. For example, such statements can define one or more access lists and tell the operating system to apply different access lists to different interfaces to provide a degree of control over the flow of packets through the router. Although the configuration file defines how to perform functions that affect the operation of the router, it is the operating system that actually does the work since it interprets and acts upon the statements in the configuration file.

The configuration file contains statements stored in ASCII. As such, its contents can be displayed on the router console terminal or on a remote terminal. It is important to note and remember this if you create or modify a configuration file on a PC attached to a network and use tftp to load the file into your router; the use of a text editor or word processor normally results in embedded control characters in a saved file that the router cannot digest. Thus, when using a text editor or word processor to create or manipulate a configuration file, be sure to save the file as an ASCII text (.txt) file. Once the configuration file is saved, it is stored in the NVRAM and loaded into upper-addressed memory each time the router is initialized. Figure 2-6 illustrates the relationship of the two key router software components with respect to router RAM.

Data Flow

The importance of configuration information can be seen by examining the flow of data within a router. See Figure 2-7, which illustrates the general flow of data within a router.

At the media interface, previously entered configuration commands inform the operating system of the type of frames to be processed. For example, the interface could be Ethernet, Token Ring, *fiber-distributed data*

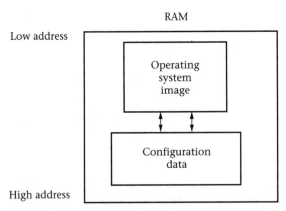

Figure 2-6 Router software components.

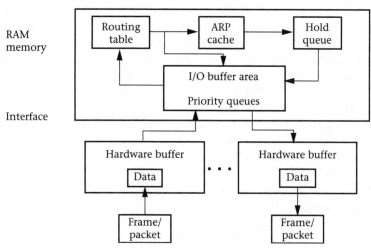

Figure 2-7 Data flow within a router.

interface (FDDI), or even a serial wide area network port such as an X.25 or frame-relay interface. In defining the interface you may be required to provide one or more operating rates and other parameters to fully define the interface.

Once the router knows the type of interface it must support, it can verify the frame format of arriving data as well as correctly form frames for output via that interface or a different interface. In addition, the router can check data integrity on received frames because once it knows the interface, it can use an appropriate *cyclic redundancy check* (CRC). Similarly, the router can compute and append an appropriate CRC to frames placed onto the media.

Within main memory, configuration commands are used to control the method by which routing table entries occur. If you configure static routing entries, the router does not exchange routing table entries with other routers. The ARP cache is an area within memory which stores associations between IP addresses and their corresponding Mac layer 2 addresses. As data are received or prepared for transmission, the data may flow into one or more priority queues where low-priority traffic is temporarily delayed in favor of the router processing higher-priority traffic. If your router supports traffic prioritization, certain configuration statements are used to inform the router's operating system how to perform its prioritization tasks. We examine prioritization and queuing in detail in Chapter 4.

As data flow into the router, the location and status are tracked by a hold queue. Entries in the routing table denote the destination interface through which the packet is routed. If the destination is a LAN and address resolution is required, the router attempts to use the ARP cache to determine the Mac delivery address as well as the manner by which the outgoing frame should be formed. If an appropriate address is not in cache, the router forms and issues an ARP packet to determine the necessary layer 2 address. Once the destination address and method of encapsulation are determined, the packet is ready for delivery to an outgoing interface port. Once again, the data may be placed into a priority queue prior to being delivered into the transmit buffer of the interface for delivery onto the connected media.

Now that we understand the two key router software components, let's look at how to develop the router configuration file.

The Router Configuration Process

The first time you take your router out of the box and power it on, or after you add one or more hardware components, you must use the setup command. This command is automatically invoked for either of the previously defined situations or it can be used later at the router's command interpreter prompt level. The interpreter is referred to as the EXEC. However, prior to running setup or issuing EXEC commands, it is important to note the cabling needed to connect a terminal device to the router's system console port.

Cabling Considerations

The system console port on a router is configured as a *data terminal equipment* (DTE) port. Since the RS-232 port on PCs and ASCII terminal devices are also configured as DTEs, you cannot directly cable the two together using a common straight-through cable because both the router's port and the terminal device transmit on pin 2 of the interface and receive data on pin 3. To correctly interface, you must have a crossover or rollover cable in which pin 2 at one end is crossed to pin 3 at the other end and vice versa. The crossover table also ties certain control signals together so it is actually a bit more than the reversal of pins 2 and 3. However, it is a readily available cable by simply specifying the term crossover or rollover. Once you install the correct cable, you should configure your terminal device to operate at 9600 baud, 8 data bits, no parity, and 1 stop bit.

Console Access

You can use a variety of communications programs to access the router via its console port. Since Windows 95 and Windows 98 include the

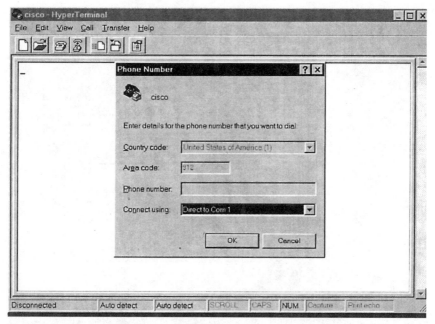

Figure 2-8 You must set the connection type to Direct when cabling a PC directly to the router console port.

HyperTerminal communications program, we briefly explore its use to configure a router. Be aware that the HyperTerminal program that is shipped with older versions of Windows contains a bug that causes it to operate incorrectly. If you are using NT to connect to the router, your connection will not work unless you upgrade the HyperTerminal program.

Figure 2-8 illustrates the use of the HyperTerminal program to create a new connection appropriately labeled Cisco by the authors. Note that since you will directly cable your computer to the Cisco console port, you need to configure the phone number entry for the use of a direct com port. In Figure 2-8, com port 1 is shown selected.

Once you select the appropriate direct connect com port and click on the OK button, the HyperTerminal program displays a dialog box labeled Port Settings. Figure 2-9 illustrates the Port Settings dialog box for the COM1 port previously configured for the connection we wish to establish to the router.

In Figure 2-9 note the Port Settings dialog box lets you define the communications settings to be used between your PC and the router port. Since the router console port's default is 9600 bps, 8 data bits, no parity, and 1 stop bit, the configuration in Figure 2-9 is set accordingly.

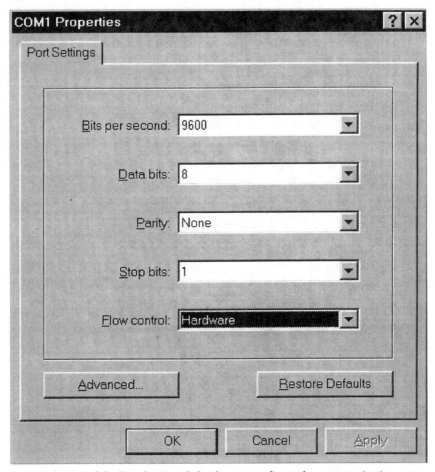

Figure 2-9 Use of the Port Settings dialog box to configure the communications parameters to be used by your computer to match those used by the router console.

Setup Considerations

Since this book serves as a guide to router performance, we only briefly mention setup, which is only run when the router is literally pulled out of the box and perhaps infrequently thereafter. However, it should be noted that to facilitate the use of the setup, you should prepare for the use of the router. You should make a list of the protocols you plan to route, determine the types of interfaces installed, and determine if you plan to use bridging. In addition, because setup will prompt you to enter a variety of specific parameters for each protocol and interface, it is highly recommended that you consult the appropriate Cisco Systems router manuals in order to determine these parameters correctly.

Included in the setup facility is the ability to assign a name to the router as well as assign both a direct connect and virtual terminal password. Once you complete setup, you are prompted to accept the configuration. Once the initial setup process is completed, you are ready to use the router's command interpreters.

Figure 2-10 illustrates an example of the use of the router setup command to review and, if desired, modify one or more previously established

Figure 2-10   An example of the use of the setup command to view an existing router configuration.

```
CISCO4000#setup
          -- System Configuration Dialog --

At any point you may enter a question mark '?' for help.
Refer to the 'Getting Started' Guide for additional help.
Use ctrl-c to abort configuration dialog at any prompt.
Default settings are in square brackets '[]'.

Continue with configuration dialog? [yes]:

First, would you like to see the current interface summary?
[yes]:
Interface       IP-Address      OK? Method   Status
    Protocol
Ethernet0       192.72.46.3     YES NVRAM    up
    down
Serial0         4.0.136.74      YES NVRAM    down
    down
Serial1         4.0.136.90      YES NVRAM    down
    down
TokenRing0      192.131.174.2   YES NVRAM    initializing
    down

Configuring global parameters:

  Enter host name [CISCO4000]:

The enable secret is a one-way cryptographic secret used
instead of the enable password when it exists.

  Enter enable secret [<Use current secret>]:

The enable password is used when there is no enable secret
and when using older software and some boot images.

  Enter enable password [abadabado]:
  Enter virtual terminal password [gobirds]:
  Configure SNMP Network Management? [yes]:
    Community string [public]:
  Configure IPX? [yes]:
  Configure bridging? [no]:
```

(Continued)

Figure 2-10 (*Continued*)

```
   Configure IP? [yes]:
     Configure IGRP routing? [no]:
     Configure RIP routing? [yes]:

Configuring interface parameters:

Configuring interface Ethernet0:
   Is this interface in use? [yes]:
   Configure IP on this interface? [yes]:
     IP address for this interface [192.72.46.3]:
     Number of bits in subnet field [0]:
     Class C network is 192.72.46.0, 0 subnet bits; mask is
255.255.255.0
   Configure IPX on this interface? [yes]:
     IPX network number [110]:

Configuring interface Serial0:
   Is this interface in use? [yes]:
   Configure IP on this interface? [yes]:
   Configure IP unnumbered on this interface? [no]:
     IP address for this interface [4.0.136.74]:
     Number of bits in subnet field [22]:
     Class A network is 4.0.0.0, 22 subnet bits; mask is
255.255.255.252
   Configure IPX on this interface? [no]:


   .  .  .  .   .  .   .
   .  .   .   .  .   .

The following configuration command script was created:

hostname CISCO4000
enable secret 5 $1$soiv$pyh65G.wUNxX9LK90w7yc.
enable password abadabado
line vty 0 4
password gobirds
snmp-server community public
!
ipx routing
no bridge 1
ip routing
!
! Turn off IPX to prevent network conflicts.
interface Ethernet0
no ipx network
interface Serial0
no ipx network
interface Serial1
no ipx network
interface TokenRing0
no ipx network
!
interface Ethernet0
ip address 192.78.46.1 255.255.255.0
ipx network 110
```

Figure 2-10   (*Continued*)

```
.   .   .   .   .
.   .   .   .   .

router rip
network 192.78.46.0
network 200.1.2.0
network 4.0.0.0
network 192.131.174.0
!
end

Use this configuration? [yes/no]:
```

configuration entries. In this example the name of the router CISCO4000 was assigned during a previous setup process so that is displayed before the prompt character. The prompt character is a pound sign (#) that indicates we are in the router's privileged mode of operation. Note the enabled password is shown as abadabado. That password must be specified after a person gains access to the router console port and enters the command enable to obtain access to privileged EXEC commands that alter a router's operating environment. In addition to the enable password, an administrator may also configure an enable secret password. The enable secret serves the same purpose as the standard enable password, except that the enable secret password is encrypted in the configuration file using MD5. When the configuration is displayed, only the encrypted version of the enable secret password is seen. This is important because it prevents anyone from determining what the enable secret password is by obtaining a copy of the router configuration file. The regular enable password may also be encrypted by using the command service password-encryption. This command also encrypts the passwords used for the vty, auxiliary, and console ports. However, the encryption used is much weaker than that used for the enable secret and many free programs are available on the Internet to crack passwords encrypted in this manner in a few seconds. The author recommends always using the enable secret password. If both the enable secret and the standard enable password are set, the enable secret password takes precedence.

To save on listing space, a portion of the router's setup configuration was eliminated from Figure 2-10 where the double rows of dots are shown. Note that you can use the question mark at each line entry level to obtain online assistance. Also note that once the configuration is completed, a command script is created by the router. This command script represents the latest configuration changes. You are then prompted to accept or reject the entire configuration.

Since the command interpreter is the key to entering router commands that control how the operating system changes router functionality, including displaying important performance-related information, let's look at this feature.

The Command Interpreter

The command interpreter, as its name implies, is responsible for interpreting router commands that are entered. Referred to as the EXEC, the command interpreter checks each command and, assuming they are correctly entered, performs the operation requested.

Assuming an administrator entered a password during the setup process, you must log into the router using the correct password prior to obtaining the ability to enter an EXEC command. In actuality, two passwords may be required to use EXEC commands, as there are two EXEC command levels: user and privileged. By logging into the router, you gain access to user EXEC commands that let you connect to another host. You can also provide a name to a logical connection, change the parameters of a terminal, display open connections, and perform similar operations that are not considered by Cisco Systems to represent critical operations.

If you use the EXEC enable command to gain access to the use of privileged commands, you can enter configuration information, turn on or off privileged commands, lock the terminal, and perform other critical functions. To use the EXEC enable command, you may have to enter another password if one was previously set with the enable-password or enable secret configuration commands.

To illustrate why the EXEC level should have its own password and why different routers should have different passwords, consider the following brief series of router operations. In this example once we obtained access to the local router's privilege mode, we initiated a telnet operation to a second router. If you assign the same password to a series of routers, one weak point can enable a hacker to enjoy restructuring your entire network with a minimum of effort!

```
Cisco7500#
Cisco7500#telnet
Host: 205.136.175.1
Trying 205.136.175.1 ... Open

          User Access Verification
          Password:
```

User-Mode Operations

Once you log into the router, you are in the user command mode. In this mode the system prompt appears as an angle bracket (>). If you previously entered a name for the router, that name will prefix the angle bracket. Otherwise the default term *router* will prefix the angle bracket.

Privileged Mode of Operation

Since you can configure a router through its privileged EXEC mode of operation, you can assign a password to this mode of operation. As previously noted, you would use the enable-password configuration command to do so, which means you enter the privileged mode without password protection to set password protection.

To enter the privileged EXEC mode, you would enter the command enable at the > prompt. You would then be prompted to enter a password, after which the prompt would change to a pound sign (#), which indicates you are in the privileged EXEC mode of operation. If you use the ? command in both user and privilege access modes, you will note that the privileged mode command set includes all user EXEC commands. In addition, the privilege user mode includes the configure command, which lets you apply configuration parameters that affect the router on a global basis.

You can configure the device from a terminal, memory, or via the network. Since a router does not have a hard disk or a floppy disk, it is common for administrators to store configuration files, including access lists, on a network. When you do so, you need to create a configuration file using a word processor or text editor and save the file in ASCII text (.txt) mode. Then you use tftp to transfer the file to the router. To accomplish this, you must install a tftp server program on your computer and indicate the location where the tftp server root directory resides. Figure 2-11 is a

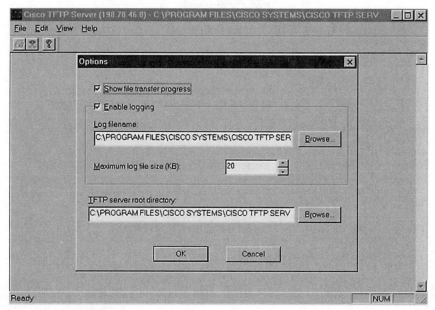

Figure 2-11   Cisco tftp server software allows you to enable or disable logging as well as specify a server root directory.

screen display of Cisco tftp server software running on an author's PC. If your organization has an appropriate account with Cisco Systems, you can download the software from the Cisco Web site.

Table 2-2 is a summary of configuration command entry methods and their operational results. Entries in this table summarize the relationship between the use of different command entry methods and the use of different types of storage for both accessing and storing configuration commands. Cisco changed the format of these commands beginning in version 10.3 of the router operating system. Both forms of the

Table 2-2   Configuration Command Entry Methods

Command	Operational Result
Configure terminal	Configures router manually from the console.
Configure memory	Loads a previously created configuration from NVRAM.
Copy startup-config	
Running-config	
Configure network	Loads a previously created configuration from a network server via tftp (trivial file transfer protocol).
Copy tftp running-config	
Write terminal	Displays the current configuration in RAM.
Show running-config	
Write network	Shares the current configuration in RAM onto a network server via tftp.
Copy running-config tftp	
Show configuration	Displays the previously saved configuration in NVRAM.
Show startup-config	
Write erase	Erases the contents of NVRAM.
Erase startup-config	
Reload	Loads the contents of NVRAM into RAM. Occurs on power-on automatically.

commands are still accepted by the router in the most current releases, although at some point it is assumed that the older version of the commands will be phased out. The newer version of the commands are shown in italics.

Configuration Command Categories

Configuration commands can be categorized into four general categories: global, which defines system-wide parameters; interface, which defines WAN or LAN interfaces; line, which defines the characteristics of a serial terminal line; and router subcommands, which are used to configure a routing protocol.

Global Configuration Commands

Global configuration commands are used to define system-wide parameters, including router interfaces and access lists that are applied to those interfaces. Some global configuration commands are mandatory if you want the router to operate. For example, you must configure your LAN and serial ports to connect to the Internet. Other configuration commands, such as creating and applying an access list, are optional. You can obtain a summary list of global configuration commands supported by the router you are using by entering the ? command after you enter the router's configuration mode. To do so, you must use the `enable` command to enter the privilege access mode as `configure` is a privilege command. Once this is accomplished, you enter the command `configure`, resulting in a router's prompt changing to `router(config)#`, where `router` is the hostname assigned to your router and `config` indicates you are in the configuration command mode. Once in the configuration command mode, you enter the ? subcommand, as illustrated in Figure 2-12 to obtain a list of global configuration commands applicable to the router used by the author.

The built-in help facility, while cryptic in some ways, can provide some information that can alleviate a trip back to the office for a reference book. For example, many times during a daily grind of configuring LAN and WAN devices, it is easy to forget blocks of numbers assigned by Cisco to different types of access lists, ICMP type codes, and similar information. By drilling down and using the ? command, you may be able to obtain the information that saves you a trip to the bookshelf. An example of this is illustrated in Figure 2-13 which shows the use of ? command parameter to obtain information about the `access list` command. In this example we obtained a listing of the numeric range associated with different types of access lists.

Figure 2-12 Using the ? command to obtain a list of global configuration commands for a particular router.

```
User Access Verification

Password:
Cisco7500>enable
Password:

Cisco7500#configure
Configuring from terminal, memory, or network [terminal]?
Enter configuration commands, one per line.  End with CNTL/Z.
Cisco7500(config)#?
Configure commands:
  aaa                         Authentication, Authorization and Accounting.
  access-list                 Add an access list entry
  alias                       Create command alias
  alps                        Configure Airline Protocol Support
  appletalk                   Appletalk global configuration commands
  arap                        Appletalk Remote Access Protocol
  arp                         Set a static ARP entry
  async-bootp                 Modify system bootp parameters
  autonomous-system           Specify local AS number to which we belong
  banner                      Define a login banner
  boot                        Modify system boot parameters
  bridge                      Bridge Group.
  bstun                       BSTUN global configuration commands
  buffers                     Adjust system buffer pool parameters
  call-history-mib            Define call history mib parameters
  cdp                         Global CDP configuration subcommands
  chat-script                 Define a modem chat script
  clock                       Configure time-of-day clock
  config-register             Define the configuration register
  controller                  Configure a specific controller
  decnet                      Global DECnet configuration subcommands
  default                     Set a command to its defaults
  default-value               Default character-bits values
  dialer                      Dialer watch commands
  dialer-list                 Create a dialer list entry
  dlsw                        Data Link Switching global configuration
                              commands
  dnsix-dmdp                  Provide DMDP service for DNSIX
  dnsix-nat                   Provide DNSIX service for audit trails
  downward-compatible-config  Generate a configuration compatible with older
                              software
  dspu                        DownStream Physical Unit Command
  dss                         Configure dss parameters
  enable                      Modify enable password parameters
  end                         Exit from configure mode
  endnode                     SNA APPN endnode command
  exception                   Exception handling
  exit                        Exit from configure mode
  file                        Adjust file system parameters
  frame-relay                 global frame relay configuration commands
  help                        Description of the interactive help system
  hostname                    Set system's network name
  interface                   Select an interface to configure
  ip                          Global IP configuration subcommands
  ipc                         Configure IPC system
```

Figure 2-13 Obtaining online help for router access lists.

```
CISCO7500(config)# access-list ?
  <1-99>       IP standard access list
  <100-199>    IP extended access list
  <1000-1099>  IPX SAP access list
  <1100-1199>  Extended 48-bit Mac address access list
  <200-299>    Protocol type-code access list
  <700-799>    48-bit Mac address access list
  <800-899>    IPX standard access list
  <900-999>    IPX extended access list
```

The interface Commands

A second category of router commands is interface commands. interface commands define the characteristics of a LAN or WAN interface and are proceeded by an interface command. Figure 2-14 illustrates the use of the show interfaces serial0/1/0 command, followed by the ? command to display a partial list of interface configuration commands that can be applied to a serial interface.

The interface command lets you assign a network to a particular port as well as configure one or more specific parameters required for the interface. For example, interface ethernet0 informs the router that port 0 is connected to an Ethernet network.

Figure 2-14 Using the interface serial command, followed by the ? command to display a list of interface configuration commands.

```
User Access Verification

Password:
CISCO7500>show interfaces serial0/1/0 ?
  accounting      Show interface accounting
  crb             Show interface routing/bridging info
  fair-queue      Show interface Weighted Fair Queueing (WFQ) info
  irb             Show interface routing/bridging info
  mac-accounting  Show interface Mac accounting info
  precedence      Show interface precedence accounting info
  random-detect   Show interface Weighted Random Early Detection (WRED)
info
  rate-limit      Show interface rate-limit info
  type            Show vlan types
  |               Output modifiers
  <cr>
```

Table 2-3   Keywords That Define the Type of Router Interface

Keyword	Interface Type
async	Port line used as an asynchronous interface
atm	Asynchronous Transfer Mode (ATM) interface
bri	Integrated services digital network (ISDN), basic rate interface (BRI)
ethernet	Ethernet 10-Mbps interface
fastethernet	Fast Ethernet 100-Mbps interface
fddi	Fiber-distributed data interface (FDDI)
hssi	High-speed serial interface
serial	Serial interface
tokenring	Token-ring interface
vg-anylan	100-Mbps VG-AnyLAN port adapter

The most common format of the `interface` command is

```
interface type number
```

where `type` defines the type of interface to be configured. Table 2-3 lists 10 examples of keywords used to define different types of router interfaces.

The `line` Commands

The `line` commands are used to modify the operation of a serial terminal line. Figure 2-15 illustrates the use of the `line` command, followed by the ? command to display a list of lines that can be configured.

The `router` Commands

The fourth category of privileged commands is router subcommands. Such commands are used to configure IP routing protocol parameters and follow the use of the `router` command. The top portion of Figure 2-16 illustrates the use of the `router` command, followed by the ? command to display a list of router subcommands supported by the router used at this point in time.

Figure 2-15 Obtaining a listing of the serial terminal lines you can configure.

```
CISCO7500(config)#line ?
  <0-6>    First Line number
  aux      Auxiliary line
  console  Primary terminal line
  vty      Virtual terminal
```

Once again, note that you can drill down to obtain information about a particular router command by entering that command and then entering that command with the ? command parameter, as illustrated in the lower portion of Figure 2-16.

Figure 2-16 Obtaining a list of `router` commands and specific information on `RIP` subcommands.

```
CISCO7500(config)#router ?
  bgp        Border Gateway Protocol (BGP)
  egp        Exterior Gateway Protocol (EGP)
  eigrp      Enhanced Interior Gateway Routing Protocol (EIGRP)
  igrp       Interior Gateway Routing Protocol (IGRP)
  isis       ISO IS-IS
  iso-igrp   IGRP for OSI networks
  mobile     Mobile routes
  ospf       Open Shortest Path First (OSPF)
  rip        Routing Information Protocol (RIP)
  static     Static routes

CISCO7500(config)#router rip
CISCO7500(config-router)#?
Router configuration commands:
  default-metric          Set metric of redistributed routes
  distance                Define an administrative distance
  distribute-list         Filter networks in routing updates
  exit                    Exit from routing protocol configuration mode
  help                    Description of the interactive help system
  maximum-paths           Forward packets over multiple paths
  neighbor                Specify a neighbor router
  network                 Enable routing on an IP network
  no                      Negate or set default values of a command
  offset-list             Add or subtract offset from IGRP or RIP metrics
  passive-interface       Suppress routing updates on an interface
  redistribute            Redistribute information from another routing
                          protocol
  timers                  Adjust routing timers
  validate-update-source  Perform sanity checks against source address of
                          routing updates
```

Abbreviating Commands

It is often not necessary to type the entire word for the router to accept a command. Generally, three or four letters of the command are enough for the router to discern what command is being requested and perform the desired action. For example, the following command:

```
Router# show interface serial0
```

could be abbreviated as

```
Router# sh int s0
```

which is certainly much easier to type! When in doubt, try abbreviating the command to the first three letters. If the first three letters are not enough for the router to determine the command you are requesting, you will get an ambiguous command error at the router prompt. You can then use the router's context-sensitive help by typing the first three letters with a question mark at the end. The router displays all of the commands that match the first three letters and then you can add as many characters as necessary to distinguish the command you want.

Remember, the ? is your friend. By using the built-in context-sensitive help, even a Cisco novice can determine the correct syntax of a command.

General Console Operations

Now that we have an understanding of general router configuration operations, look at some specific operations. In this section we first examine how to control router general operations such as assigning a hostname, generating a banner message, and setting the day and date. Once this is accomplished, we examine how to tune our console and, if desired, log messages. The operations we examine provide us with an appreciation for the use of privileged commands as well as how to use a router's display to verify the execution of different router commands.

Hostname Assignment

The assignment or reassignment of a name to your router is accomplished by using of the hostname command. Since the hostname command is a configuration command, you must be in the privilege user mode to set or reset the hostname. Figure 2-17 illustrates entering the privilege user mode followed by the use of the configure command, the use of the hostname command, and the ? parameter to obtain online assistance about the use of the command. Note that online assistance informs you that you should enter a word which will be used as the system's network

Figure 2-17 Using the `hostname` command to set and reset the name assigned to a router.

```
User Access Verification

Password:
router>enable
Password:
router#configure
Configuring from terminal, memory, or network [terminal]?
Enter configuration commands, one per line.  End with CNTL/Z.
router(config)#hostname ?
  WORD  This system's network name

router(config)#hostname beverly
beverly(config)#hostname gilbert
gilbert(config)#hostname Macon7500
Macon7500(config)#exit
```

name. In the example in Figure 2-17 we assume that no hostname was previously assigned, resulting in the default name of router being assigned. The `hostname` command was then followed by the word `bev-erly` to change the name to beverly. Next, the `hostname` command was followed by the word `gilbert` to change the name of the router to gilbert. While the preceding changes are nice for the ego of the author and his wife, in reality hostnames should be meaningfully assigned, especially when you have a complex network. The last use of the `hostname` command in Figure 2-17 illustrates the use of a more meaningful name, with Macon7500 used since this better describes the location and type of router. Although Figure 2-17 shows the use of the `enable` command to enter the privilege mode, in subsequent examples throughout the book we assume we made our point about the use of the `enable` command and simply show the # prompt after a hostname to indicate we are in privilege mode.

Banner Creation

A banner is a message displayed when a certain type of initial activity is performed. In a Cisco router environment several types of banner messages can be displayed. Figure 2-18 illustrates the use of the `banner` configuration command, followed by the ? parameter to display a list of the types of banner messages supported on the authors' router. In Figure 2-18 note that `line` is not a banner option. Instead, it is how you enter a banner-text message. For example, to display the message Welcome, you enter it within a pair of delimiting characters, such as the pound (#) sign, result-

Figure 2-18 Using the banner ? command to display the types of banner messages supported by a router.

```
Cisco7500#configure
Configuring from terminal, memory, or network [terminal]?
Enter configuration commands, one per line.  End with CNTL/Z.
Cisco7500(config)#banner ?
  LINE             c banner-text c, where 'c' is a delimiting character
  exec             Set EXEC process creation banner
  incoming         Set incoming terminal line banner
  login            Set login banner
  motd             Set Message of the Day banner
  prompt-timeout   Set Message for login authentication timeout
  slip-ppp         Set Message for SLIP/PPP
```

ing in the line entry becoming #Welcome#. You should carefully select your delimiter character since that character cannot be used in the banner message.

The banner exec command is used to display a message when a line is activated, an incoming vty connection occurs, or a similar EXEC process occurs. In comparison, the banner login command results in the display of a message when you connect to a router facility that requires a login, such as a telnet connection. Thus, the banner login command results in a message display before the result of any banner exec command message. Other banner command options listed in Figure 2-18 include incoming, motd, prompt-timeout, and slip-ppp.

A banner incoming message results in the display of a message when an incoming connection initiated from the network side of a router occurs. The motd subcommand permits you to specify a message of the day. An motd banner is displayed whenever any type of connection to the router occurs. Thus, you should consider its use when you have information to convey that affects all users. For example, the command banner motd #Router will be taken offline from 21:00 to 23:00 tonight for hardware upgrade# would represent a common type of use for this banner.

The prompt-timeout subcommand permits a message to be displayed if a login authentication process times out. Finally, the slip-ppp subcommand results in the display of a message for access via those protocols.

Note that banners are displayed in a particular order regardless of the sequence of commands you use to set banners. The banner motd, if set, will be displayed first, followed, if previously configured, by the banner incoming. If a user login occurs, the banner exec, if configured, will then be displayed.

Figure 2-19   Using the banner command to configure text displays at login and when an EXEC process occurs.

```
CISCO7500(config)#banner exec #Welcome#
CISCO7500(config)#banner login #Hello#
CISCO7500(config)#exit
CISCO7500#exit

Hello

User Access Verification

Password: Welcome
CISCO7500>enable
Password:
CISCO7500#configure
Configuring from terminal, memory, or network [terminal]?
Enter configuration commands, one per line.  End with CNTL/Z.
```

To illustrate the creation and display of two messages, see Figure 2-19. The upper portion shows the use of two banner commands. The first command, banner exec, associates the message Welcome with the occurrence of an EXEC process. The second command, banner login, associates the message Hello with an incoming connection. The results of the two banner commands are illustrated in the lower portion of Figure 2-19. Before moving on, a word about misconfiguration of messages and their erasure is warranted. If you use an improper delimiter, such as cWelcomec, you will not get the message display you desire. Because of the manner in which Cisco routers buffer data, it is sometimes not a simple solution to just redo the message. Instead, it is far better to use the "no" version of a banner command to delete the previous entry. For example, entering a no banner exec command followed by the no banner login command would suppress the previous entries. A "no" version of each command is usually available to either return a router parameter to its default or counteract the effect of a previously issued command.

DAY/TIME SETTINGS

Cisco routers support several commands that affect the system calendar and system clock. You can use the calendar set command to set a 7000 or 4500 series system calendar by entering the command followed by the time and date in either of the following two formats:

hh:mm:ss day month year

hh:mm:ss month day year

You enter the day as a numeric and the month by full name, allowing the operating system to automatically distinguish between the two formats. Once you set the system calendar, you can configure your router to be the authoritative time source for a network. To do so, you would use the clock calendar-valid global command.

A second date/time related–command to note is the clock set command. This command has the same format for parameter entries as the calendar set command. Instead of setting the system calendar, the clock set command sets the system clock.

Figure 2-20 provides several examples of the use of the clock and calendar commands. Note that the first two examples simply list options supported for each command. A show calendar command was then used to display the system calendar, which was found to be rather dated. Next, the calendar set command was used to update the system calendar and another show command verified our setting. We then used the clock read-calendar command to read the hardware calendar values into the system clock and used two additional show commands to display our results.

Depending on your router, you may be able to use other date/time commands. Some commands enable your system to automatically switch to daylight savings time, while another command allows you to perform a reverse of the clock read-calendar. That is, the clock update-calendar command enables Cisco 7500 or 4500 routers to have their calendar set from the system clock.

Figure 2-20 Setting the system calendar and system clock.

```
Cisco7500#clock ?
  read-calendar    Read the hardware calendar into the clock
  set              Set the time and date
  update-calendar  Update the hardware calendar from the clock

Cisco7500#calendar ?
  set  Set the time and date

Cisco7500#show calendar
18:38:24 UTC Wed Aug 6 1997

Cisco7500#calendar set 10:55:00 28 september 1999
Cisco7500#show calendar
10:55:09 UTC Tue Sep 28 1999

Cisco7500#clock read-calendar
Cisco7500#show clock
10:58:23.415 UTC Tue Sep 28 1999
Cisco7500#show calendar
10:59:18 UTC Tue Sep 28 1999
```

Terminal Customization

Similar to the way we feel about food products and other topics, probably no one terminal setting makes everyone happy. Recognizing this, you can change terminal parameters to meet your specific preference through the use of the terminal command.

Once you connect to your router, you can obtain information about the current terminal line through the use of the show terminal command. Figure 2-21 illustrates an example of the show terminal command and its resulting display. By carefully examining the entries in the display, you can determine not only information about the setting of your terminal parameters but also information about system settings. For example, you will note from Figure 2-21 that idle session disconnect warning is not set at the system level. Thus, it might be a good idea to give users a warning.

Figure 2-21   Using the show terminal command to display information about the terminal configuration parameters for the current line.

```
Cisco7500>show terminal
Line 2, Location: "", Type: "vt100"
Length: 24 lines, Width: 80 columns
Baud rate (TX/RX) is 9600/9600
Status: PSI Enabled, Ready, Active, No Exit Banner
Capabilities: none
Modem state: Ready
Special Chars: Escape  Hold  Stop  Start  Disconnect  Activation
               ^^x     none   -      -       none
Timeouts:      Idle EXEC    Idle Session    Modem Answer   Session
Dispatch
               00:10:00        never                        none     not
set
                            Idle Session Disconnect Warning
                            never
                            Login-sequence User Response
                            00:00:30
                            Autoselect Initial Wait
                            not set
Modem type is unknown.
Session limit is not set.
Time since activation: 00:06:27
Editing is enabled.
History is enabled, history size is 10.
DNS resolution in show commands is enabled
Full user help is disabled
Allowed transports are pad v120 mop telnet.  Preferred is telnet.
No output characters are padded
No special data dispatching characters
Cisco7500>
```

Figure 2-22   Displaying a list of commands that affect the hardware and software parameters of the current terminal line.

```
Cisco7500#terminal ?
    data-character-bits      Size of characters being handled
    databits                 Set number of data bits per character
    default                  Set a command to its defaults
    domain-lookup            Enable domain lookups in show commands
    download                 Put line into 'download' mode
    editing                  Enable command line editing
    escape-character         Change the current line's escape character
    exec-character-bits      Size of characters to the command exec
    flowcontrol              Set the flow control
    full-help                Provide help to unprivileged user
    help                     Description of the interactive help system
    history                  Enable and control the command history function
    international            Enable international 8-bit character support
    ip                       IP options
    length                   Set number of lines on a screen
    monitor                  Copy debug output to the current terminal line
    no                       Negate a command or set its defaults
    notify                   Inform users of output from concurrent sessions
    padding                  Set padding for a specified output character
    parity                   Set terminal parity
    rxspeed                  Set the receive speed
    special-character-bits   Size of the escape (and other special) characters
    speed                    Set the transmit and receive speeds
    start-character          Define the start character
    stop-character           Define the stop character
    stopbits                 Set async line stop bits
    terminal-type            Set the terminal type
    transport                Define transport protocols for line
    txspeed                  Set the transmit speeds
    width                    Set width of the display terminal
```

You can easily display a list of commands to change the hardware and software parameters of the current terminal line. To do so, you use the command `terminal ?`, as illustrated in Figure 2-22.

To illustrate some common examples of terminal parameter alteration, let's assume you wish to set the terminal width to 132 columns and the number of lines to 32. First, you use the `terminal width` command, followed by the number of columns for your setting. Thus, your entry would be as follows:

```
Router>terminal width 132
```

To set the number of lines on the screen to 32, you use the `terminal length` command, indicating the number of lines you desire in the command as follows:

```
Router>terminal length 32
```

For both commands the "no" prefix (terminal no width, terminal no length) restores applicable settings to a default of 80 columns and 24 lines.

Some of the terminal parameters are rather dated and represent an era of electromechanical devices. For example, the terminal padding command governs the generation of null bytes after a specified character. The generation of nulls was commonly used during the 1980s when many terminals required extra time for an electromechanical print head to move back to the leftmost position on the next line. However, unless your organization uses antiquated equipment in an era of CRT displays, it is doubtful if you would ever use this parameter setting. Similarly, many other settings are interesting too, but may not be applicable to most readers.

Logging

The ability to observe the changing condition of a router through its message logging facility is an important feature often overlooked by many persons. In this section we look at message logging and the commands associated with this feature.

Message logging is controlled through the EXEC privilege mode. Once in that mode, you can use one or more logging subcommands within the global configuration command. Figure 2-23 illustrates the display of logging subcommand options supported by a particular router. Note that we are in the privilege mode (#) and first entered the command configure to display the prompt config which allowed us to enter logging ? to display the various logging options supported.

To enable or disable message logging, you enter the logging on command or its "no" version. The two commands are shown here and although they appear simple, they require a bit of explanation.

```
logging on
no logging on
```

Figure 2-23   Logging subcommand options.

```
Cisco7500(config)#logging ?
  Hostname or A.B.C.D  IP address of the logging host
  buffered             Set buffered logging parameters
  console              Set console logging level
  facility             Facility parameter for syslog messages
  history              Configure syslog history table
  monitor              Set terminal line (monitor) logging level
  on                   Enable logging to all supported destinations
  source-interface     Specify interface for source address in logging
                       transactions
  trap                 Set syslog server logging level
```

The logging on command enables message logging to all supported destinations other than the console. The no logging on command reverts logging to the console terminal and turns off logging to a previously selected destination other than the console.

In examining the message logging options listed in Figure 2-23 note that logging to a specified hostname results in messages being sent to a syslog server host. For those not familiar with the terminology, a *syslog server* is a UNIX host that captures and saves messages. Thus, you would enter logging *hostname* or an IP address to specify the UNIX host to be used as a syslog server. Like most EXEC commands, the no logging *hostname* command deletes the prior operation, removing the syslog server with the specified address from the list of syslogs.

The logging buffered configuration command permits messages to be written to memory. Figure 2-24 illustrates the various options available by using this command, and they are also applicable to the logging console, monitor, history, and trap subcommands. In Figure 2-24 note that you can use the logging buffered command to set logging to memory and assign an amount of memory for message logging. Also note that you can specify eight types of messages to be logged. Earlier versions of IOS used both level numbers and different keywords to allow you to limit logging messages to be sent to the console or another area. Last, but not least, once again the "no" version of the command cancels the use of the buffer and reverts message writing to the console terminal.

You can use the logging trap command to limit the amount of messages transmitted to a syslog server. To do so you follow the command with one of the keywords previously listed in Figure 2-24, which limits logging messages transmitted to those with a level at or above the level of the keyword.

The logging monitor subcommand is similar to the trap subcommand, since it is used to limit messages sent to terminal lines referred to

Figure 2-24 Observing logging message options.

```
Cisco7500 (config)#logging buffered ?
  <4096-2147483647>  Logging buffer size
  alerts             Immediate action needed
  critical           Critical conditions
  debugging          Debugging messages
  emergencies        System is unusable
  errors             Error conditions
  informational      Informational messages
  notifications      Normal but significant conditions
  warnings           Warning conditions
  <cr>
```

as monitors. Messages are logged based on being at or above the keyword entered after the command. The keywords listed in Figure 2-24 that are applicable for a `trap` are also applicable for the `monitor` command.

You can also set up monitoring for a specific interface by using the `logging source-interface` subcommand. In doing so, you specify an interface after the command such as `serial0`.

One nifty feature of logging is the ability to log messages of a particular area of interest such as the authorization system. To accomplish this, you use the `logging facility` subcommand, followed by the facility type you want to log.

In concluding our overview of monitoring, let's look at an additional monitoring-related command. That command is the `show logging` command, and its use enables you to view the state of logging. An example of the use of this command is shown in Figure 2-25 where we first used the `show logging` command and observed that buffer logging is disabled. Next, we entered the `configure` command and used the `logging buffer` command to initiate recording messages to memory. After we exited the `config` mode, we used another `show logging` and saw that buffer logging had been enabled. Note that toward the bottom of Figure 2-25 the log buffer, by default, is assigned 65536 bytes of storage. As previously noted in Figure 2-23, there are limits to the minimum and maximum buffer area that can be used.

Figure 2-25   Viewing the state of logging on the router.

```
Cisco7500#show logging
Syslog logging: enabled (0 messages dropped, 0 flushes, 0 overruns)
    Console logging: level debugging, 97 messages logged
    Monitor logging: level debugging, 0 messages logged
    Buffer logging: disabled
    Trap logging: level informational, 105 message lines logged
Cisco7500#configure
Configuring from terminal, memory, or network [terminal]?
Enter configuration commands, one per line.  End with CNTL/Z.
Cisco7500(config)#logging buffer
Cisco7500(config)#end
Cisco7500#show logging
Syslog logging: enabled (0 messages dropped, 0 flushes, 0 overruns)
    Console logging: level debugging, 98 messages logged
    Monitor logging: level debugging, 1 messages logged
    Buffer logging: level debugging, 1 messages logged
    Trap logging: level informational, 106 message lines logged

Log Buffer (65536 bytes):

4d01h: %SYS-5-CONFIG_I: Configured from console by vty0 (198.78.46.8)
```

Now that we have an appreciation for Cisco router hardware and software to include the use of basic user mode and privilege mode commands, we are ready to move on. In Chapter 3 we will turn our attention to basic LAN and WAN metrics, examining LAN frames, frame fields, and the manner by which data flows on a WAN interface. Similar to the intent with this chapter, Chapter 3 is included in this book to provide readers with a variety of backgrounds with a common base of knowledge.

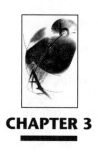

CHAPTER 3

LAN and WAN Metrics

This chapter focuses on *local area network* (LAN) and *wide area network* (WAN) metrics that can be used to determine the level of performance on each network. We will first discuss LANs—Ethernet and token-ring LANs, including a brief overview of each LAN access method, followed by the composition of network frames and the fields in each frame. Using this information as a base will then enable us to describe and discuss various network error conditions and related performance metrics.

In the second half of this chapter, we discuss WANs, including the various types of serial encapsulation supported by Cisco routers, the manner by which a serial interface is specified, the types of WAN transmission facilities you can consider using, and the effect of framing on different transmission facilities, which affects the overall level of potential performance on a WAN. Similar to Chapter 2, the information in this chapter is presented to ensure that readers with a diverse background obtain a common foundation of knowledge that will be useful as we probe deeper into router performance in subsequent chapters in this book.

LAN Metrics

This section examines a core series of local area network metrics that can be used to categorize LAN performance by focusing on Ethernet and token-ring LANs since they are, by far, the most frequently used LAN interface with Cisco routers.

Ethernet

Since the best method for becoming familiar with the characteristics of a network is to examine its frame composition, we do so in this section; however, prior to doing so, a few words describing how Ethernet operates in terms of its access protocol are in order. By first describing and discussing Ethernet's access protocol, we can better understand how this local area network operates. Thus, let's turn our attention to how Ethernet operates before moving on to the composition of the Ethernet frame.

NETWORK ACCESS

Ethernet can be considered as a listen first, then talk access protocol. That is, a station with data to transmit that is connected to an Ethernet network first listens for network activity. If no activity is noted, the station can then proceed to transmit its data. If activity is noted, the station waits until a period of inactivity occurs prior to transmitting its data.

COLLISIONS

Since it takes time for an electric signal to propagate down a transmission medium, it's possible for one station to listen to the network and hear no activity while another station is in the process of transmitting data. This situation is illustrated in Figure 3-1, where station A listened to the network, but did not hear the frame being transmitted by station C. Assuming there is no network activity, station A begins its transmission, resulting in a collision.

The official name of the Ethernet network access method is *carrier sense multiple access with collision detection* (CSMA/CD). Although Ethernet includes a broadband version that uses *radio frequency* (rf) modems for transmission, the most popular types of Ethernet are its various baseband type of networks where only one signal at a time can flow on the network. Since a baseband LAN does not use a carrier, a station cannot listen for a carrier to determine if transmission is occurring on the network. For a

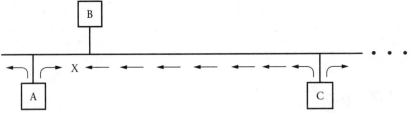

Figure 3-1   Ethernet collisions result from a station that is listening to the network not hearing a signal that is propagating toward it. Station A listens to the network and hears no activity. Station C has commenced transmission and the frame is flowing but has not propagated to station A. Station A assumes no activity is occurring on the network and transmits a frame, resulting in a collision. X = collision.

baseband LAN an Ethernet station listens for voltage, since Manchester coding, used by Ethernet LANs transmit data, results in a positive voltage placed on the network to specify coding for a binary 1 value. When a collision occurs, a similar listening process is used to determine this event. That is, when a collision occurs on a baseband Ethernet network, the voltage level rises above the nominal level associated with normal data transmission. Thus, the presence of voltage and its value or height is used to determine that there is activity on an Ethernet network and to determine that a collision occurred.

JAM PATTERN

Once a collision is detected, the transmitting station ceases its transmission of data and initiates the transfer of a special signal referred to as a *jam pattern*. The jam pattern consists of 32 to 48 bits that can have any value other than the *cyclic redundancy check* (CRC) value that corresponds to the partial frame transmitted prior to the jam. The function of the jam signal is to ensure that the collision lasts long enough to be detected by all stations on the network. In addition, a second function of the jam signal ensures that the nontransmitting stations that could become transmitting stations wait until the jam signal ends prior to attempting to transmit, alleviating the potential for additional collisions to occur.

WAITING TIME

Once a collision is detected, the transmitting station waits a random number of slot times before attempting to retransmit. Here the term *slot* represents 512 bits on a 10-Mbps Ethernet network, or a minimum frame length of 64 bytes. The actual number of time slots a station waits is governed by a randomization process, which is referred to as a *truncated binary exponential back-off algorithm*. Under this randomization process, a random integer *n* is used to define the number of slot times a station wants before again listening to the media. Once the back-off time expires, the station listens to the media, and if a lack of activity is noted, retransmits the frame while listening for the possible occurrence of another collision.

COLLISION ON RETRANSMISSION

If an Ethernet station successfully transmits the frame and has additional data to transmit, it again listens to the media as it prepares another frame for transmission. If a collision occurs on a retransmission attempt, a slightly different process occurs. That is, after a jam signal is transmitted, a station doubles the previously generated random number and then waits the prescribed number of slot intervals before attempting a retransmission. Up to 16 retransmission attempts can occur before the station aborts the transmission and declares the occurrence of a multiple collision error condition. When this condition occurs, some hubs turn the port off as the condition is typically caused by a hardware problem on a network adapter cabled to the hub. Other hub manufacturers ignore the condition. Both situations comply with the Ethernet standard since excessive collisions are only defined in the standard, leaving it to vendors to determine how their equipment should react to this situation.

LATE COLLISIONS

A special type of collision, referred to as a *late collision,* detects a collision after a station transmits a complete frame onto a network. Since an Ethernet network is structured to enable all stations to hear some activity within the transmission of 64 byes of data, a late collision is detected by a transmitter after the first slot time of 64 bytes and is applicable only for frames whose length exceeds 65 bytes. The detection of a late collision occurs in exactly the same manner as a normal collision; however, true to its name, it happens later than normal. The primary cause associated with a late collision is an excessive network segment cable length. If a network segment cable length exceeds the specification for an Ethernet network, the time required for a signal to propagate from one end of a segment to another part of the segment exceeds the time required to place a complete frame on the network. The result of this situation is that two devices on the network could communicate at the same time without either being able to listen to the other's transmission until their signals collide. In addition to an excessive segment cable length, other potential causes of late collisions include faulty connectors, an excessive number of repeaters in a network, and a defective Ethernet network adapter. However, since the most frequent primary cause of late collisions is an excessive cable length, this area is a good first step for investigation in attempting to isolate and correct the cause of late collisions. Now that we understand how stations on an Ethernet LAN gain access to the network and how collisions occur, let's look at the composition of the Ethernet frame and the fields within the frame.

The Ethernet Frame

Since Ethernet was developed before the *Institute of Electrical and Electronics Engineers* (IEEEE) standardized the technology, some slight differences exist between pure Ethernet and the IEEE 802.3 standard. In our examination of the basic Ethernet frame, we focus attention on the IEEE 802.3 frame format, indicating, when applicable, the differences between the original Ethernet frame and the IEEE 802.3 frame.

Figure 3-2 illustrates the fields in the IEEE 802.3 version of Ethernet. As we examine the function of each field within the frame, we can better understand how an Ethernet LAN operates.

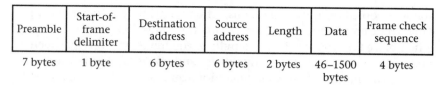

Preamble	Start-of-frame delimiter	Destination address	Source address	Length	Data	Frame check sequence
7 bytes	1 byte	6 bytes	6 bytes	2 bytes	46–1500 bytes	4 bytes

Figure 3-2   The IEEE 802.3 Ethernet frame.

PREAMBLE FIELD

The Preamble field announces the presence of a frame flowing on an Ethernet LAN. The Preamble field contains a repeating pattern of bits that enable each station on the network to synchronize themselves to the flow of the frame.

Under the original Ethernet standard, the Preamble field was 8 bytes (64 bits) in length and consisted of the alternating pattern of a binary 1 followed by a binary 0. Under the IEEE version of Ethernet, the Preamble field was subdivided into Preamble and Start-of-Frame Delimiter fields, with the new Preamble exactly the same as the original Ethernet version, but now only 7 bytes in length.

START-OF-FRAME DELIMITER FIELD

This 1-byte field is only applicable to the IEEE 802.3 version of Ethernet and can be viewed as an extension of the Preamble field. The Start-of-Frame Delimiter field is similar to the Preamble field, which consists of an alternating pattern of binary 1's and 0's, and contains the same sequence for the first 6 bits in the 8-bit field. However, the sequence terminates with the bit settings of 1 followed by another 1, resulting in the Start-of-Frame Delimiter pattern and alerting the receiver that frame data follows.

The use of a Preamble and Start-of-Frame Delimiter field results in a degree of confusion concerning the possible length of an Ethernet frame. In Figure 3-2, if you count the length of each field in an IEEE 802.3 Ethernet frame, you will note that the frame length can vary between a minimum length of 72 bytes and a maximum length of 1526 bytes, with the exact length dependent on the number of characters contained in the data field.

Some magazine and journal articles refer to an Ethernet frame that varies in length between 64 and 1518 bytes. While it is easy to become confused when you see different references to the minimum and maximum length of an Ethernet frame, there is a reason for this confusion. When referring to a frame formed within a *network interface card* (NIC), there is no Preamble or Start-of-Frame Delimiter field since those fields are added to a frame when it is placed on the media and removed when a frame is copied off the media. Thus, when referring to a frame within an NIC, the frame length will vary between 64 and 1518 bytes; however, when placed on the media, the length of the frame will vary between 72 and 1526 bytes, a fact that many articles and books fail to mention. Now that we can mimic a famous radio announcer and say that "we know the rest of the story," let's look at the next field in the frame.

DESTINATION ADDRESS FIELD

The Destination Address field identifies the recipient of the frame. This 6-byte field consists of a 46-bit address and two 1-bit subfields, as illustrated in Figure 3-3. In Figure 3-3, note that this field format is applicable for both Source and Destination Address fields, with the first 1-bit field set to a 0 in the Source Address field. For each type of address, the actual address represents a network adapter card.

ADDRESS REPRESENTATION

Both Source and Destination Address field values are commonly displayed by network monitors in hexadecimal, with the first 3 bytes separated from the last three by a colon (:) or every pair of hex characters separated from every other pair by a dash (-). For example, the source address 0350BC14FE01 could be displayed either as 0350BC:14FE01 or 03-50-BC-14-FE-01. As we shortly note, the first 3 bytes or 6 hex characters, identify the manufacturer of a network adapter card, while the last 3 bytes represent a specific adapter manufactured by the vendor. An understanding of the type of address and the method used to generate the address requires us to examine the first two subfields shown in Figure 3-3, so let's do so.

I/G Subfield

The 1-bit I/G subfield is only applicable to a destination address as this field is always set to a value of 0 in the Source Address field. In the Destination Address field this subfield is set to a 0 to indicate that the frame is destined to an individual station, or to a binary 1 to indicate that the frame is destined to more than one station. The latter situation is referred to as a *group address* and results in each member of the group copying the frame off the network.

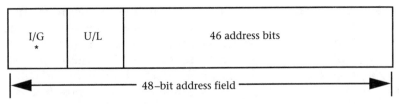

Figure 3-3   Source and Destination Address field formats. * is set to 0 in Source Address Field.

One special example of a group address is the assignment of all 1's to the Address field. The assignment of all 1's results in a destination address of hex FF-FF-FF-FF-FF-FF which is recognized as a broadcast address. Upon receipt of this address, each station on the network copies the frame off the network.

As you might surmise by now, Ethernet supports three types of addresses with respect to their number of recipients. When a destination address specifies a single station, the address is referred to as a *unicast address*. When the address is a group address that defines multiple stations, the address is referred to as a *multicast address*. The third type of destination address is a group address that specified all stations on a network, and is referred to as a *broadcast address*.

U/L Subfield

The setting of the U/L subfield indicates the method used to generate the address. That method can be either universally administrated addressing when the U/L field is set to 0 or locally administrated addressing when the value of the field is set to 1.

The unique address burned into *read-only memory* (ROM) on each network interface card is referred to as a *universally administrated address*. The assignments of universally administrated addresses are the function of the IEEE, which assigns a unique 3-byte prefix to each NIC manufacturer. The manufacturer then uses the prefix and assigns unique numbers to the last 3 bytes to uniquely identify each adapter. If the manufacturer runs out of numbers, they would then apply to the IEEE for another manufacturer ID prefix.

Although the use of universally administrated addressing ensures there will never be a duplicate address, it does not provide flexibility in addressing. When mainframes were originally connected to LANs, the communications software in the mainframe required coding that indicated the layer 2 address of each station on the network that required access to the big computer. Since the purchase of network adapters at different periods of time can result in obtaining adapters with different blocks of layer 2 addresses, it is difficult, if not impossible, to predict the addresses you would obtain. This resulted in the need to reprogram the mainframe communications processor with the addresses on the new network adapter cards, a process that required communications to be disrupted since software had to be recompiled and reloaded. Since organizations might have thousands of stations connected to a mainframe, this process typically occurred on weekends and was not very responsive when a new employee station was added to a network. The use of locally administrated addressing provides a solution to this problem since you can set the address of each station in software by overriding the universally administrated address with an address stored in the station's configuration file. Since you can plan in advance for additional addresses, those addresses can be coded into the mainframe communications processor, allowing you to simply add new stations to the network without having to take down the network. While this provides greater flexibility, you must be sure to not assign duplicate NIC addresses. In comparison, when universally administrated addressing is used, you do not have to worry about the possibility of duplicate addresses.

SOURCE ADDRESS FIELD

The Source Address field identifies the station that transmitted the frame. Similar to the Destination Address field, the Source Address field is 48 bits in length. Like the Destination Address field, the first 3 bytes of the Source Address field identify the adapter manufacturer, while the fourth through sixth bytes identify the product number produced by the manufacturer.

Since most network monitoring products are capable of reading source and destination addresses, they can also be programmed to compare the first 3 bytes of each address to a table of manufacturers' IDs obtained from the IEEE. This explains how some network monitoring products let you display the manufacturers of different network adapter cards.

TYPE/LENGTH FIELD

This 2-byte field was originally known as the Type field when used by the Ethernet standard. This field identifies the higher-level protocol contained in the data field, in effect informing the receiving device how the data field should be interpreted. For example, a value of hex 0800 defines the Internet protocol (IP), while a value of hex 0806 identifies the data field as an address resolution protocol (ARP) frame.

When the IEEE standardized Ethernet, the Type field was converted into a Length field. Here the Length field defines the number of bytes contained in the following Data field. Since the minimum-length Ethernet frame must be 72 bytes when flowing on the media and the frame has 26 bytes of overhead, this means the minimum length is 46 bytes. Since the maximum length of the Data field is 1500 bytes, the maximum value of the Length field is hex 05DC. If a value in this field exceeds 05DC, this would indicate that instead of a Length field (IEEE 802.3), the field is a Type field (Ethernet).

DATA FIELD

As indicated by our prior examination of the Length field, the Data field must be a minimum of 46 bytes in length and a maximum of 1500 bytes in length. When an application has 46 bytes or less data to transmit, a PAD character or characters are added to this field to ensure a minimum length frame is formed.

FRAME CHECK SEQUENCE FIELD

The Frame Check Sequence field (FCS) provides a mechanism for error detection. Each network adapter card contains a chip set which computes a cyclic redundancy check that covers the Destination and Source Address fields, Type/Length field, and the Data field. This computed CRC is placed in the 4-byte FCS field.

The computation of the CRC is based on treating the previously mentioned fields as one long binary number. The n bits to be covered by the CRC are the coefficients of a polynomial $M(x)$ of degree $n-1$. Here the first bit in the Destination address field corresponds to the term X $n-1$, while the last bit in the Data field corresponds to the X term. Next, $M(x)$ is multiplied by X^{32} and the result of that multiplication process is divided by the following polynomial:

$$G(X) = X32 + X26 + X23 + X22 + X16 + X12 + X11 + X10 + X8 + X7 + X5 + X4 + X2 + X + 1$$

Note that for the preceding polynomial, the term x^n represents the setting of a bit to a 1 in position n. Thus, the prior polynomial could be represented in binary as

$$100000100110000010001110110110111$$

The division process results in a quotient and a remainder. The quotient is discarded, while the remainder becomes the CRC and is placed in the FCS field.

Once a frame reaches its destination, the receiver uses the same fixed polynomial to generate a local CRC. If the locally computed CRC matches the CRC contained in the FCS field, the frame is considered to have arrived error-free and is accepted. Otherwise, the frame is assumed to have one or more bits in error and is discarded. In addition to a CRC mismatch, there are two additional conditions under which a receiver will discard a frame: (1) if the frame does not contain an integral number of bytes or (2) if the length of the data field does not match the value contained in the length field. In these two cases, an error is assumed to have occurred and the frame is discarded.

FRAME VARIATIONS

Since the initial IEEE 802.3 frame does not identify the type of data carried, it would normally allow only one type of protocol to be transported, which limits your ability to use this frame to transport multiple protocols. Recognizing this limitation, the IEEE defined a frame format variation that places an Ethernet-type code within the Data field. This frame variation is referred to as an Ethernet *subnetwork access protocol* (SNAP) frame.

The Ethernet SNAP Frame

The Ethernet SNAP frame is a variation of the IEEE 802.3 frame. The use of the SNAP frame provides a mechanism for obtaining a Type field identifier associated with a pure Ethernet frame, thus enabling the Ethernet SNAP frame to transport multiple protocols at the same time. The result is that many organizations configure their software to support this protocol instead of the original IEEE 802.3 version of Ethernet.

To obtain a Type code, the Ethernet SNAP frame subdivides the Data field, as illustrated in Figure 3-4. The first two fields, destination services access point (DSAP) and source services access point (SSAP), are each 1 byte in length. The DSAP field is used to indicate the destination upper-layer protocol carried in the frame, while the SSAP specifies the source upper-layer protocol. Both DSAP and SSAP addresses are either assigned by the IEEE or are manufacturer-implemented and should always be the same since destination and source protocols must be the same. For example, DSAP and SSAP values of hex 06 indicates that the Data field is transporting IP. Although DSAP and SSAP fields provide flexibility in specifying protocols, they were used in a *logical link control* (LLC) protocol data unit which formed the basis for the Ethernet SNAP frame, but which is not actually used by the frame. Instead, the value hex AA is placed in the DSAP and SSAP fields to denote that the frame is a revised LLC frame known as an Ethernet SNAP frame.

The control field that follows the SSAP field indicates the type of service and protocol format in the original LLC frame on which the Ethernet SNAP frame is based. The value of this field is fixed at hex 03 for an Ethernet SNAP frame to indicate a connectionless service unnumbered format, which is the only format supported by a SNAP frame. Thus, the first 3 bytes of the Data field in an Ethernet SNAP frame have the fixed value of hex AA:AA:03.

The Organization Code field indicates the organization that assigned the value contained in the following Ethernet Type field. This field permits compatibility with the original Ethernet frame format and Type

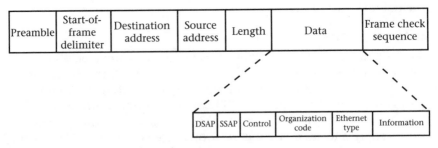

Figure 3-4 Ethernet SNAP frame format.

codes originally defined by Xerox Corporation. For example, an organization code value of hex 00-00-00 indicates that Xerox assigned the following Type field value. This enables Ethernet Type field values to match those values originally specified by Xerox when that company, in conjunction with Intel and Digital Equipment Corporation, developed the original Ethernet standard.

FRAME DETERMINATION

Due to the manner in which entries occur in the Type/Length field, it is possible for a receiving station to determine the type of frame it is receiving. This, in turn, allows the receiver to correctly interpret the values of the fields contained within the frame.

Since all Ethernet frames are similar through the Source Address field, a receiver will examine the value of the field following that field in order to determine the specific frame type. For example, if the value of the Type/Length field exceeds a 1500 decimal, the field must be a Type field and the frame is a true Ethernet frame. If the value of the 2 bytes following the Source Address field is decimal 1500 or less, the field is a Length field, and the 2 bytes following that field must be examined to determine the specific type of Ethernet frame. If the next 2 bytes have a value of hex AA-AA, the frame must be an Ethernet SNAP frame. Thus, this is how it becomes possible for a receiver to automatically determine the type of frame being transported on a network.

UTILIZATION

Ethernet uses a CSMA/CD access protocol, and stations delay themselves a random amount of time when encountering a collision. Thus, the degree of network utilization that is tolerable prior to encountering a possible undesirable level of performance is less than encountered on a deterministic network such as a token-ring LAN. The actual level of utilization that is tolerable depends on the operational environment of the LAN. For example, a network used primarily for file transfer can accept random delays associated with a high level of collisions that commonly increase in tandem with network utilization. In comparison, if your organization installed a voice over IP gateway on an Ethernet network, a high level of utilization could result in random delays that adversely affect reconstructed voice.

You will probably encounter various guidelines about when to upgrade or segment a network based upon its level of utilization. More than likely hardware vendors will propose a lower level of network utilization as a point to upgrade or segment a network than publications authored by network users. Unfortunately, there is no magic number concerning when to upgrade or segment an Ethernet network as the decision is best made based on one's application environment. This said, one general guideline is worth mentioning. Under the general guideline, you should consider upgrading or segmenting an Ethernet network if utilization often exceeds 50 percent and definitely upgrade when the level of utilization exceeds 70 percent; however, the preceding metrics are for shared media Ethernet networks. If your organization is operating a switch-based network, you should examine packet loss due to blocking when two sources attempt to transfer data to a common destination and the switch queue is full. If packet loss begins to exceed a few percent, this indicates that the connection to servers and routers on the switch should be examined for possible upgrade. Now that we understand the operation of Ethernet, we look at token-ring networks.

Token Ring

Although token-ring LANs are not as commonly used as Ethernet, they still account for approximately 10 percent of all local area networks. Thus, we examine token-ring operations in this section to become acquainted with the use of different fields in the frame as well as access control, error checking, and the flow of data between networks.

ACCESS CONTROL

Token Ring uses a special frame referred to as a *token frame* that governs access to the network. If the token bit is set to a value of 0, the token, under certain situations that will be described shortly, can be acquired by a station and turned into a frame. If the value of the token bit is 1, it is in use and a station with data to transmit can make a reservation to acquire the token. Since the token frame flows around the network in a circular manner, a station with data to transmit either directly acquires a free token or waits until one becomes available. Thus, unlike an Ethernet network where access is based on the CSMA/CD protocol, a token-ring network uses token passing as the access protocol. This eliminates the possibility of collisions as well as the need for a back-off algorithm.

UTILIZATION

Since the ability of a station to acquire a token from a frame and transmit data onto the media follows a predefined procedure, a token-ring network is a deterministic network. This means that each station with data to transmit will, at most, have to reserve a token and wait until its reservation is honored. Due to this method of access control, it's theoretically possible to run a token-ring LAN at 100 percent utilization without encountering significant throughput problems that this level of utilization would encounter on an Ethernet LAN. As a general guideline, due to the fact that not all reservations are immediately honored, a token-ring network should be segmented when utilization exceeds 90 percent.

FRAME FORMATS

A token-ring network supports three types of frames—a token frame, an abort frame, and a complete frame. Each is illustrated in Figure 3-5. The token format in Figure 3-5a provides the mechanism by which a station obtains access to the ring. Note the token consists of 3 bytes, with the Starting and Ending Delimiter fields common to each type of token-ring frame, with the access control byte providing stations with the ability to directly acquire a frame or to reserve a frame. The access control byte has 3 bits that serve as a priority indicator and 3 bits used as a reservation indication. Thus, Token Ring supports eight levels of reservation. One bit is the token bit, whose setting indicates if the token is free (0) or if it is in use (1). When the value of the token bit is set to 1, the token is transporting

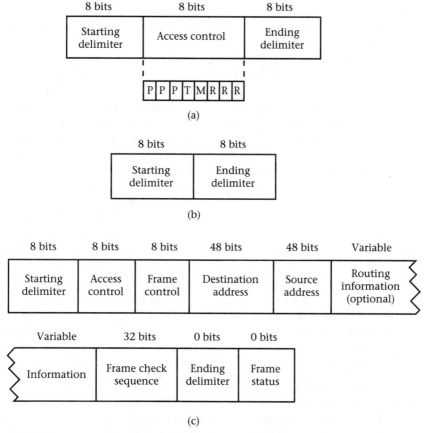

Figure 3-5 Token-ring networks support three types of frames: (*a*) token; (*b*) abort frame; and (*c*) complete frame.

information and is converted into a frame, as indicated in Figure 3-5c. The monitor bit is set by a device referred to as the active monitor, since a frame flows around the ring. This enables the active monitor to discard a frame if its monitor bit is set, which prevents a token from continuously flowing around a network if its destination is not active of if another error condition occurs. This limits the ability of a frame to reach its destination.

In the middle portion of Figure 3-5, you will note an abort token. In actuality, there is no token, since this format is defined by an ending delimiter immediately following a starting delimiter. The transmission of an abort token is used to abort a previous transmission. Since all three frame formats have common fields, let's investigate the fields in the token frame which include the fields used by the other two frame formats.

Starting/Ending Delimiters

The purpose of the starting and ending delimiters are twofold: (1) they provide synchronization since they consist of a predefined bit pattern and (2) they are used to mark the beginning and logical end of a frame which may or may not be its physical end. The latter is true because a Frame Status field follows a token frame's ending delimiter.

Both Starting and Ending delimiter fields consist of a bit pattern that includes several nondata symbols that represent code violations that cannot occur in actual data. By examining the composition of these fields, a receiver can determine if a framing error occurred as the symbols used for each field repeat. Thus, an electrical disturbance of short duration will allow a receiver to recognize an error occurred in the framing of the frame.

One special bit position in the ending Delimiter field warrants discussion. That bit position is the last bit in the field which is referred to as the E or error bit. As a frame flows around the ring, each station on the fly checks the transmission for errors. To do so, the station computes a CRC and compares the locally computed CRC to the CRC in the Frame Check Sequence field. If the two do not match, the station that first detects an error sets the E bit to a value of 1. Since stations keep track of the number of times they set the E bit to a value of 1, it becomes possible to use this information as a guide for possibly locating cable problems. For example, assume one station on a token-ring LAN accounted for a very high percentage of E bit settings in a network. Since tokens and frames flow downstream, this indicates that the cabling of the station's nearest upstream neighbor to the network should be checked as a loose connector or crimped cable could be the cause of the E bit settings.

Access Control Field

As illustrated in Figure 3-5, the Access Control field consists of four subfields. The first 3 bits in the Access Control field represent the Priority subfield whose value can range from 0 to 7. Workstations on a token-ring network have a default priority of 3, while bridges have a default priority of 4.

The last subfield, which consists of 3 bytes, is the Reservation field. To reserve a token, a station attempts to insert its priority value into the Reservation field. Unless another station with a higher priority bumps the requesting station's reservation assignment, the reservation is honored and the requesting station obtains the token. If the token bit is set to 1, this indicates that the token is in use and was converted into a frame.

A station that has data to transmit at a given priority can use any available token that has a priority level either equal to or less than the priority level of the frame to be transmitted. When a token of equal or lower priority is not available, the station requiring a token can reserve a token of the required priority through the use of the reservation bits. In doing so, the station must comply with two rules: (1) if a passing token has a higher level desired by the workstation, the station cannot alter the contents of the reservation field; (2) if the reservation bits are not set or if they indicate a lower priority than that required by the requesting station, the station can now set the reservation bits to the required priority level.

When a frame is transmitted on a token-ring network, it is copied by its destination, but flows back to the originating station with a Frame Copy bit in its Frame Status field set to indicate it was received by the destination. When the frame returns to the originator, the reservation bits are checked. If the bits have a nonzero value, a new token is pending. Then the originating station removes the frame from the network and generates a nonzero priority token. The actual value in the priority field is based upon the priority used by the station in generating the recently transmitted frame, the reservation bit settings received upon the return of the frame, and any stored priority from the station receiving the returned frame.

Now that we have discussed the priority and reservation fields, the two additional subfields left in the Access Control field are the monitor bit and token. As previously noted, the monitor bit is set by the active monitor to prevent frames from endlessly circulating a token-ring network. The active monitor is selected by each station broadcasting its layer 2 media access control (Mac) address every 7 seconds. The station with the highest Mac address becomes the active monitor while all other stations become standby monitors. Thus, if a user turns off his or her workstation (representing the active monitor on the network), within 7 seconds a standby monitor would take over. Since we previously discussed the use of the Token Bit field, we can now move on to the next field in a token-ring frame.

Frame Control Field
The Frame Control field identifies the type of frame flowing on the network. In this field are the setting of the Frame Control information and responses on an LLC frame transporting data. Within the Frame Control field, 3 bits are used to identify various types of Mac frames. For example,

values can indicate a request to remove a station from the ring, a Beacon condition, Claim token, ring purge, and active monitor present and standby monitor present frames. Many of these functions are related to one another. For example, the active monitor issues an *active monitor present* (AMP) Mac frame every 7 seconds to inform the standby monitors that the active monitor is operational. If the active monitor fails to issue an AMP within the prescribed time interval, the standby monitor with the highest network address will continuously issue claim token Mac frames in an attempt to become the active monitor. Once a standby monitor becomes the active monitor, it issues a Purge Mac frame. A Beacon frame indicates a serious problem on the network. For example, if a station fails to receive a frame or token, it transmits a Beacon Mac frame. If this frame can flow back to the originator, it then removes itself from the ring and performs a series of tests to determine if it should attempt to reinsert itself into the ring.

Destination and Source Address Fields

Token Ring's Destination and Source Address fields are similar to those used by Ethernet. That is, each is 48 bits in length. The Destination Address has a 1-bit *individual/group* (I/G) and a 1-bit *universal/locally administrated* (U/L) subfield. Token-ring addresses are similar to Ethernet addresses in that they are administrated by the IEEE, with the first 3 bytes indicating the manufacturer ID and the next 3 bytes indicating a specific unit manufactured by a vendor.

Routing Information Field

The Routing Information field (RIF) is optional and is included when bridging is employed by a token-ring network to interconnect networks. When bridging occurs, the RIF frame will include the ring number and bridge number of up to eight distinct ring/bridge connections from source to destination. To determine the actual route for data transfer, a token-ring station issues a discovery frame that is forwarded by all bridges onto all paths other than the path on which the frame was received. As the frame is forwarded toward its destination, the ring number and bridge number traversed are entered into the RIF field. Upon receipt of the first discovery frame, the destination reverses the path to form a response. Up to 16 bridges can be used to join any two rings in a token-ring network.

Information Field

The Information field has a maximum length which depends upon the ring speed. A 4-Mbps network supports an Information field up to 4.5 bytes, while a 16-Mbps network supports an Information field up to 18 kB. The minimum length of the Information field is 1 byte, which results in a minimum frame length of 22 bytes due to the 21 bytes of overhead in a frame.

Frame Check Sequence Field

This field functions in a similar manner to Ethernet; however, the first station to note a CRC error sets the E bit in the Ending Delimiter field which functions as a mechanism to note cabling problems since the number of E bit settings by each workstation can be retrieved.

Frame Status Field

The Frame Status field indicates the results of the circulation of a frame around a ring back to the station that initiated the frame. This field has two distinct subfields that are repeated since the field resides outside the CRC checking area. One subfield denotes whether the destination address was recognized. The second subfield indicated whether the frame was copied at its destination. Thus, it is possible to note that a frame reached its destination but was not copied off the network, with the most likely cause being an E bit set to 1 which indicates a CRC error.

WAN Metrics

Since most commonly used types of wide area network (WAN) transmission facilities only provide a fraction of the bandwidth obtainable on a LAN, a majority of performance problems can be expected to occur on WAN transmission facilities. Thus, the first portion of this section looks at the flow of data on a WAN transmission facility, including an examination of the composition of the workhorse of WAN connections, the T1 circuit. Once this is accomplished, we discuss and describe encapsulation methods used to transmit data over WAN transmission facilities and methods you can consider to enhance the transmission efficiency associated with moving information over a wide area network.

The T1 Circuit

The T1 circuit is the most commonly used wide area network transmission facility for interconnecting geographically separated routers. The design of the T1 circuit was based on a desire to reduce cable congestion in urban areas and dates to the 1960s when the first T1 circuits were installed by communications carriers. That design was based on multiplying 24 voice circuits onto a copper wire. Since each voice circuit used *pulse code modulation* (PCM) voice digitization, a T1 circuit was designed to transport a series of 8 bits from each of 24 voice channels 8000 times per second, with the rate of 8000 samples per second the sampling rate used by PCM. To provide a synchronization capability between transmitter and receiver, a framing bit is added to each frame transporting a sequence of 24 8-bit bytes. Figure 3-6 illustrates the formation of a standard T1 frame.

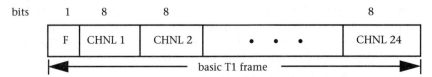

Figure 3-6 The basic T1 frame repeats 8000 times per second.

CHANNEL RATE FOR DATA

In Figure 3-6, note that the basic T1 frame length is 8 × 24 + 1 or 193 bits and repeats 8000 times per second. Each of the 24 voice channels is referred to as a digital signal level 0 (DS0) channel. Since each DS0 consists of 8 bits repeated 8000 times per second, each channel appears capable of transporting data at 64 kbps (8 bits/sample × 8000 samples per second). While this is usually true, there are some exceptions to this, especially when a T1 circuit's last mile is routed over an old copper access line that has one or more repeaters, and the central office serving your organization does not have the latest equipment to provide repeaters with a minimum 1's density. Under such circumstances, equipment used by the communications carrier sets the seventh bit in the sixth and twelfth frame to a binary 1 to ensure that repeaters have a sufficient number of 1 bits, referred to as a one's density, to stay in synchronization with the data stream. While this technique, which is referred to as *binary 7 zero suppression* (B7ZS) does not adversely affect received voice, it would adversely affect data. For this reason, 1 bit in a DS0 on older access lines cannot be used for data transmission, limiting the data transfer capability of the DS0 to 7/8 × 64 kbps or 56 kbps. This also explains why an organization located in one area may be able to obtain a 64-kbps access line while an office in another location may only be able to obtain a 56-kbps access line when they request a lower-speed digital leased line.

Returning to Figure 3-6, if we assume that a newer technique, referred to as B8ZS, is used to provide repeaters with a minimum 1's density, then 1's are generated by replacing a byte consisting of a sequence of eight zeros with bipolar violations that are removed at the other end of the access line. This technique does not require the use of a bit in any byte, and enables a data transmission rate of 64 kbps to be obtained on each DS0. Thus, the data rate obtainable on a T1 where the metallic access line uses B8ZS coding or on a fiber access line that does not have repeaters becomes 64 kbps × 24, or 1.536 Mbps, with 8000 bytes used for framing.

TYPES OF T1 CIRCUITS

Two basic types of T1 circuits are available: channelized and nonchannelized. A *channelized* T1 is structured by the communications carrier to transport 24 separate DS0s and is commonly used to connect a PBX to the voice packet-switched data network (PSDN). In comparison, a *nonchannel-ized* T1 circuit is used to provide a transmission path for end-user equip-ment that normally bypasses the PSDN, such as connecting geographically separated routers.

FRAMING FORMATS

Two popular types of T1 framing formats are D4 and EFS.

D4 Framing

Under D4 framing, the basic frame of 193 bits is formed into what is referred to as a *superframe*. This superframe consists of 12 frames, with the framing bit altered to enable the receiving device to maintain syn-chronization with the received data. That receiving device and the device that forms the framing bits are referred to as *service channel units* (CSUs). Figure 3-7 illustrates the relationship between a pair of routers, CSUs, and a T1 circuit used to interconnect two geographically separated networks.

The D4 superframe was primarily used as the T1 framing format during the 1970s through the mid-1980s, and was gradually replaced by a newer framing format referred to as the *extended superframe* (ESF). Under D4 framing, the repeating pattern formed by CSUs is illustrated in Figure 3-8. Note that the odd numbered frames provide the sequence 1010..., while the even numbered frames provide the alternating sequence 000111.... By counting the repeating pattern formed by the framing bit, equipment always knows where a specific DS0 signal is in the bit stream. For example, assume that the received frame bit pattern for the last four frames is 0010. From Figure 3-8, the next frame that will be received must be F7, since the 0010 pattern only occurs in frame bits 3 through 6.

Although D4 framing provides a mechanism for synchronization, it only provides an indirect measurement of line quality through the moni-toring of frame bits. A second limitation of D4 is that it lacks the ability to provide a communications capability between devices without using data

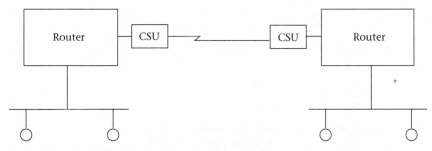

Figure 3-7   Networking using a T1 transmission facility.

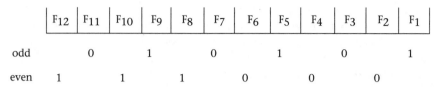

F_{12}	F_{11}	F_{10}	F_9	F_8	F_7	F_6	F_5	F_4	F_3	F_2	F_1
odd		0		1		0		1		0		1
even	1		1		1		0		0		0	

Figure 3-8 D4 superframe synchronization pattern.

bits from the channel. Perhaps as a result of these problems, ESF framing was developed.

ESF Framing

ESF framing extends the D4 superframe to 24 consecutive frame bits (F1 through F24). The sequence of 24 framing bits are subdivided into three types of bits: (1) d bits that transport data between two devices via framing bits, (2) c cyclic redundancy bits that enable an error rate to be computed, and (3) F framing bits. Table 3-1 indicates the ESF framing pattern.

Table 3-1 ESF Framing Pattern

Frame	Bit Composition	Frame	Bit Composition
1	d	13	d
2	c1	14	c4
3	d	15	d
4	0	16	0
5	d	17	d
6	c2	18	c5
7	d	19	d
8	0	20	1
9	d	21	d
10	c3	22	c6
11	d	23	d
12	1	24	1

Note: d represents data bits. c1 through c6 represents CRC-6 bits. 001011 represents actual framing.

In examining the entries in Table 3-1 note that since 12 d bits are used to communicate between devices via framing bits, the data rate becomes 12/24 × 8,000 bps, or 4000 bps. The protocol used for d-bit transmission is a variation of *higher-level data link control* (HDLC) referred to as BX.25. The framing bits, which are indicated by 0's and 1's in Table 3-1, represent the 8-bit sequence 001011, which repeats 6/24 × 8000 or 2000 times per second. Finally, the c bits, denoted as c1 through c6, in Table 3-1 are used to form a CRC-6 check sum. The CRC-6 is recomputed by receiving equipment to provide a measurement of the error rate on a T1 circuit and represents 2 kbps of the 8-kbps framing rate. Unlike a CRC used by many protocols as an indication for the receiver to request the retransmission of a frame, a mismatch between a locally computed CRC-6 and the CRC-6 transported in ESF framing is limited to computing a line error rate.

Since a router does not directly connect to a T1 circuit, the command interface will not normally display CRC-6 error rate information. An exception to this is a line interface, which includes a built-in CSU. When you use this type of hardware, it then becomes possible to use the router's show command to display the CRC-6 error rate, as we note in Chapter 4. If your router does not have a built-in CSU, you can obtain related error information based on the protocol used to transmit data over the WAN. Thus, let's turn our attention to this topic.

Serial Encapsulation

The serial interface on a Cisco router can support a variety of WAN transmission protocols. Some of those protocols may require special hardware to operate at a high data rate. Table 3-2 lists the serial encapsulation methods supported by a router the author was using when he wrote this book.

The specific method of serial encapsulation is set using the encapsulation subcommand, followed by a keyword that defines a specific encapsulation method. Thus, the format of the command is

```
encapsulation encapsulation-type
```

where the encapsulation-type is a keyword in the left column of Table 3-2.

By specifying a particular type of encapsulation method for use on a T1 transmission facility, you can obtain an indirect measurement of the quality of the T1 circuit by monitoring the serial interface, because a Cisco router keeps track of CRC errors occurring in terms of the line encapsulation method used. As we note in Chapter 4, from the use of the show interfaces command, we can display a count of CRC mismatches as well as count associated frame errors, overrun conditions, and similar problem areas that can be used to determine if the inability of a packet to flow from source to destination is due to a transmission line problem or

Table 3-2 Common Cisco Router Encapsulation Methods

Router command entry	Description
atm-dxi	ATM-DXI encapsulation
bstun	Block serial tunneling
frame-relay	Frame relay
hdlc	Serial higher-level data-link control
lapb	Link access protocol B (E.25 level 2)
ppp	Point-to-point protocol
sdlc	Synchronous data-link control (SDLC)
sdlc-primary	SDLC (primary)
sdlc-secondary	SDLC (secondary)
smds	Switched megabit data service (SMDS)

the inability of the router to service arriving data in a timely manner. Thus, examining the reason for a packet's inability to flow end to end can provide clues about different methods to resolve a recurring problem.

The CRC in the encapsulation method should not be confused with the CRC in a T1 line ESF framing format. Although they are created in a similar manner via a polynomial, the polynomials differ, with most WAN encapsulation methods using either a 16-bit or 32-bit CRC in comparison to the T1 6-bit CRC. A second difference is the reaction to a CRC error. Here the encapsulated protocol will on detection of a CRC error issue a request to the originator to retransmit the packet. In comparison, a CRC error occurring on a T1 using ESF framing is simply recorded as an error count. Now that we understand how to use serial encapsulation CRC errors to obtain an indirect measurement of the quality of a wide area network transmission facility, we conclude our discussion of WANs by focusing on how we can prioritize traffic routed over serial ports.

Priority Output Queuing

Although Cisco routers support priority queuing for all interfaces, because serial interfaces normally operate at a fraction of the rate of LANs, this feature is best used on relatively low bandwidth serial ports. The rationale behind priority output queuing is to provide LAN administrators and network managers with a mechanism to differentiate between different protocols or applications with respect to their eventual transmission via a serial port. The term *eventual* is used because the use of priority output queuing results in the assignment of protocols or applications to one of four types of queues. Depending upon the assigned queue, the protocol or application first flows into the queue where it waits for the extraction and placement onto the serial interface, with the actual time spent waiting dependent on the priority queue specified and other activity flowing through the router.

Cisco routers support four types of priority output queues: high, medium, normal, and low, with all unclassified packets by default other than keep-alives assigned to the normal queue. Keep-alives originated by a router are extremely important and are assigned to the high-priority queue.

Priority Assignment

Two basic methods are available for the assignment of a specific priority. First, you can assign a priority based on a protocol where you can specify a specific application since you can include a TCP or UDP port to equate an application with a priority. A second method is to assign a priority based on the interface from which a packet entered a router. In this section we examine both methods as well as how to assign a default priority.

PRIORITY BASED ON PROTOCOL

You can use the `priority-list` command to establish priority output queuing based on the protocol transported in a packet. The format of this command is shown below:

```
priority-list list protocol protocol-name queue-keyword [arguments]
```

where the argument list is an arbitrary integer between 1 and 10 used to identify the list you are creating. The keyword `priority-list` identifies the command as a global configuration command for setting queuing priorities. The argument `protocol-name` specifies the protocol to be associated with a queue. In an IP environment you would specify IP as the protocol. The argument `queue-keyword` is the priority queue and would be replaced by high, medium, normal, or low. Last, but not least, the optional arguments let you specify the assignment of a protocol into a queue based on the number of bytes in a packet, the IP access-list number previously configured for an interface, or the TCP or UDP port number in a datagram. Table 3-3 lists the optional arguments you can specify in a `priority-list` global command.

Table 3-3 Optional `priority-list` Global Command Arguments

Argument	Description
`gt byte-count`	Assigns a priority level when a packet's length, including layer 2 encapsulation, exceeds the specified byte count.
`lt byte-count`	Assigns a priority level when a packet's length, including layer 2 encapsulation, exceeds the specified byte count.
`bridge list list-number`	Assigns a priority level to bridge traffic based on the Ethernet type code access-list number assigned by an access-list global command.
`list list-number`	Assigns a priority level based on an IP access-list number assigned by an access-group list interface command.
`tcp port`	Assigns a priority level based on a TCP segment originating from or destined to the specified port.
`udp port`	Assigns a priority level based on a UDP datagram originating from or destined to the specified port.

In examining the entries in Table 3-3 you might not be aware of the fact that some arguments provide the answer to many routing problems. For example, assume your organization is considering implementing real-time fax over IP, an application that is very time-dependent. If your organization is evaluating several products, it is highly likely that each product uses a different port number since at the time this book was written, there was no standard governing the port number for fax over IP applications. Thus, if you wanted to prioritize real-time fax, you would have to enter a series of `priority-list` commands. As an alternative, you could scan the manual for each product and determine the largest length UDP packet used to convey real-time fax. Since just about all real-time fax over IP applications use very short datagrams, you could then use one `priority-list` command. Assuming the longest packet is 80 bytes, you could then use the following command to assign all packets with a length less than 81 bytes to the high-priority queue:

```
priority-list 1 protocol ip high lt 81
```

If you prefer to be more specific, let's assume two real-time fax over IP applications use UDP ports 5758 and 6132. Then you could use the following statements to assign specific applications based on their port numbers instead of packet length to high-priority queues:

```
priority-list 1 protocol ip high udp 5758
priority-list 1 protocol ip high udp 6732
```

Now that we understand the assignment of priority based on protocol type, let's turn our attention to how we can assign a priority based on the interface through which packets entered a router.

PRIORITY BASED UPON INTERFACE

We can use a modified version of the `priority-list` global configuration command to establish queuing priorities based on the interface a packet used to enter a router. This version of the `priority-list` command can simplify the setting of queue priorities if you configure your network such that time-dependent applications reside on a specific interface. For example, Figure 3-9 illustrates the use of a voice gateway connected to a PBX and LAN, with the LAN in turn connected to port E0 on the router. In this example, port E1 is connected to a LAN that supports various data applications such as an FTP server and a Web server as well as individual workstations. Thus, any mechanism that permits you to prioritize traffic entering the router on interface E0 for priority queuing onto serial port S0 in effect permits you to prioritize voice over IP traffic.

To establish queuing priorities based on the interface a packet used to enter a router requires the use of the `priority-list` global command

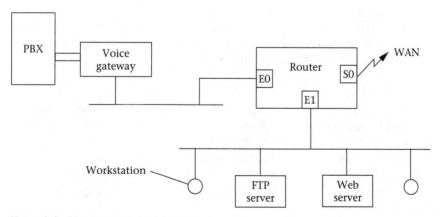

Figure 3-9   Using a voice over IP gateway.

with the keyword `interface`. The format of this command is indicated here:

```
priority-list list interface interface-name queue-keyword
```

where `list` is the same as a `priority-list` by protocol command. That is, it is an arbitrary integer between 1 and 10 that identifies the priority list.

The argument `interface-name` identifies the specific interface, such as E0, E1, and so on. Similar to establishing a priority list based on protocol, the argument `queue-keyword` identifies the priority queue name such as high, medium, normal, or low.

Returning to our example in Figure 3-9, the following statement uses the `priority-list interface` command to set any packets entering the router on `interface` e0 to a high priority:

```
priority-list 1 interface ethernet0 high
```

Now that we understand assigning priority output queues based on the interface through which a packet entered a router, let's continue our examination of priority queuing with how default priorities are established.

ASSIGNING A DEFAULT PRIORITY

As you might expect, the `priority-list` command is also used to assign a default priority queue for packets that do not match other entries in a priority list. This version of the `priority-list` global command includes the keyword `default` and its format is shown here:

```
priority-list list default queue-keyword
```

where `list` is an integer between 1 and 10 that defines a specific priority list and the argument `queue-keyword` denotes the specific default queue such as high, medium, normal, and low.

To illustrate the use of this command, assume you want to set any packet without an assigned priority to the low-priority queue. To do this, you enter the following command:

```
priority-list 1 default low
```

Although we now understand how we can assign packets to queues, we have not considered until now the fact that such queues are finite. Thus, we need a mechanism to adjust the size of priority queues based on our operational requirements. That mechanism can be obtained through the use of another version of the `priority-list` global configuration command which includes the keyword `queue-limit`. Thus, let's look at this command.

ADJUSTING PRIORITY QUEUE LENGTHS

When you use a `priority-list` command, you associate packets based on protocol or the interface on which they arrived to specify queues. Those queues have a default length that you can adjust through the use of the keyword `queue-limit` in a `priority-list` global command. By default, the `queue-limit` for high-, medium-, normal-, and low-priority queues are 20, 40, 60, and 80 packets. If a priority queue overflows, excess packets flow to the great bit bucket in the sky, a condition that may not be satisfactory, especially because the high-priority queue has by default the lowest queue limit value. To specify the maximum number of packets that can reside in each priority queue, you would use the keyword `queue-limit` in a `priority-list` global command. The format of this command is shown here:

```
priority-list list queue-limit high limit medium limit normal limit low limit
```

where `list` is an integer between 1 and 10 that identifies the priority list and each limit (high, medium, normal, and low) identifies the revised length of a queue in terms of packets.

For example, assume you want to revise the default of 20 packets for the high queue to 40, with the default values for the other queues being retained. Then you would enter the following command:

```
priority-list 1 queue-limit 40 40 60 80
```

ASSIGNING A PRIORITY LIST

Until now, we examined the creation of a priority list but have not discussed how we can assign the list to a specific interface. Thus, let's conclude this chapter by looking at this topic and the relationship of an `interface` queue to a priority queue.

Once you create a priority list, you would use the `priority-group` `interface` command to assign a priority list to an interface. The format of the `priority-group` command is shown here:

```
priority-group list
```

where `list` once again represents an integer between 1 and 10 that identifies a priority list. To illustrate the use of the `priority-group` command, let's assume we want to assign packets entering interface S0 in Figure 3-9 to a high-priority queue while all other packets are assigned by default to a low-priority queue. Let's further assume that we want to be able to store up to 60 packets in the high-priority queue and will assign priority queuing to serial port 0. Based on this information, we would enter the following commands:

```
interface serial0
priority-group 1
 :
 :
priority-list 1 interface 30 high
priority-list 1 default low
priority-list 1 queue-limit 60 40 60 80
 :
```

In concluding our discussion of priority queues we would be remiss if we did not discuss the hold queue associated with each interface. Thus, we conclude this chapter with this topic.

THE INTERFACE HOLD QUEUE

Each network interface has a queue that represents a temporary storage area. In actuality, memory is split to store inbound and outbound packets, thus a network interface has two queues. The input queue is a temporary storage area into which packets arriving via a LAN or serial interface are placed. If the router is busy performing other operations, the input queue alleviates the discarding of a packet. The output queue is the inverse of the input queue. That is, instead of placing a packet directly onto the media, the router stores the packet in an output queue. Then, if a collision just occurred, current activity on an Ethernet network is noted, or if another ongoing operation prevents the direct placement of a packet onto the media, the packet is stored in the output queue until it can be placed onto the media.

Both the input and output queues are finite in length, with the default input queue length set to 75 packets, while the output queue length is set to 40 packets. If either queue is full when a packet arrives, the packet is discarded. You can alter the hold queue length with the use of the `hold-queue` interface command. The format of this command is shown here:

```
hold-queue length [in|out]
```

Although we examine different router interfaces in Chapter 4 and can determine the number of dropped packets and use that metric to consider adjusting the output queue, the output queue is not applicable if we are using priority queuing. When priority queuing is employed, you set the length of four output queues using the `priority-list` global configuration command. Since you are now specifying the output queue with the `priority-list` command, you cannot use the `hold-queue` command.

CHAPTER 4

Accessing External Performance Measurements

This chapter provides information about different methods that can be used to access various router performance measurements. Since the overall level of performance of a router depends on both its external interfaces and internal operation, it is important to consider both. However, to better focus on the different performance measurements, those measurements are divided into two distinct categories: internal and external. This chapter covers external performance measurements, by examining how to observe the state of router interfaces and determine how LANs and WANs connected to a router are operating. Since the operational state of networks connected to router interfaces have a direct bearing on the ability of the device to transfer information, the state of router interfaces is an important area to consider. In doing so, we look at the "Swiss knife" of observing performance measurements, the show command and its interfaces subcommands.

Examining the Interface Status

This section examines the use of the show interfaces command. This command can be used to display the status of a specific interface or can be used to display information about each router interface.

Although a Cisco router can support many different types of interfaces, we focus on four specific types in this section: Ethernet, Fast Ethernet, Token Ring, and serial. Since such interfaces probably represent 95 percent or more of all router interfaces, we will not examine less frequently employed interfaces such as 100VG-AnyLAN. However, as we examine these four interfaces, note that the resulting display for each interface is essentially the same, even when an entry for one type of interface is impossible. An example of the latter is the inclusion of an entry for collisions when we display the status of a token-ring interface, even though a token-ring network cannot have collisions. Cisco routers use some entries in the display of the status of an interface for different purposes, although the field label remains the same, such as the field labeled Collisions that is displayed when you show the status of a token-ring interface. Now that we have a general understanding of the interfaces command, let's examine the use of the show interfaces command, including its options.

The show interfaces **Command**

The show interfaces EXEC command lets you display various statistics and general information for a specific interface or all interfaces on a router. The general format of this command is shown here:

```
show interfaces [interface-type#][accounting]
```

The interface-type# defines a specific interface and its location in the router. If the interface is built into the router, the type# may be simply a 0 or 1, whereas on a series 7500 router the type# can represent the slot/port-adapter/port location.

If you do not specify an interface-type#, statistics on all interfaces are displayed. If you include the option accounting, the result displays the number of packets of each protocol type transferred through an interface.

Table 4-1 lists the interface-type values supported by different types of Cisco routers. Note that many keywords of popular interfaces, such as Ethernet, Fast Ethernet, and serial are supported across all Cisco products.

Since you can abbreviate commands, some articles refer to a show interface command that is used to display information about a specific interface. Although Cisco 7500 series routers do support this command, it can really be considered as an abbreviation of the keyword interfaces. Depending on the model of the router in use, you may encounter some interesting capabilities not available on other routers. For example, if you enter the command show interfaces fastethernet on a Cisco 7200 series router without specifying a particular slot/port argument, you obtain a listing of all interfaces. Similarly, entering show interfaces tokenring or show interfaces serial also results in a display of information about all router interfaces, which may not be your intention. Now that we understand the show interfaces command, let's put it to use and view the status of several specific types of router interfaces.

Table 4-1 Interface Types

Keyword	Description
async	asynchronous
atm	Asynchronous Transfer Mode*
bri0	Basic Rate Interface (ISDN)
e1	European e1 circuit operating at 2.048 Mbps†
ethernet	Ethernet 10 Mbps
fastethernet	Fast Ethernet 100 Mbps
fddi	Fiber Data Distributed interface
hssi	High Speed Serial Interface
loopback	loopback
null	null interface used for testing
serial	serial interface
t1	T1 circuit operating at 1.544 Mbps†
token	Token-Ring‡
tokenring	Token-Ring

*4500 series and 7000 family routers
†4000 series and 7000 family routers
‡4000 series routers

VIEWING AN ETHERNET INTERFACE

Since 10BASE-T is still one of the most popular types of LAN interfaces, if not *the* most popular, we begin our examination of interface information with the Ethernet interface. Figure 4-1 illustrates the use of the show interfaces ethernet command to display the status of a specific Ethernet interface.

We noted previously that, in general, Cisco routers display a common set of items when you use the show interfaces command, regardless of the type of interface you wish to display information about. Thus, to understand the display shown in Figure 4-1, which can serve as a foundation for examining additional types of router interfaces, let's examine each of the fields in the display in detail.

Figure 4-1   Displaying information about the status of an Ethernet interface.

```
Router#show interface ethernet4/1/1
Ethernet4/1/1 is up, line protocol is up
  Hardware is cxBus Ethernet, address is 0010.7936.a889 (bia 0010.7936.a889)
  Internet address is 205.131.176.1/24
  MTU 1500 bytes, BW 10000 Kbit, DLY 1000 usec,
     reliability 255/255, txload 3/255, rxload 39/255
  Encapsulation ARPA, loopback not set
  Keepalive set (10 sec)
  ARP type: ARPA, ARP Timeout 04:00:00
  Last input 00:00:02, output 00:00:07, output hang never
  Last clearing of "show interface" counters 1w2d
  Queuing strategy: fifo
  Output queue 0/40, 63 drops; input queue 0/75, 0 drops
  5 minute input rate 1540000 bits/sec, 227 packets/sec
  5 minute output rate 149000 bits/sec, 201 packets/sec
     67474772 packets input, 2918914911 bytes, 0 no buffer
     Received 483898 broadcasts, 0 runts, 0 giants, 0 throttles
     80 input errors, 80 CRC, 0 frame, 0 overrun, 0 ignored
     0 input packets with dribble condition detected
     61027904 packets output, 1487025680 bytes, 0 underruns
     1035 output errors, 1035 collisions, 0 interface resets
     0 babbles, 0 late collision, 1966186 deferred
     0 lost carrier, 0 no carrier
     0 output buffer failures, 0 output buffers swapped out
```

Interface and Live Status

In Figure 4-1 the display indicates that the hardware interface is active and the software process that handles the line protocol believes the interface is usable. If the hardware interface was taken down by a router operator, the first field would display the message *is administratively down*: If the router receives over 5000 errors within a keepalive interval, the term *Disabled* will appear in this field to show that the router automatically disabled the interface. The Line protocol field also displays one of the three previously mentioned descriptions: up, down, or administratively down. If the field entry is up, it indicates the software process that handles the line protocol believes the interface is usable since it is receiving keepalives. A *keepalive* is a signal placed on a line every so often which indicates that the device on one end of a connection is still alive and kicking. The goal of a keepalive is so other devices can determine if an idle connection is still active or alive. For an Ethernet interface the default value of keepalives is 10 s. As we will note shortly, the setting of keepalives is obtained through the use of the show interfaces command for a particular interface. You can change the keepalives setting through the use of the keepalive interface command whose format is shown here:

```
keepalive seconds
```

Hardware

The Hardware field informs you of the type of hardware that provides the interface. In Figure 4-1 the hardware is a *Cisco Extended Bus* (CxBus) Ethernet, a 533-Mbps data bus for interface processors. Thus, the Hardware field informs us that a high-speed CxBus interface processor is used for supporting the Ethernet connection. Also note that the Display field includes the Mac address of the interface. As we noted in Chapter 3, Mac addresses are 48 bits in length. The address shown in Figure 4-1 consists of 12 hex digits, which is 48 bits. Since the first 24 bits of a Mac address represent the manufacturer ID, hex 00-10-79 is the identification assigned by the IEEE to Cisco.

Internet Address

If an interface is configured for IP routing, it is assigned an Internet address. That address is followed by its subnet mask. In Figure 4-1 the IP address is 205.131.176.1. The slash (/) 24 indicates that the first 24 bits of the address represent the network, which is equivalent to a subnet mask of 255.255.255.0.

MTU

The maximum transmission unit (MTU) indicates the maximum number of bytes that the Information field of the protocol operating on the interface supports. Since the maximum length of the Ethernet frame's Information field is 1500 bytes, its MTU is shown as 1500 bytes. For just about all Ethernet applications, the default MTU of 1500 bytes should be sufficient. For Token Ring, the default MTU value is 8192 bytes; however, you should note that in RFC 1191 MTU values of 17,914 for 16-Mbps Token Ring and 4464 bytes for 4-Mbps Token Ring are recommended.

The minimum MTU is 64 bytes and the maximum value is 65,535 bytes. If an IP datagram exceeds the maximum MTU, it will be fragmented, which adds to overhead since each resulting datagram contains its own header. While you normally do not have to worry about the overhead associated with fragmentation on a high-speed LAN connection, it can be a more serious problem on a relatively low-speed serial connection. You can change the default MTU by using the `MTU interface` command whose format is shown below:

```
mtu bytes
```

where the number of bytes can range from 64 to 65,535.

BW

The bandwidth (BW) of an interface actually refers to the operating rate of the interface in kilobits per second. Since Ethernet operates at 10 Mbps, the BW value is shown as 10,000 kb.

You can use the `bandwidth` command to set an informational bandwidth value, which is not actually used to adjust the bandwidth of an interface because for certain types of media, such as Ethernet, the bandwidth is fixed. For other media, such as a serial line, you normally adjust hardware to adjust its operating rate, for example, by setting a different clock rate on a DSU/CSU to increase or decrease the operating rate of the serial interface. Thus, the primary purpose of the bandwidth command is to communicate the current bandwidth to the higher-layer protocol.

You can set the bandwidth value via the following command format, where kilobits indicate the intended bandwidth in kilobits per second.

```
bandwidth kilobits
```

DLY

This field indicates the delay of the interface in microseconds. For Ethernet the delay (DLY) is 1000 s. You can set a delay value for an interface through the use of the delay interface command. The format of this command is shown here:

```
delay tens-of-microseconds
```

Reliability

The Reliability field indicates the reliability of the interface as a fraction of 255. The value displayed in this field is computed by an exponential average over a 5-min period. Since the Ethernet interface computes a CRC for each frame, the reliability is based upon a CRC error rate and not a bit error rate. In Figure 4-1, a reliability of 255/255 indicates that for the 5-min period the interface is 100 percent reliable.

While there is no reliability command, an important command to consider using periodically is the clear counters EXEC command. The function of this command is to clear or reset the interface counters. The general format of the command depends upon the router being used. The second format shown here is for Cisco 7000 series products:

```
clear counters [type number]
clear counters [type slot/port]
```

where type indicates a specific interface type. If you do not specify a specific interface, counters for all interfaces will be cleared.

Load

Both transmit and receive loading on the interface are displayed as a fraction of 255. Similar to the Reliability field, the Load field is computed as an exponential average over a 5-min period. From Figure 4-1 the transmit (txload) load is indicated as 3/255 and the receive (rxload) load is shown as 39/255. Since Ethernet operates at 10 Mbps, you can obtain a general indication of the activity of the interface by multiplying the operating rate by each fraction. This is because each Ethernet frame has at least 26 overhead bytes and when an Information field is less than 45 bytes, it results in PAD characters added to the Information field.

Encapsulation

This field indicates the encapsulation method assigned to the interface. In Figure 4-1 the encapsulation method is shown as ARPA, which is the standard Ethernet version 2.0 encapsulation method. Other encapsulation methods can include the keyword iso1 for IEEE 802.3 Ethernet and the keyword snap (subnetwork access protocol) frame variation of the IEEE 802.3 frame.

Loopback

The Loopback field indicates whether or not the interface is in a loopback mode of operations. If loopback is set, this explains a common problem that occurs when a technician places an interface into loopback for testing during the evening and forgets to reset the loopback, resulting in some interesting calls to the control center the next morning.

You can use the `loopback interface` configuration command to set an interface into its loopback mode of operation. The `loopback` command has no parameters and you should use the `no loopback` command to remove or disable loopback. The following example illustrates the setting of an Ethernet interface into a loopback mode.

```
interface ethernet4/1/1
loopback
```

You can view the state of loopbacks by using the `show interfaces loopback EXEC` command. If your router has a large number of interfaces and your technicians perform periodic testing, it is a good idea to use that command early in the morning to avoid unnecessary problems.

ARP Type

This field indicates the type of address resolution protocol (ARP) assigned. In an IP environment the ARP type is ARPA. By default the ARPA keyword is used with an Ethernet interface to specify ARP encapsulation on an IP interface. You can change the encapsulation to either HP Probe or SNAP via the use of the `arp interface` command whose format is shown here:

```
arp {arpa|probe|snap}
```

Note that HP Probe is used by IOS to attempt to resolve an IEEE 802.3 or Ethernet local data-link address. You would set the ARP type to `probe` to enable one or more router interfaces to communicate transparently with HP IEEE 802.3 hosts that use an address resolution technique referred to as *virtual address request and reply.*

ARP Time-Out
This field indicates the length of time an ARP entry will be retained in cache before being purged when inactive. The default value of ARP time-out is 4 h, which is shown in Figure 4-1.

You can adjust the length of time an ARP cache entry will stay in cache by using the `arp timeout` command. The format of that command is shown here:

```
arp timeout seconds
```

Last Input and Output
This field indicates the number of hours, minutes, and seconds since the last packet or frame was successfully received or transmitted by the interface. You can use the value in this field to determine if an active interface is still alive or when a dead interface failed. In terms of the former, entering a second `show interfaces` command 10 s or 1 min after the prior command would indicate a new last input for the interface, which would also indicate that if a problem is occurring, it is not due to an inability to receive packets. For example, in Figure 4-1 the last successful input occurred 2 s ago. If we wait a few seconds and issued another `show interfaces` command, we can expect to obtain an update to this counter.

The last output value functions the same as the Last Input field. That is, it indicates the number of hours, minutes, and seconds since the last packet was successfully transmitted by the interface.

Output Hang
The Output Hang field denotes the time since the interface was last reset due to a transmission that took too long. The value of this field is specified in hours, minutes, and seconds or the word never is displayed if a hang condition has not occurred. If the number of hours from the last reset exceeds 24, the number of days and hours will be displayed until the field overflows. When this situation occurs, asterisks (*) are displayed in this field.

Last Clearing
This field indicates the time at which the counters for an interface that measure cumulative statistics were last reset to zero. Clearing affects all statistics, except those that affect routing such as load and reliability.

The actual value displayed for last clearing is based upon the use of a 32-bit ms counter. A display of asterisks indicates the elapsed time is too large to be displayed, while a display of 0:00:00 indicates the counters were cleared more than 2^{31} ms and less than 2^{32} ms ago. On many routers this last clearing value will be displayed in terms of weeks and days or days and hours. For example, in Figure 4-1 the last clearing of the `show interface` counters is indicated as 1w2d.

Queuing Strategy

This field indicates the queuing strategy assigned to the interface. The default is *first in-first out* (FIFO). If you previously assigned priority queuing to the interface, that queuing method would be listed in this field.

Queue Information

For output and input queues a pair of numbers of the form m/n is shown, followed by the number of packets dropped due to a full queue. Here the value substituted for m indicates the number of packets in the queue, while the value substituted for n indicates the maximum size of the queue in packets. By examining the number of drops and the relationship between m and n over a period of time, you can determine if an adjustment to the queue length for a particular interface is advisable to reduce packet drops. However, you should also consider the level of utilization of the media connected to the interface to determine if an adjustment to an output queue length will be beneficial. A heavily used media is most likely the cause of drops occurring from the output queue: The router will experience difficulty in being able to transmit data, resulting in output packet queuing which, in turn, results in drops when the output queue is filled and another packet arrives for transfer via the interface onto the media. In the input direction packet drops and a large value of m with respect to n indicates that the router is too busy doing other work to expediently process inbound packets. If this situation occurs over a prolonged period of time, it generally indicates that a more powerful router is required to satisfy the workload. Normally, this situation is observed by having a large number of packet drops in the inbound direction for many, if not most or all, router interfaces.

The Queue Information field values in Figure 4-1 show no packets currently in either queue. In addition, although 63 packets were dropped due to a full output queue, no packets were dropped due to an input queue. The latter is a common situation since most routers, unless overconfigured, should not have a problem processing inbound data.

Five-Minute I/O Rate

The next field displays the average number of bits and packets transmitted and received over the interface during the past 5 minutes. There are several items you must consider when interpreting the data displayed in this field. First, you must consider the operating mode of the interface and the configuration of the network to which the interface is connected. For example, if the interface is a LAN interface, it can operate either in promiscuous mode where it reads every frame on the LAN or a nonpromiscuous mode, where it only reads broadcast frames and frames directly addressed to the interface.

If the interface is in promiscuous mode, it reads all packets and provides a measurement of the data flow on the network. If the interface is not in promiscuous mode, it only senses traffic it sends and receives, which could be a small percentage of all traffic on the network.

In terms of network configuration, if the interface is connected to a LAN with only one station, such as a Web server, then all traffic flows to and from the router interface. This means you can obtain a relatively accurate measurement of network activity regardless of the mode the interface is in.

One other item that warrants consideration is the fact that the 5-min I/O rates represent exponentially weighted averages with a time constant of 5 min. Thus, any one 5-min I/O rate is an approximation of traffic per second for the period. However, a timespan of four 5-min periods results in an average that will be within 2 percent of the instantaneous rate of a uniform stream of traffic for a 20-min period.

Since packets are variable lengths, the bits per second rate is normally more useful for examining the activity on an interface with respect to the transmission media. In Figure 4-1 the input rate of 1,540,000 bps represents approximately one-sixth of the operating rate of the interface. In the event you are curious as to why the input rate is approximately an order of magnitude greater than the interface output rate, the answer lies in the connection of the interface. In this particular router utilization environment the Ethernet interface was connected to a 10BASE-T LAN with one other station on that network, a corporate Web server. Requests for Web pages flow in the form of *uniform resource locators* (URLs), while responses to URL requests are Web pages; this explains the disproportionate level of traffic with respect to inbound and outbound transmission directions. Now that we understand the 5-min I/O rate, let's examine specific packet input and output information that can be displayed about an interface.

Packets and Bytes Input
This field first indicates the total number of error-free packets received by the router. Next, it indicates the total number of bytes in the error-free packets received by the router.

If you divide the number of packets by the number of bytes, you obtain the average packet length, in bytes. This information can be used to provide a general indication of the type of traffic flowing over the interface. For example, relatively short packets commonly transport interactive query/response traffic, while relatively long packets commonly transport files that could include Web pages and the graphics contained on most of those pages.

No Buffers
The No Buffers field indicates the number of packets received on the interface that had to be discarded due to a lack of buffer space in the router. This buffer space should not be confused with internal buffers on the interface. When you have a recurring No Buffers situation, it usually indi-

cates the router needs more memory. However, if you periodically encounter a No Buffers value, it may be the result of broadcast storms on a LAN or bursts of noise on a serial port. You can determine if the reason for a No Buffers value is due to broadcasts by examining the next field.

Received Broadcasts
This field indicates the total number of broadcast or multicast packets received on the interface. It is important to note that many broadcasts are part of the natural communications process. For example, the ARP, which is used to resolve a layer 3 IP address into a layer 2 MAC address, depends upon issuing a broadcast to query each station on a LAN for the layer 2 address associated with the layer 3 address it must obtain in order to correctly form a frame to deliver the packet. Similarly, in a Novell IPX environment servers broadcast *service advertising protocol* (SAP) packets every 30 s. These define the services provided by the server.

If you are strictly an IP environment, a good portion of broadcasts more than likely result from ARP requests. If you have time-dependent applications, you can literally kill two problems with one action by setting fixed entries into the router's ARP cache for stations that operate time-dependent applications. Doing so not only eliminates the necessity for the router to perform an ARP operation, it also allows the resolution process to occur via checking memory which is much faster than waiting for the response to a broadcast. Since data traffic is suspended during an ARP broadcast, the reduction in ARP broadcasts results in an increase in information transfer capability via the interface. Since ARP tables are maintained internally in a router, we discuss this topic in more detail in Chapter 5 when we examine internal performance measurements.

Runts
A Runt is an error-condition term associated with a packet whose length is less than the minimum length associated with a protocol. In an Ethernet environment the minimum packet length is 64 bytes in the adapter and 72 bytes on the LAN. Thus, if an interface receives an Ethernet packet less than 72 bytes, it is an error condition and the packet is discarded. Typically, a collision causes the generation of a Runt, although a failing adapter can also cause this situation to occur.

Giants
A Giant packet is another error condition, indicating that the packet exceeded the protocol's maximum packet length. In an Ethernet environment the maximum packet length is 1518 bytes in an adapter and 1526 bytes when flowing on the network. Thus, an Ethernet packet whose length, including the Preamble and Start of Frame Delimiter fields, exceeds 1526 bytes is considered a Giant. Such packets are also sent to the great bit bucket in the sky and the Giant count indicates the number of

packets discarded due to this situation. A common cause of Giant packets is a late collision or a failing adapter.

Throttles

Although rare, if a router senses buffer or processor overload, it will shut down its receiver. This condition is referred to as a Throttle and is not actually a communications problem. Instead, it is a router-capacity problem that requires you to examine the state of the system's buffers and its processor. If your use of the `show interfaces` command denotes both a large number of No Buffers and Throttles, it normally indicates you should consider adding memory to the router. In Chapter 5 we look at the internal aspects of router performance, including memory and CPU utilization.

Input Errors

The Input Errors field is a summary of packets with various types of errors received at an interface. Input errors include Runts, Giants, No Buffers, CRC, Frame, Overrun, and Ignored counts, with the latter four types of error conditions denoted in the four fields that follow this field. It is important to note that the Input Error count may not always equal the sum of the error counts in the previously mentioned fields. This results from the fact that other input-related errors can cause this counter to increase. In addition, some packets can have more than one type of error. In examining Figure 4-1, note that the Input Errors counter exactly matches the CRC error counter; however, as previously mentioned, this may not always be true.

CRC Errors

As indicated in Chapter 3, under the discussion of LAN and WAN metrics, most protocols compute a cycle redundancy check (CRC) that is appended to a frame or packet placed on the media. A receiver also computes a CRC on the received data, using the same algorithm. When the locally generated CRC does not match the received CRC, the CRC error counter is incremented and the packet is discarded.

You can use the ratio of CRC errors to packets input to determine the packet error rate. That is, the packet error rate in percent is

$$\frac{\text{CRC errors}}{\text{packets input 1 CRC errors}} \times 100$$

Although it is normal to receive some CRC errors because of collisions on an Ethernet LAN or noise on a WAN, a relatively high percentage of errors normally indicates a problem with the media, such as electromagnetic interference in the form of lightning adversely affecting a WAN or machinery that is too close to the media adversely affecting both LANs and WANs.

Frame Errors

A Frame error occurs when a packet has a noninteger number of bytes and an erroneous CRC. The typical cause of a Frame error is a failing adapter card or the occurrence of collisions on an Ethernet network.

Overrun

The Overrun counter indicates the number of packets the interface had to ignore due to the input rate exceeding a receiver's ability to process the received data.

Since most LANs are shared media networks, this means that a network operating at m bps with n stations has as an average where each station operates at m/n bps. Although most interfaces can support a data transfer at m bps, they cannot do so for a sustained period of time, resulting in streaming data such as a long file transfer periodically causing an overrun condition. This is usually a normal part of communications unless the overrun counter indicates a large number of such conditions.

Ignored

The Ignored counter indicates the number of received packets that the interface's receiver ignored due to a lack of internal buffers. Although this buffer problem is different than the lack of buffer space in the main system of a router, the two are related. This is because a lack of main system buffer area denoted by the No Buffers count adversely affects the ability of an interface to process inbound packets from the interface buffer area into the router's main buffer area. Thus, you should examine both the No Buffers and Ignored counters as they can be related to one another as previously noted.

Input Packets with Dribble Condition Detected

A Dribble is a frame that is slightly too long, usually by a single bit, that could be line noise. Assuming the CRC is in order, the router accepts a Dribbled Frame and increments this Error counter for informational purposes.

Packets and Bytes Output

The Packets and Bytes Output is the first of a series of counters associated with the transmit side of the interface. Here Packets Output is a counter that denotes the total number of packets transmitted by the router through the interface while Bytes is the total number of bytes transferred through the interface.

You can compute the average packet length by dividing the total number of bytes by the total number of packets. As indicated earlier in this chapter when we did this for the input traffic, we can use the average packet length as a general indication of the type of activity being performed.

Underruns

An Underrun condition is the situation where packets passed through the router do not reach the interface at the rate it can transfer data onto the media. Thus, this counter is an inverse of the Overrun counter.

Output Errors

The Output Errors counter is a sum of all possible error conditions that prevent the transmission of packets through the interface and onto the attached media. Although there are six specific Output Error counters, which we will shortly examine, the sum of those errors may not match the value of the Output Errors counter. This is because some packets can have multiple errors, while other packets may have an error that is tracked but not specifically tabulated as a separate entity.

Collisions

Collisions adversely affect transmitted frames as well as received data. Thus, this counter indicates the number of frames on an Ethernet network that were retransmitted due to a collision adversely affecting the transmission of a prior frame. Although some collisions can always be expected to occur on an Ethernet LAN, a high percentage of collisions, typically more than a few percent, commonly indicates a network whose cabling distance exceeds its design specification. For example, in a 10BASE-T Ethernet network each station should be wired to a hub using a cable length equal to or less than 100 m, with the distance between any two stations connected to the network equal to or less than 200 m. If you exceed these cabling distances, the Ethernet Collision window widens beyond normal tolerance. This means you have a higher probability that one station with data to transmit will listen to the network and not hear a transmission in progress, resulting in the listening station then transmitting data, which results in a collision. Thus, if you observe a large number of retransmissions, you may wish to examine the cable length associated with each station's connect to a hub as well as the maximum span distance between the pair of stations that are most distant from one another.

Another possible cause of collisions is a violation of the Ethernet 3-4-5 rule in which transmission between two stations on a network should not traverse more than three populated segments, four repeaters, or a maximum of five segments. It is important to note that a populated segment is a segment with more than two connected nodes, while a repeater can be both a hub and a stand-alone device that regenerates a transmitted signal. Although the violation of this rule will not cause a network to fail, it results in an increase in collisions and is another area to check.

Interface Resets

This counter indicates the number of times the specified interface was reset. This condition can occur as a result of several situations. First, when an interface is placed into loopback or shut down, the Interface counter is incremented. Thus, this counter does not necessarily indicate a problem.

Another cause of interface resets results when packets queued for transmission cannot be transmitted, resulting in a timer expiring which results in an automatic interface reset. This condition commonly occurs on a serial line, where the attached CSU turns off its transmit clock either due to a failure of the transmission line or a failure of the CSU. Since it is also possible that the interface lost synchronization with the CSU's transmit clock, the interface is automatically reset.

Another cause of interface resets results when a carrier signal is detected on a serial line but the line protocol is down. This situation indicates that the line is up but the protocol is down and the router automatically performs an interface reset in an attempt to restart the transfer of information. Since you should know when you or another employee performs a loopback or shut down operation, you should be able to discount those occurrences and determine the number of interface resets, if any, that result from error conditions.

Babbles
This counter is only applicable to Ethernet interfaces. Each time the transmit jabber timer expires, the Babbles counter is incremental.

Late Collisions
As the name of this counter implies, its value indicates the number of late collisions and is only applicable to shared Ethernet network connections. As previously noted in Chapter 3, a late collision represents the detection of a collision after the station transmits a complete frame onto a network. Since the primary cause of late collisions is an excessive network segment cable length, you should first verify the length of station-to-hub cables and the maximum span length between the two most distant stations connected to the network. If cable lengths are within specification, you then turn your attention to other possible causes of late collisions such as faulty connectors, an excessive number of repeaters in the network, and a defective network adapter.

Deferred
The Deferred counter indicates the number of times the interface transmitter had to wait to transmit a frame due to the carrier being asserted. Because another station can be expected to periodically transmit data when the router interface has data to transmit, it is quite natural to expect a large value for this counter. For example, Figure 4-1 indicates a Deferred counter value of 1,966,186. However, because the total number of packets output was 61,027,904, the Deferred count is only a small percentage of total packets transmitted. Similar to the counters for collisions and late

collisions, the Deferred counter is only applicable to Ethernet network interfaces to include Fast Ethernet.

Lost Carrier

The Lost Carrier counter is applicable only for a serial WAN interface. Each time a carrier is lost during transmission, this counter value is incremented.

No Carrier

Similar to the Lost Carrier counter, the No Carrier counter is also only applicable to a serial WAN interface. This counter is incremented when a carrier is not present during an attempted transmission.

Output Buffer Failure

The Output Buffer Failure counter indicates the number of times a packet could not be output from a hold queue because of a shortage of shared memory. Thus, this counter display can provide information concerning a potential router memory problem.

Output Buffers Swapped Out

This counter indicates a situation where the output queue was full and packets were stored in main router memory to prevent them from being dropped. Thus, the value of the counter can be expected to be high when a long burst of output traffic occurs that exceeds the ability of the output queue to hold packets.

Custom Output Queuing

A variation of the previously described interface shown in Figure 4-1 occurs when Custom Output Queuing is enabled. When this situation occurs, information about the input and output queues is also displayed similar to the following:

```
Last clearing of 'show interface' counters 0:00:15
Input queue: 0/75/0 (size/max/drops); Total output drops: 24
Output queues: (queue #: size/max/drops)
    0: 5/20/12 1: 0/20/5 2: 0/20/23 0:20/0 4: 0/20/2 5: 0/20/0
```

Note that when custom queuing is enabled, the resulting number of packets drops in output queues are a result of bandwidth limitations. For each queue number (queue #) in the display, three metrics are shown using the format $m/n/0$, where n is the current size of the queue, m is the maximum size, and 0 represents the number of packets discarded.

Now that we understand the fields displayed when a show interfaces ethernet command is issued, let's continue our examination of the command and view information about other popular types of interfaces. In doing so, we focus primarily on key fields applicable to each interface that differ from the fields displayed in Figure 4-1, were added for a specific interface, or previously described that warrant attention due to a new use for the field.

VIEWING A FAST ETHERNET INTERFACE

This section continues an examination of different types of router interfaces by focusing on Fast Ethernet. Figure 4-2 illustrates the use of the show interfaces fastethernet command.

In comparing the fields shown in Figure 4-2 with those in Figure 4-1, you will note they are very similar. Since Fast Ethernet operates 10 times faster than Ethernet, its Bandwidth (BW) field reflects this fact. Similarly, the Delay (DLY) field value is one-tenth that of Ethernet, or 100 μsec. After the Keepalive field, you will note a new field that was not shown on the prior interface so let's look at that field.

Half-Duplex

The line that begins with half-duplex indicates several operating conditions associated with this particular Fast Ethernet interface. First, a Fast Ethernet interface can support either half- or full-duplex transmission, with the former associated with a connection of the interface to a shared media network, while the latter indicates the connection of the interface to a switch port that supports full-duplex transmission. Since full-duplex

Figure 4-2   Displaying information about a Fast Ethernet interface.

```
Router#show interface fastethernet1/0
FastEthernet1/0 is up, line protocol is up
  Hardware is cyBus FastEthernet Interface, address is 0010.7936.a820
(bia 0010.7936.a820)
  Internet address is 205.131.175.2/24
  MTU 1500 bytes, BW 100000 Kbit, DLY 100 usec,
    reliability 255/255, txload 1/255, rxload 13/255
  Encapsulation ARPA, loopback not set
  Keepalive set (10 sec)
  Half-duplex, 100Mb/s, 100BaseTX/FX
  ARP type: ARPA, ARP Timeout 04:00:00
  Last input 00:00:00, output 00:00:02, output hang never
  Last clearing of "show interface" counters 3w5d
  Queuing strategy: fifo
  Output queue 0/40, 0 drops; input queue 0/75, 0 drops
  5 minute input rate 5407000 bits/sec, 719 packets/sec
  5 minute output rate 482000 bits/sec, 631 packets/sec
    621146139 packets input, 3448439771 bytes
    Received 21039744 broadcasts, 0 runts, 0 giants, 0 throttles
    0 input errors, 0 CRC, 0 frame, 0 overrun, 0 ignored
    0 watchdog, 0 multicast
    0 input packets with dribble condition detected
    510267201 packets output, 490611473 bytes, 0 underruns
    0 output errors, 4167605 collisions, 0 interface resets
    0 babbles, 0 late collision, 14104915 deferred
    0 lost carrier, 0 no carrier
    0 output buffer failures, 0 output buffers swapped out
```

transmission permits data flow in both directions at the same time, you can enhance performance when a router is configured to a switch that supports full-duplex transmission. The following two values indicate the operating rate of the interface and the particular type of Fast Ethernet connection since there are three types of such connections.

Watchdog
If you look at the seventh line from the bottom in Figure 4-2, you will note two new fields. The first field is for a counter labeled Watchdog. This counter is incremented whenever a Receive Watchdog time expires. When a Preamble is encountered, the interface sets the Watchdog timer, which then begins to decrement. If a packet is still being received when the timer expires, it indicates that the length of the packet is in error.

Multicast
The Multicast counter indicates the number of multicast packets received at the interface. Since multicasts are commonly associated with audio or video conferences, some network managers and LAN administrators look at this metric when there is a high level of network utilization. The reason for this is the fact that many multicast transmissions are not the type of activity that an organization expects of its employees.

Since the remaining Fast Ethernet fields can be used the same way as those corresponding Ethernet fields, we will not re-examine those fields. Instead, we look at another popular type of LAN and examine the use of the show interfaces tokenring command.

VIEWING A TOKEN-RING INTERFACE
As previously noted, use of the show interfaces command results in the display of a common core set of counters and their associated values, even when those counters are not directly applicable to a particular interface. If you examine the fields in the display of a token-ring interface, you will note a counter for collisions, even though they are only applicable to Ethernet and Fast Ethernet networks. However, if this puzzles you, be assured that Cisco is not implying that you can encounter collisions on a token-ring network. Instead, as we will shortly note, this field is used for a different purpose.

Figure 4-3 illustrates the display of information about a particular token-ring interface through the use of the show interfaces tokenring command. Since the operation of a token-ring network differs considerably from that of an Ethernet network, review the different fields within the display of a token-ring interface.

Token-Ring Status
When you see the display Token Ring is up, it indicates that the interface is currently active and a participant is on a ring. Other options that can be displayed for this field are listed in Table 4-2.

Figure 4-3   Displaying information about a token-ring interface.

```
Router#show interface tokenring4/0/0
TokenRing4/0/0 is up, line protocol is up
  Hardware is cxBus Token Ring, address is 0008.9e6c.1501
    (bia 0008.9e6c.1501)
  Internet address is 205.131.174.2/24
  MTU 4464 bytes, BW 16000 Kbit, DLY 630 usec,
    reliability 255/255, txload 6/255, rxload 3/255
  Encapsulation SNAP, loopback not set
  Keepalive set (10 sec)
  ARP type: SNAP, ARP Timeout 04:00:00
  Ring speed: 16 Mbps
  Duplex: half
  Mode: Classic token ring station
  Single ring node, Source Route Transparent Bridge capable
  Group Address: 0x00000000, Functional Address: 0x08000000
  Ethernet Transit OUI: 0x000000
  Last Ring Status 3w5d <Soft Error> (0x2000)
  Last input 00:00:00, output 00:00:00, output hang never
  Last clearing of "show interface" counters 3w5d
  Queuing strategy: fifo
  Output queue 0/40, 191 drops; input queue 0/75, 0 drops
  5 minute input rate 231000 bits/sec, 70 packets/sec
  5 minute output rate 397000 bits/sec, 84 packets/sec
    39345013 packets input, 2741510461 bytes, 0 no buffer
    Received 47219 broadcasts, 0 runts, 0 giants, 0 throttles
    0 input errors, 0 CRC, 0 frame, 0 overrun, 0 ignored, 0 abort
    36977576 packets output, 1985333208 bytes, 0 underruns
    0 output errors, 0 collisions, 0 interface resets
    0 output buffer failures, 0 output buffers swapped out
    0 transitions
```

Table 4-2   Token Ring Status Field Options

Display	Description
Up	The interface is a participant on the ring.
Down	The interface is inactive and not part of the ring.
Reset	A hardware error occurred.
Initializing	The interface is in the process of being inserted into the ring.
Administratively Down	The interface was taken down by a router administrator.

Line Protocol
Similar to Ethernet, this field indicates the status of keepalive signals or if the protocol was taken down by the router administrator. Thus, the Line protocol field has an up, down, or administratively down entry.

Hardware Type
This field indicates the type of board used to provide a token-ring interface. In Figure 4-3 a CxBus is indicated. This field also notes the MAC address of the interface in terms of 12 hex characters.

Internet Address
If IP was configured for the interface, an IP address is assigned. Similar to our discussion on the Ethernet Internet address, the subnet mask is denoted indirectly via the use of the slash (/) character followed by the number of bits associated with the network portion of the address.

MTU
The MTU is the longest Information field frame supported. As indicated in Figure 4-3,this value is set to 4464 bytes for the interface.

BW
This field indicates the bandwidth of the interface. Since the operating rate of the token-ring network to which the interface is connected is 16 Mbps, this field shows a value of 16,000 kb for informational purposes.

DLY
This field indicates the delay of the interface in microseconds. As indicated in Figure 4-3, this field for a 16-Mbps token-ring interface has a value of 630 μsec.

Reliability
Similar to Ethernet, this field indicates the reliability of the interface as a fraction of 255, calculated as an exponential average over 5 min. Thus, a reliability of 255/255 indicates a 100 percent level of reliability.

Transmit and Receive Load
The Transmit (txload) and Receive (rxload) load fields provide the same information as their Ethernet counterparts. From Figure 4-3 it is apparent that the token-ring network interface is not heavily taxed.

Encapsulation
In this example the interface is configured to support SNAP token-ring frames. Since the next few fields, such as loopback, ARP type, and ARP time-out, function in the same way as those for an Ethernet interface display, let's jump to the Ring Speed field, which is unique to a token-ring interface.

Ring Speed
The Ring Speed field indicates the type of Token Ring. Thus, this field is set to 4 or 16 Mbps.

Mode
This field indicates the type of connection between the interface and a token-ring network. In Figure 4-3, the field value of Classic Token-Ring Station indicates that the connection is to a standard type of ring and not a switch port. If the interface is used in a bridging environment, the mode either appears as single ring or multiring. The former indicates that the optional *routing information field* (RIF) in a token-ring frame is not supported, while multiring indicates it is supported.

Group Address
This field indicates by a nonzero entry that the interface is part of a group. Thus, the nonzero entry then indicates the group address, which serves as a multicast address for a token-ring network.

Functional Address
In a token-ring environment a Functional Address indicates the function associated with a destination address. Thus, this field indicates the function associated with the token-ring interface, which in this example is a simple participant on a ring.

Last Ring Status
This field indicates when the status of the ring last changed and the reason for the change. In Figure 4-3 the ring status changed 3 weeks and 5 days ago because of a soft error.

Last Imput/Output (I/O)
Both the Last Input and Last Output fields denote the number of hours, minutes, and seconds since a packet was successfully received or transmitted. Since these fields, as well as the remaining fields shown in Figure 4-3, function similar to those in Ethernet, we focus on certain differences between field values in a token-ring environment. Those differences include some frame-related errors that we now discuss.

Runts
In a token-ring environment the minimum length frame is 22 bytes. Thus, a Runt is a misformed frame shorter than 22 bytes in length.

Giants
A Giant packet is a frame that exceeds the maximum length. Since the MTU is 4464 bytes and a frame has 21 bytes of overhead, it indicates a frame greater than 4485 bytes in length if no RIF field is present.

Collisions
Although a token-ring network cannot have Collisions, Cisco uses this field to indicate an unusual condition that can represent frames being queued or dequeued by the system software, which more than likely indicates excessive activity that cannot be compensated for by the bandwidth of the media when frames are being transmitted.

Transitions

The last field shown in Figure 4-3 is unique to Token Ring. This field indicates the number of times the ring went from an up to down state or a down to up state. If you see a large number of transitions, it normally indicates a problem either on the ring or at the interface. Now that we understand the display of token-ring interface information, we look at a fourth popular type of interface, the serial interface.

VIEWING THE SERIAL INTERFACE

Cisco routers support several types of serial WAN interfaces. Some interfaces include a built-in CSU, enabling a show interfaces command to display several types of T1 line errors, such as B8ZS coding violations, CRC-6 errors, and T1 line framing errors. Other types of serial interfaces do not include a built-in CSU and do not provide such statistics. In this section we first examine the display of interface information from a conventional serial WAN interface. Once this is accomplished, we cover additional fields you can expect to see when you use the show interfaces serial command to view the state of a serial interface with a built-in CSU.

Figure 4-4 illustrates the use of the show interfaces serial command to display information about the status of a serial WAN interface

Figure 4-4   Displaying information about a serial interface.

```
Router#show interface serial0/0/0
Serial0/0/0 is up, line protocol is up
  Hardware is cyBus Serial
  Description: MCI MGBC673F00010002
  Internet address is 4.0.156.2/30
  MTU 1500 bytes, BW 1544 Kbit, DLY 20000 usec,
     reliability 255/255, txload 245/255, rxload 29/255
  Encapsulation HDLC, crc 16, loopback not set
  Keepalive set (10 sec)
  Last input 00:00:00, output 00:00:00, output hang never
  Last clearing of "show interface" counters 3w5d
  Input queue: 0/75/0 (size/max/drops); Total output drops: 156004
  Queuing strategy: weighted fair
  Output queue: 52/1000/64/156004 (size/max total/threshold/drops)
     Conversations  18/205/256 (active/max active/max total)
     Reserved Conversations 0/0 (allocated/max allocated)
  5 minute input rate 180000 bits/sec, 176 packets/sec
  5 minute output rate 1486000 bits/sec, 196 packets/sec
     132341296 packets input, 463322459 bytes, 0 no buffer
     Received 0 broadcasts, 0 runts, 1 giants, 0 throttles
     957 input errors, 957 CRC, 0 frame, 0 overrun, 0 ignored, 0 abort
     153303195 packets output, 3998661221 bytes, 0 underruns
     0 output errors, 0 collisions, 0 interface resets
     0 output buffer failures, 53551646 output buffers swapped out
     2 carrier transitions
     RTS up, CTS up, DTR up, DCD up, DSR up
```

that does not include a built-in CSU. In examining the display we focus primarily on fields that differ from previously described fields or fields whose values warrant a few words of explanation.

Examining Transmit and Receive Loads
In examining the field entries in Figure 4-4 note that the Internet address in this example has a subnet mask of 30 bits. Also note that the Bandwidth (BW) field is 1544 kb, which is a T1 transmission line.

If you compare the Transmit (txload) and Receive (rxload) loads, you will note a significant imbalance, with the Transmit load approaching 100 percent occupancy. Normally, such an imbalance could be a cause for concern; however, in this situation the T1 line is an Internet connection and another interface provides a connection to a popular Web server. Because of this configuration a majority of inbound transmissions are URL requests, while transmit or outbound traffic are Web pages, thus explaining the imbalance. Thus, instead of a cursory view, you need to examine the previously described metrics with respect to the configuration of your network, including the general data flow characteristics resulting from the use of servers and gateways. To paraphrase a famous general, "in network analysis, there is no substitute to understanding your network."

Encapsulation
Continuing our examination of the serial interface display shown in Figure 4-4, note that the encapsulation is set to HDLC. As previously indicated in Chapter 3, a serial interface can be configured to support many types of protocols. In this particular example the HDLC protocol with a 16-bit CRC was configured for use.

Queuing Strategy
This field indicates the queuing strategy. The default is first in-first out (FIFO), with other strategies supported being priority list, custom list, and weighted fair.

Output Queue
As noted in Figure 4-4, this field contains four numbers. The first number denotes the number of packets in the queue. Following the first slash, the next number indicates the maximum size of the queue. This is followed by a threshold value and the number of packets dropped due to a lack of buffer storage at the interface. Although it appears that the interface display in Figure 4-4 has a large number of packet drops, you need to compare that value to the number of packets output. If you do so, you will note the number of packets dropped is a very small fraction of packets transmitted.

Input/Output Rate
Since a T1 line uses 8 kbps for framing bits, its maximum data transfer rate is 1.536 Mbps. Thus, when viewing the output and input data rates you

should view the displayed rate in comparison to 1.536 Mbps and not 1.544 Mbps, since the latter includes 8 kbps of framing bits.

Control Signals

The last line in Figure 4-4 depicts the state of five control signals: *request to send* (RTS), *clear to send* (CTS), *data terminal ready* (DTR), *data carrier detected* (DCD), and *data set ready* (DSR).

RTS is passed from the interface to an attached CSU, which returns a CTS if the line is operational. The CSU also supplies a DCR signal when a carrier signal in the form of line variations is noted. Similarly, the CSU returns a DSR signal. When the interface is ready, it provides a DTR signal to the CSU. When everything is working correctly, the state of all five control signals are up. If one or more are down, you cannot transmit and receive data and an analysis of those signals can assist in isolating a problem. For example, if DCD is down, it normally indicates a line problem. Now that we understand basic serial interface display fields, look at several fields that are displayed when a CSU is built into the serial interface.

CV Errors

The Coding Violation (CV) counter indicates the number of coding violations that occurred on a digital transmission facility. CV errors are counted when a bipolar violation error occurs, such as two positive or two negative voltages in succession instead of alternating positive and negative voltages. The cause of bipolar violations can include faulty repeaters or noise on the line. Usually you can expect a very small percentage of coding violations.

CRC-6 Errors

The CRC-6 counter is applicable to the ESF framing format and indicates the number of superframes received in error. As noted in Chapter 3, an ESF superframe consists of a sequence of 24 frames. Thus, a CRC-6 error indicates that at least 1 bit in the sequence of 24 frames was received in error. Although a CRC-6 error rate cannot be directly equated to a bit error rate, you can use this counter as a general indication of the quality of the digital transmission facility. That is, a relatively high counter value indicates that there is a high error rate on the transmission line. You can verify this fact by examining the CRC rate associated with the line protocol. Since the protocol is carried by the transmission line, the CRC counter should rise in tandem with the CRC-6 counter. This would tell you that a low level of throughput and the filling of buffers and dropping of packets would be attributed to the transmission line.

Frame Errors

The Frame Errors counter indicates the number of framing errors encountered. Although a periodic framing error can simply be a bit error, a high framing error rate would indicate that the transmitting and receiving devices are losing synchronization, resulting in a lower throughput on the transmission facility.

Alarm Signals

In addition to the CV errors, CRC-6 Errors and Frame Errors counter, a built-in CSU lets you monitor alarm signals that can occur on a digital transmission facility. Those alarm signals are generated by the setting of a bit pattern which indicates a particular alarm or an absence of a signal. On an interface with a built-in CSU there are six alarm fields. Those fields include *receive loss of signal alarm* (rxLOS), *receive loss of frame alarm* (rxLOF), *receive loss of payload alarm indication signal* (rxPAIS), *receive loss of physical alarm indication signal* (rxAIS), *receive remote alarm indication signal* (rxRAIS), and *receive high bit error rate alarm* (rxHBER). For each of these fields the display is either active or inactive.

To appreciate what these alarms mean, it is important to note that most do not follow industry notation. Thus, let's equate the labels of the fields used by Cisco to industry notation.

Red Alarm

When a receiver loses frame alignment, it generates what is referred to as a Red alarm. Under D4 framing, a Red alarm is set by placing bit 2 to a value of 0 in all 24 data channels and the frame bit to 1 in frame 12. If ESF framing is used, a Red alarm is generated by a repeated pattern of eight zeros, eight ones on the data channels. Thus, a loss of frame alarm (rxLOF) is a Red alarm and its composition depends upon the type of T1 framing.

Yellow Alarm

When a Red alarm is received by a distant device, it returns a Yellow alarm, which denotes the distant device noted that the receiver at the opposite end of the T1 line reported a loss of frame alignment and resynchronization is required between the two devices. The composition of a Yellow alarm generated by a receiver depends on the framing format of the T1 line. Under D4 framing, bit 2 is set to 0 for 255 consecutive channels and the framing bit is set to 1 in frame 12. Under ESF, a Yellow alarm is indicated by 16 patterns of eight zeros and eight ones on the data link.

Blue Alarm

A third type of alarm on a T1 transmission facility that warrants attention is a Blue alarm, which is also referred to as an *alarm indication signal* (AIS). Since T1 lines are multiplexed onto T3 lines by a communications carrier, the failure of a T3 line results in 28 T1 lines becoming inoperative. Rather than have technicians dispatched to 28 locations when the failure resulted from a higher-order system, a Blue alarm, in effect, says there is a problem, but its not your fault. A Blue alarm is normally generated after 150 ms of loss of an incoming signal and the higher-order system, such as a T3 multiplexer, generates a continuous pattern of ones across all 24 data channels to indicate the condition. Thus, if the receive loss of payload alarm indication signal (rxPAIS) or the receive loss of physical alarm indication signal (rxAIS) field displays the word active, it indicates that the higher-order system failed. Now that we understand the various types of fields associated with a serial interface, we conclude our examination of the use of the show interfaces EXEC command by examining the use of the accounting subcommand.

DISPLAYING ACCOUNTING INFORMATION

If you use the accounting subcommand with a show interfaces EXEC command, you can display the number of packets of each protocol type that has been transmitted and received via a specific interface or all interfaces. However, to obtain meaningful results, you must first enable accounting. Since we are primarily concerned with the IP, we enable IP accounting. To do so, you first enter the privileged mode of the router. Thus, to enable IP accounting, you enter the following sequence of router commands:

```
Router>enable
Password:
Router#config
Configuring from terminal, memory, or network [terminal]?
Enter configuration commands, one per line (End with CNTL/Z.
Router(config)#interface ethernet4/1/1
Router(config-if)#ip accounting
Accounting will exclude mls traffic when mls is enabled.
Router (config-if)#end
```

In examining the preceding sequence of statements used to enable IP accounting, note that once it is enabled for one interface, accounting is enabled on all interfaces, a situation which we shortly view. Also note that mls refers to multiprotocol label switching, a technique where routing occurs based on the association of a label appended to a packet and a port or interface instead of a router examining its routing tables to check the destination IP address associated with a packet. Since packets expediently flow through the router without checking their contents, protocol information is not captured.

Once you enable IP accounting, you can view accounting data for a specific interface or all interfaces. For example, you would enter one of the following two commands to display accounting information about a specific Ethernet interface or all interfaces:

```
show interfaces ethernet4/1/1 accounting
show interfaces accounting
```

Figure 4-5 illustrates the use of the show interfaces accounting command. In examining the resulting display note that per-packet information is displayed for each router interface. If an interface is disabled, the display indicates this situation. In addition, if an interface is active but no traffic is flowing across the interface, this situation is also noted in the resulting display.

Figure 4-5   Using the accounting subcommand.

```
Router#show interfaces accounting
Serial0/0/0 MCI MOBC673F00017002
                Protocol    Pkts In    Chars In    Pkts Out   Chars Out
                      IP   13241557  1277296414    15154016  4010340737
                     CDP       4637     1530210        9286     2609366
Serial0/0/1 MCI MOBC673F00027002
                Protocol    Pkts In    Chars In    Pkts Out   Chars Out
                      IP   13242791  1277771248    15103785  3869196623
                     CDP       4637     1530210        9285     2609085
Interface Serial0/0/2 is disabled

Interface Serial0/0/3 is disabled

FastEthernet1/0
                Protocol    Pkts In    Chars In    Pkts Out   Chars Out
                      IP   62780905  3213851805    52891396   638177273
                 DEC MOP          0           0         468       36036
                     ARP      26657     1603058        7898      473880
                     CDP       4639     1489119        9282     2835651
Interface FastEthernet1/1 is disabled

TokenRing4/0/0
                Protocol    Pkts In    Chars In    Pkts Out   Chars Out
                      IP    2985770  1046229457     2942059  1300690432
                     ARP        649       32450         716       35800
                     CDP          0           0        4642     1401884
TokenRing4/0/1
                Protocol    Pkts In    Chars In    Pkts Out   Chars Out
No traffic sent or received on this interface.
Interface TokenRing4/0/2 is disabled

Interface TokenRing4/0/3 is disabled
```

DEC MOP

Cisco routers are currently capable of maintaining per-packet accounting information on 16 protocols, ranging from Apollo and AppleTalk to ARP, CLNS, DECnet, IP, and various bridging protocols. Although we previously turned on IP accounting, which explains the display of ARP packets on a LAN interface, you might be a bit puzzled by the appearance of DEC MOP packets when a router is not supporting DECnet. Cisco routers use DEC MOP packets to advertise their existence. Thus, a Cisco router periodically broadcasts MOP packets even when DECnet is not actively being used. If you examine Figure 4-5, note that DEC MOP is an insignificant amount of traffic. Since the accounting subcommand can be used to provide a breakdown of traffic by general protocol, it can provide information that may be useful to determine if a network should be subdivided. For example, if your organization was operating a few Novell servers that were primarily accessed by a limited number of employees, it might be practical to place the servers and employees on a separate segment if the level of LAN utilization is high. However, because accounting information does not provide a detailed breakdown on applications, its overall value may be limited.

CDP

The second protocol you might be puzzled about is *Cisco Discovery Protocol* (CDP). CDP runs on all Cisco manufactured equipment, including routers, communications servers, and switches. CDP enables you to view information about other Cisco devices as well as use management tools to discover Cisco devices that are neighbors of known devices. CDP operates by transmitting or advertising its presence. You can use the show cdp command to view the status of the configured CDP settings. The following example shows the use of the show cdp command:

```
Router # show cdp
Global CDP information:
Sending CDP packets every 60 seconds
Sending a holdtime value of 180 seconds
Sending CDP advertisements is enabled
```

You can control the interval between CDP advertisements through the use of the cdp timer command. The holdtime is the amount of time, in seconds, that a device directs a neighbor to hold a CDP advertisement prior to discarding it. The value of this field is controlled by the cdp holdtime command. The last line indicates whether or not advertisements are enabled or disabled and is controlled through the use of the cdp advertise command.

If you are concerned about bandwidth, you should consider changing the CDP update time from its default of 60 s to a higher value. For example, to reduce CDP updates by one-half, you could use the following command:

```
cdp timer 90
```

IP Environment Consideration

In an IP environment you can obtain more detailed traffic information by using the show ip traffic command. Through the use of this command, you can obtain much more detailed information than from the show interfaces accounting command. As indicated in Figure 4-6, you can note both raw traffic as well as specific error conditions and the number of specific functions performed, such as the fragmentation and reassembly of packets. By carefully examining the display of statistics with respect to your network configuration, you can determine if an adjustment to your organization's network should be considered. For example, because fragmentation requires more processing power than routing, an excessive number of fragmentations along with a high level of CPU uti-

Figure 4-6   Using the show ip command to display detailed IP statistics.

```
Router#show controllers ?
  cbus       Cbus interface internal state
  fddi       FDDI interface internal state
  pos        POS framer state
  tokenring  Show TokenRing controllers
  vip        Show vip-card related information
  |          Output modifiers
  <cr>
 Router#show controllers cbus utilization


CYOBus utilization for five seconds: 5%; one minute: 5%; five minutes: 5%
CY1Bus utilization for five seconds: 4%; one minute: 4%; five minutes: 4%


Router#show controllers
TokenRing4/0/0: state up
  current address: 0008.9e6c.1501, burned in address: 0008.9e6c.1501
  Last Ring Status: 1w3d <Soft Error> (0x2000)
    Stats: soft: 0/33, hard: 0/0, sig loss: 0/0
           tx beacon: 0/0, wire fault 0/0, recovery: 0/0
           only station: 0/0, remote removal: 0/0

  Port is operating in : half-duplex


  Monitor state: (active), chip f/w: '000001.CT17C4 ', [bridge capable]
    ring mode: 0, internal enables:
    internal functional: 08000000 (08000000), group: N/A (00000000)
    Internal controller counts:
      line errors: 0/9, internal errors: 0/0
      burst errors: 0/36, ari/fci errors: 0/0
      abort errors: 0/0, lost frame: 0/3
      copy errors: 0/0, rcvr congestion: 0/255
      token errors: 0/0
    Microcode TX errors:
      pci read 0/0, icdb read parity 0/0
      icdb write parity 0/0, icdb address parity 0/0
      status write 0/0, fifo underrun 0/0
      fifo parity 0/0
    Microcode RX errors:
      pci read parity 0/0, internal read parity 0/0
      internal write parity 0/0, internal address bfr parity 0/0
      fifo parity 0/0, no buffer 0/0
      pci write 0/0, fifo overrun 0/0
      receive parity error 0/0
      receive mpc error 0/0
      received implicit aborted frame 0/1, explicit aborted frame 0/0
      received giant mac frame 0/0
    Internal controller smt state:
      Adapter MAC:    0008.9e6c.1501, Physical drop:    00000000
      NAUN Address:   0006.29aa.f78c, NAUN drop:        00000000
      Last Source     0000.f651.9074, Last poll:        0000.f651.9074
```

(Continued)

Figure 4-6 (*Continued*)

```
      Last MVID:        0006,      Last attn code:       0006
      Txmit priority:  0003,      Auth Class:           7B7F
      Monitor Error:   0000,      Interface errors      0003
      Correlator:      0000,      Soft Error Timer:     00DC
      Local Ring:      0000,      Ring Status:          0000
      Beacon rcv type: 0000,      Beacon txmit type:    0000
      Beacon type:     0000,      Beacon NAUN:          0008.9e6c.1501
      Beacon drop:     00000000,  Reserved:             0000
      Reserved2:       0000
Ring sampling/1000:    0
```

lization, if unchecked, could result in the requirement for a new router. Instead of making a salesperson happy, you could examine your network since you might be able to limit the need to fragment by limiting the length of the Information field transported in frames. In fact, one of the built-in features associated with a token-ring network is the ability to set the maximum frame length on a ring. Similarly, you can adjust the MTU at layer 3. Through such adjustments, it may be possible to reduce the need for fragmentation.

A careful examination of the entries in Figure 4-6 shows that while a significant improvement over a raw packet count, UDP, and TCP statistics are cumulative segment and datagram counts, they do not provide a breakdown of activity by application. Thus, you should consider a network monitoring tool, such as a *sniffer*, if you need a detailed breakdown of IP datagrams to determine the amount of Web, FTP, email, and similar application data.

EXAMINING CONTROLLERS

In concluding this chapter, we examine the show controllers command, which can be used to display specific information about the controllers present in a router.

Figure 4-7 illustrates several examples of the show controllers command. In the top portion of Figure 4-7, the use of the command followed by a question mark (?) results in the display of the various options supported. If you enter an option followed by a question mark, a display of the options for the selected option appears. Thus, you can drill down to obtain information about less frequently used IOS commands that you may not be familiar with.

Returning to Figure 4-7, the second example shows the use of the utilization option to display information about the level of utilization of all CBUS controllers in the router. Note that the resulting display indi-

Figure 4-7   Using the show controllers command.

```
Router#show controllers ?
  cbus        Cbus interface internal state
  fddi        FDDI interface internal state
  pos         POS framer state
  tokenring   Show TokenRing controllers
  vip         Show vip-card related information
  |           Output modifiers
  <cr>
Router#show controllers cbus utilization


CY0Bus utilization for five seconds: 5%; one minute: 5%; five minutes: 5%
CY1Bus utilization for five seconds: 4%; one minute: 4%; five minutes: 4%


Router#show controllers
TokenRing4/0/0: state up
  current address: 0008.9e6c.1501, burned in address: 0008.9e6c.1501
  Last Ring Status: 1w3d <Soft Error> (0x2000)
    Stats: soft: 0/33, hard: 0/0, sig loss: 0/0
           tx beacon: 0/0, wire fault 0/0, recovery: 0/0
           only station: 0/0, remote removal: 0/0


  Port is operating in : half-duplex


  Monitor state: (active), chip f/w: '000001.CT17C4 ', [bridge capable]
    ring mode: 0, internal enables:
    internal functional: 08000000 (08000000), group: N/A (00000000)
    Internal controller counts:
      line errors: 0/9, internal errors: 0/0
      burst errors: 0/36, ari/fci errors: 0/0
      abort errors: 0/0, lost frame: 0/3
      copy errors: 0/0, rcvr congestion: 0/255
      token errors: 0/0
    Microcode TX errors:
      pci read 0/0, icdb read parity 0/0
      icdb write parity 0/0, icdb address parity 0/0
      status write 0/0, fifo underrun 0/0
      fifo parity 0/0
    Microcode RX errors:
      pci read parity 0/0, internal read parity 0/0
      internal write parity 0/0, internal address bfr parity 0/0
      fifo parity 0/0, no buffer 0/0
      pci write 0/0, fifo overrun 0/0
      receive parity error 0/0
      receive mpc error 0/0
      received implicit aborted frame 0/1, explicit aborted frame 0/0
      received giant mac frame 0/0
    Internal controller smt state:
      Adapter MAC:    0008.9e6c.1501, Physical drop:     00000000
      NAUN Address:   0006.29aa.f78c, NAUN drop:         00000000
```

(Continued)

Figure 4-7 (*Continued*)

```
        Last Source       0000.f651.9074, Last poll:          0000.f651.9074
        Last MVID:        0006,           Last attn code:     0006
        Txmit priority:   0003,           Auth Class:         7B7F
        Monitor Error:    0000,           Interface errors    0003
        Correlator:       0000,           Soft Error Timer:   00DC
        Local Ring:       0000,           Ring Status:        0000
        Beacon rcv type:  0000,           Beacon txmit type:  0000
        Beacon type:      0000,           Beacon NAUN:        0008.9e6c.1501
        Beacon drop:      00000000,       Reserved:           0000
        Reserved2:        0000
   Ring sampling/1000:    0
```

cates a relatively low level of CBUS utilization for the past 5 min. This means that a throughput problem would not be the result of an overloaded controller in this example, at least during the past 5 min.

The third example shown in Figure 4-7 illustrates the use of the show controllers command without any options. Since the router used by the author had its token-ring interfaces fabricated on CBUS controllers, the result displayed detailed information about each token-ring interface. For the sake of brevity, only the display of TokenRing4/0/0 is shown in Figure 4-7.

Although a portion of the display of information about the TokenRing4/0/0 interface is similar to what you obtain by using a show interfaces command, the use of the controllers subcommand provides more detailed information. If you examine Figure 4-7 you will note that specific types of microcode transmit and receive errors as well as detailed information concerning the internal controller state. Thus, if you are experiencing a problem with a particular interface that is fabricated on a controller, you should consider the use of the show controllers command to obtain a more detailed level of information.

CHAPTER 5

Accessing Internal Performance Measurements

For anyone familiar with Cisco routers, there is little doubt they consist of highly sophisticated hardware and software. From a hardware perspective a router is similar to a personal computer, with a microprocessor providing the internal computing capability required to move packets from one interface through the router to another interface. Like a personal computer, a router is commonly expanded by using expansion boards; however, those boards typically include on-board processors so a router can perform I/O operations with a minimal impact on its central processing unit.

From a software perspective there are probably hundreds of thousands of lines of code that make up a router's operating system whose execution makes it possible to move data between interfaces, convert packet formats, and perform numerous additional functions. Some of these functions occur by default while others, such as data compression, must be enabled through the use of different EXEC commands.

This chapter focuses first on accessing internal router performance measurements by examining the different commands that let us observe the state of various router functions and other commands that help us alleviate potential or actual bottlenecks. In terms of the latter, we are concerned with improving the performance level of a router, so we do not limit our efforts to simply observing the state of router functions. Thus, when applicable we examine the use of router commands to enable functions that enhance the performance of this communications device as well as describe and discuss how those functions enhance router performance.

Since a router is a collection of sophisticated hardware and software modules, many areas can be examined that indicate various aspects associated with both the overall level of router performance and specific areas of router performance. For this reason, we examine performance-related areas within a router in this chapter. Those areas begin with the display of different types of memory through the use of the show memory command. Since we need a mechanism to verify memory problems as well as to adjust or reallocate available memory, we also examine the use of the show buffers and buffers commands, with the latter used to adjust buffer memory.

Next, we use the show processes command to display information about active processes. This command also results in the display of CPU utilization at the beginning of the display.

After we examine the use of the previously mentioned commands, we look at the other commands used to enhance the overall level of router performance. We examine functions that can be enabled or disabled by using different router commands, including address resolution protocol (ARP) table entries, compressing TCP headers, and switching functions that can have a significant impact upon the flow of data.

Displaying Memory Information

You can display a variety of information about memory utilization by using the show memory command. For example, you can display a memory dump, show the state of allocating processes and memory failures, or display statistics about the use of different types of router memory.

The format of the show memory command is indicated here:

```
show memory type
```

where type defines the memory type to be displayed. If you do not specify a memory type, information about all types of memory installed in your router is displayed, which can result in an extensive list. Thus, you are probably well advised to display information concerning specific types of memory.

Figure 5-1 illustrates the use of the show memory command with the question mark (?) to display a list of available memory display options. Note that there are 11 primary options you can use with the show memory command. Some options, such as the dump of memory, are more useful for troubleshooting when a problem exists in hardware and software, and a Cisco Systems employee will typically ask customers to dump a specific area of memory to assist their problem-resolution effort. Other memory display command options that provide summary statistics are more useful for organizations operating Cisco routers that wish to deter-

Figure 5-1   Memory display options.

```
Router#show memory ?
  <0-4294967294>      Dump memory starting at <address>
  allocating-process  Show allocating process name
  dead                Memory owned by dead processes
  failures            Memory failures
  fast                Fast memory stats
  free                Free memory stats
  io                  IO memory stats
  multibus            Multibus memory stats
  pci                 PCI memory stats
  processor           Processor memory stats
  summary             Summary of memory usage per alloc PC
  |                   Output modifiers
  <cr>
```

mine if their equipment is performing. Thus, this section focuses primarily on the latter.

Since any discussion of the use of the show memory command requires an understanding of the different types of memory used by Cisco routers, a brief review of router memory is in order. In addition, because different routers use different types of memory at different locations, a discussion of memory maps is also in order.

Router Memory Review

A Cisco router can contain different types of memory that is used to store microcode, configuration files, and memory images. Unfortunately, those locations typically differ from router to router, based upon the specific router model and the type of memory installed in the device. Although there is no such thing as a typical Cisco router since even two of the same models can differ because of customization, this section focuses on learning about the different types of router memory and how such memory is used. There are four general categories of router memory, so let's examine each.

DYNAMIC RANDOM ACCESS MEMORY (DRAM)

Dynamic random access memory (DRAM) is the basic type of memory used by all routers. Information in DRAM depends on the power-on state of the router, and all information in this type of memory is lost when power is turned off.

DRAM is used for two functions: main memory and shared memory. Although Cisco literature refers to this as two types of memory, in actuality there is only one type of DRAM that is used for two different functions. *Main memory,* which is also referred to as *primary or processor memory,* is reserved for use by the processor to execute *Internetwork Operating System* (IOS) software and to hold the running router configuration and routing tables. Similar to many PCs that partition memory for use by the processor and video, Cisco partitions DRAM for use by the processor and for I/O operations. Thus, the second type of DRAM is referred to as *I/O memory* or *shared memory.* This memory area of DRAM is used as a buffer area for data destined for transmission via an interface or received via an interface.

ERASABLE PROGRAMMABLE READ ONLY MEMORY (EPROM)

Erasable programmable read-only memory (EPROM) holds information when a router is shut down or rebooted. That information is semipermanent, as it can be erased. EPROM is often referred to as ROM, although this is not technically correct since ROM cannot be erased. The purpose of EPROM is to hold the ROM monitor, which provides a user interface when the router cannot locate a valid image and the boot loader. The latter enables the router to boot when an IOS image cannot be located in Flash memory.

Nonvolatile Random Access Memory (NVRAM)

Nonvolatile random access memory (NVRAM) is similar to DRAM; however, information is retained when power is lost or a system rebooted. Although NVRAM is similar to EPROM memory, a key difference between the two is information access speed, since data stored in NVRAM can be retrieved faster than information stored in EPROM. NVRAM is used to store the startup configuration file for all routers other than members of the 7000 family of products, which uses an environment variable to denote the location of the startup configuration. A second function of NVRAM contains the software configuration register associated with all modern routers. This register, which was used as a physical register on older router models, indicates which configuration image to use during the router initialization or booting process.

FLASH

A fourth type of memory available on Cisco routers is Flash memory. Depending upon the router model, Flash memory may be implemented on EPROMs as *single in-line memory modules* (SIMMs) or Flash memory cards. Flash memory cards are inserted into a PC card slot in the router in a manner similar to that by which a PC card modem is inserted into a PC card slot in a notebook computer.

The use of Flash memory, as well as the type of Flash memory supported, depends on the particular router being used. On some platforms you can use internal Flash memory with one or two banks of SIMMs. Other routers include one or more PC card slots. Regardless of the type of Flash memory, their functionality is similar. That is, Flash memory can be used to copy a system image from a router to a network server via tftp or from a server into Flash memory. For certain routers, such as the Cisco 4500 series and 7000 family of products, you can also boot a router from a system image stored in Flash memory. For those products you can transfer a boot image to a network server or load the image into Flash memory from a server.

Because of the high degree of functionality of Flash memory, Cisco IOS software has a series of commands that facilitate working with this type of data storage. These commands range from formatting Flash for initial use to storing, erasing, deleting, and recovering files. In fact, some commands are similar to DOS, providing a well-recognized operating environment for those readers who worked with PCs prior to Windows and became familiar with its command structure. Because of the capability such commands provide, let's briefly digress and examine a core set of commands prior to resuming our discussion of router memory.

FLASH REFERENCE

Depending on the router in use, it has either one or two PC card slots into which Flash memory cards can be inserted. When a router only has one slot, such as a Cisco 1600 series device, Flash memory is referenced using the term flash:, with the colon (:) always following the reference to the device. For Cisco 3600 routers the device can have internal Flash memory in the form of SIMMs or Flash Memory PC cards. Internal Flash is referenced as flash:, while PC card Flash is referenced as slot0: or slot1: to distinguish one PC card module from another. For Cisco 7000 family routers you can have internal Flash memory referenced as bootflash: or Flash memory PC cards inserted in one or both PC card slots and referenced as slot0: and slot1:.

FORMATTING FLASH

Similar to DOS, IOS has a format command, which can be used in privileged mode. The following example illustrates the use of the format command to initialize a Flash memory card inserted in slot 0. Note that because the command erases all information previously stored, IOS provides a suitable prompt to make you think about your pending action:

```
Router#format slot0:
Running config file on this device, proceed? [confirm]y
All sectors will be erased, proceed? [confirm]y
Enter volume id (up to 31 characters): Return
Formatting sector1 (erasing)
Format device slot0 completed
```

Once you have initialized your Flash memory, it is ready for use. At this point, several IOS commands can be used to manage Flash memory. First, you could use the `cd` command, which in DOS means *change directory* to specify the default Flash memory device similar to a default directory. The format of this command is

```
cd device:
```

Thus, to set the default device to the Flash memory card previously inserted into slot 0, you enter

```
cd slot0:
```

If you are in doubt as to the current working device specified by a previously issued `cd` command, you can use the `pwd` command to obtain this information. The following example of the `pwd` command is equivalent to determining the default directory:

```
Router> pwd
Slot0
Router>
```

In addition to the `cd` and `pwd` commands, there are commands to partition Flash memory (`partition`), download a configuration into Flash memory (`copy`), display information stored in Flash (`dir`), erase a file stored in Flash memory (`erase`), delete a file (`delete`), and recover or undelete a previously deleted file (`undelete`), as well as permanently delete files (`squeeze`). An erased file cannot be recovered; it is permanent removal. In comparison, a deleted file can be recovered or permanently deleted through the use of the `squeeze` command. Since the primary focus of this chapter is on examining internal router performance measurement metrics, we do not probe deeper into Flash memory commands at this time. Thus, let's now return to memory and continue by examining how memory is used.

Memory Maps

A memory map is a guide to the use of actual and expandable memory for a particular router. Since routers are designed at different periods of time for different end-user operating environments, techniques were used to create each hardware platform that resulted in a nonstandard use of memory by different products. Thus, the allocation of memory for one router will more than likely differ from that of another router. In addition, although two routers can have the same basic memory map, the actual utilization of memory between routers can differ if one router has different types of optional memory not used by another router. Thus, a mem-

Table 5-1   Cisco 7000 Router Memory Map

Hex Address	Function
11110100	System status register
11110400	Flash memory card status
11110C00	I/O address base
11120024	Timer control register
11120200	Environmental monitor control-16 bits
11120300	Environmental monitor status-32 bits
11130000	Diagnostic bus
11131000	ID PROM
11140000	NVRAM
1115FC00	Environmental monitor NVRAM base address
1115FFFF	Real-time calendar bit
11200000-11FFFFFF	Reserved
12000000	Onboard Flash memory
14000000	External Flash memory

ory map is a guide to the potential use of memory instead of the actual use of memory.

Table 5-1 lists the memory map for a Cisco 7000 router. Note that the addresses listed in Table 5-1 represent high memory locations. Most Cisco routers use low memory for system DRAM which holds the operating version of IOS and the current configuration file and whose actual availability depends upon the number and capacity of memory modules installed in the router. Older routers, such as the Cisco 3104 and 4500 products, support 8-, 16-, and 32-Mbyte modules. Newer routers may also support 64 Mbyte modules.

It is extremely important to review Cisco literature for the IOS release you are running, the platform on which you are running the release, and the feature set you are operating so you can determine the minimum required code memory to store information in Flash as well as the minimum amount of required main memory. For example, a Cisco 7500 Series router running IOS version 11.2 with the IP set should have a 16/20-MB Flash memory card and 32 MB of RAM. You can determine the minimum amount of memory required for a particular router operating environment from the manual or CD-ROM shipped with the router or from the Cisco Web site through an appropriate search. Now that we understand memory maps, let's return to the show memory command.

The show memory Options

Figure 5-1 showed the variety of options that can be used with the show memory command. Thus, let's probe a bit deeper into the use of this command and examine the use of several show memory subcommands.

Figure 5-2 illustrates the use of two show memory subcommands, show memory allocating-process and show memory dead. The top portion

Figure 5-2   Using different show memory command options.

```
Router#show memory allocating-process
             Head   Total(b)   Used(b)    Free(b)  Lowest(b)  Largest(b)
Processor  61418C40  46035904   6112848   39923056   36991856   37103368
    Fast   613F8C40    131072     95032      36040      36040      35996


Router#show memory dead
             Head   Total(b)   Used(b)    Free(b)  Lowest(b)  Largest(b)
Processor  61418C40  46035904   6112732   39923172   36991856   37103368
    Fast   613F8C40    131072     95032      36040      36040      35996



Dead Proc Summary for: Processor

pc = 0x601EAB8C, count = 0022, name = Virtual Exec
pc = 0x601EAB98, count = 0022, name = Virtual Exec
pc = 0x60283D38, count = 0022, name = Virtual Exec
pc = 0x60707D4C, count = 0020, name = Virtual Exec
pc = 0x602CD2C4, count = 0008, name = Virtual Exec
pc = 0x605C57D8, count = 0008, name = RIP sw subblock
pc = 0x6044E510, count = 0007, name = Virtual Exec
pc = 0x60249204, count = 0006, name = TTY timer block
pc = 0x60358594, count = 0006, name = remote filesys
pc = 0x60707B38, count = 0005, name = Virtual Exec
pc = 0x60397E98, count = 0005, name = Slave Server
pc = 0x605C7288, count = 0004, name = RIP ndb
pc = 0x60446300, count = 0004, name = Router Init
pc = 0x605C6E1C, count = 0004, name = RIP rdb
pc = 0x60707B20, count = 0003, name = Virtual Exec
```

Figure 5-2 (*Continued*)

```
pc = 0x601EB288, count = 0003, name = Virtual Exec
pc = 0x601EB294, count = 0003, name = Virtual Exec
pc = 0x6028072C, count = 0003, name = Virtual Exec
pc = 0x60B656C0, count = 0003, name = Virtual Exec
pc = 0x603D6248, count = 0003, name = Virtual Exec
pc = 0x609B3320, count = 0003, name = SWIDB_SB: SRB Info
pc = 0x603ACB1C, count = 0002, name = IPC Name String
pc = 0x602282D0, count = 0002, name = Virtual Exec
pc = 0x603A8414, count = 0002, name = IPC Port
pc = 0x60227EE8, count = 0001, name = Virtual Exec
pc = 0x60227FE4, count = 0001, name = Virtual Exec
pc = 0x605C6264, count = 0001, name = RIP pdb info
pc = 0x60227F84, count = 0001, name = Virtual Exec
pc = 0x60228060, count = 0001, name = Virtual Exec
pc = 0x602280B0, count = 0001, name = Virtual Exec
pc = 0x60718768, count = 0001, name = Virtual Exec
pc = 0x6024D914, count = 0001, name = Virtual Exec
pc = 0x60B56C48, count = 0001, name = Virtual Exec
pc = 0x602491A8, count = 0001, name = TTY timers array
pc = 0x60B56C70, count = 0001, name = Virtual Exec
pc = 0x6071877C, count = 0001, name = Virtual Exec
pc = 0x60B56C30, count = 0001, name = Virtual Exec
pc = 0x602A6670, count = 0001, name = RIP WorkQ
pc = 0x60B656C0, count = 0001, name = Router Init
pc = 0x602A6670, count = 0001, name = FIB default path chunk
pc = 0x603D6248, count = 0001, name = Router Init
pc = 0x602A6670, count = 0001, name = NAT Port Range Chunks
pc = 0x602A6670, count = 0001, name = IPnat DNS RR ptrs
pc = 0x602A66D4, count = 0001, name = IPnat DNS RR ptrs
pc = 0x602A66D4, count = 0001, name = FIB default path chunk
pc = 0x602B6F78, count = 0001, name = Watched Queue
pc = 0x608BF668, count = 0001, name = Virtual Exec
pc = 0x608BF680, count = 0001, name = Virtual Exec
pc = 0x602A6670, count = 0001, name = NAT Entry Chunks
pc = 0x602A6670, count = 0001, name = NAT Address Chunks
pc = 0x6023B530, count = 0001, name = Priority List
pc = 0x6022CEF4, count = 0001, name = Virtual Exec
pc = 0x602A6670, count = 0001, name = FIB maximum path chunk
pc = 0x602A66D4, count = 0001, name = FIB maximum path chunk
```

    Processor Memory

Address	Bytes	Prev.	Next	Ref	PrevF	NextF	Alloc PC	What
61429914	72	614298C8	61429988	1			603ACB1C	IPC Name String
61429F2C	64	61429ED8	61429F98	1			60707B20	Virtual Exec
6142A040	124	61429FEC	6142A0E8	1			605C7288	RIP ndb
6142BAF8	24	6142BAB4	6142BB3C	1			60227EE8	Virtual Exec
614B52EC	52	614B5218	614B534C	1			60707D4C	Virtual Exec
614B534C	52	614B52EC	614B53AC	1			60707B38	Virtual Exec
Address	Bytes	Prev.	Next	Ref	PrevF	NextF	Alloc PC	What
614B53AC	52	614B534C	614B540C	1			60707D4C	Virtual Exec
614B540C	52	614B53AC	614B546C	1			60707B38	Virtual Exec
614B9D38	112	614B9CEC	614B9DD4	1			6044E510	Virtual Exec

(*Continued*)

Figure 5-2 (*Continued*)

Address	Bytes	Prev.	Next	Ref	PrevF	NextF	Alloc PC	What
6153E950	24	6153E90C	6153E994	1			60227FE4	Virtual Exec
6159E85C	32	6159E4AC	6159E8A8	1			60397E98	Slave Server
6159E8A8	32	6159E85C	6159E8F4	1			60397E98	Slave Server
615AACE4	28	615AABE0	615AAD2C	1			60446300	Router Init
615AB114	44	615AB090	615AB16C	1			60249204	TTY timer
block								
615AB274	112	615AB204	615AB310	1			60358594	remote
filesys								
615AB310	44	615AB274	615AB368	1			60707D4C	Virtual Exec
615AB4BC	160	615AB410	615AB588	1			605C6264	RIP pdb info
6169F8FC	24	6169F8B8	6169F940	1			60227F84	Virtual Exec
616A6568	36	616A365C	616A65B8	1			60228060	Virtual Exec
616AEDA4	24	616AED10	616AEDE8	1			602280B0	Virtual Exec
61823D5C	44	61823D18	61823DB4	1			60707D4C	Virtual Exec
618289D0	24	6182898C	61828A14	1			60707D4C	Virtual Exec
61828B88	24	61828B44	61828BCC	1			60707B20	Virtual Exec
6183C8F4	300	6183C8AC	6183CA4C	1			602CD2C4	Virtual Exec
6183E0F4	112	6183E0AC	6183E190	1			60358594	remote
filesys								
6183E190	40	6183E0F4	6183E1E4	1			605C6E1C	RIP rdb
6183E1E4	100	6183E190	6183E274	1			605C6E1C	RIP rdb
6183E274	44	6183E1E4	6183E2CC	1			60249204	TTY timer
block								
Address	Bytes	Prev.	Next	Ref	PrevF	NextF	Alloc PC	What
.....	..	..	...		...		....	...

of Figure 5-2 shows the use of the first command and the resulting display. Note that the use of either command results in the display of a two-line table that provides a breakdown of processor and fast memory usage. However, the use of the show memory dead command follows that initial table with a comprehensive table of *program counter* (pc) information.

As a result of the show memory allocating-process and show memory dead commands, in the first two pairs of tables in Figure 5-2 you will note they provide the same summary information. This information can be quite valuable to review periodically so let's do so. First, the entries under the column labeled Head indicate the hexadecimal address of the beginning or head of the memory allocation chain. This is the area where IOS begins to store data.

If you examine the next five headings you will note the suffix (b) after each heading, where (b) indicates that the entry for each heading is provided in terms of bytes.

The second column is labeled Total and indicates, in bytes, the sum of the next two column entries. That is, total bytes = the amount of memory used + the amount of free memory that is not being used at the present time. By examining the amount of free or available memory, you can quite often determine ahead of time the need to upgrade your router.

Returning to our examination of Figure 5-2, note that the use of the show memory dead command first provides a summary of dead processes. That summary includes the current program counter (pc) value, count, and process name. For space conservation purposes, only a portion of that summary table is shown. That table is followed by a second table, labeled Processor Memory. This table can be displayed by using several show memory command options, including show memory without any following options.

In examining the Processor Memory table you will note nine columns. The first, labeled Address, indicates the hexadecimal address of the block. The second column, labeled Bytes, indicates the size of the memory block in bytes. The next column, which is labeled Prev., indicates the address of the previous memory block. For all entries other than the first, this field should have a value that matches the value in the Address field on the previous line. The exception is the first entry which has no previous block and is set to 0. As you might expect, the column or field labeled Next contains the address of the next block, which should match the value entered in the Address field for the next line.

The column labeled Ref is a reference count for each memory block. Thus, the value in the Ref field indicates how many different processes are using a particular memory block. The following column, labeled PrevF, indicates the address of the previous free memory block if one is available. Similarly, the column labeled NextF contains the address of the next free block if one is available. The last two columns, labeled Alloc PC and What, indicate the address of the system call that allocated the block and the name of the process that owns the block. In terms of the latter, other possible entries in the column labeled What can include (fragment) if the block is a fragment or (coalesced) if the block was coalesced from adjacent free blocks.

Continuing our examination of different versions of the show memory command, Figure 5-3 illustrates the use of the show memory io command. The top portion of Figure 5-3 illustrates the various show memory io command options. The lower portion of Figure 5-3 illustrates a portion of the results obtained when the show memory io command is used without options, resulting in a full summary of the use of memory IO blocks.

It is quite possible that a router administrator may never have to display information about memory usage. However, if you begin to experience unexplained throughput problems once in a while, it is possible to isolate the cause of a problem by using a show memory command. For example, consider the count values for the program counter. Since the table is sorted by block size, you would have to scroll through the table in an attempt to determine if any one or series of blocks have an unusually large count value. If you encounter this situation, it is quite possible that an enabled function might be better set as disabled if not essential.

Figure 5-3 Using the show memory io command.

```
Router#show memory io ?
  allocating-process  Show allocating process name
  dead                Memory owned by dead processes
  free                Free memory stats
  |                   Output modifiers
  <cr>

Router#show memory io
Allocator PC Summary for: Processor

pc=0x602731A8, size=001605468, count=000879, name=*Packet Data*
pc=0x602A6670, size=001481532, count=000086, name=List Elements
pc=0x602C979C, size=000642916, count=000089, name=Interrupt Stack
pc=0x602A66D4, size=000620940, count=000009, name=Adjacency chunk
pc=0x60273178, size=000516992, count=000879, name=*Packet Header*
pc=0x602B6F78, size=000161388, count=001213, name=Watched Boolean
pc=0x602F8480, size=000122924, count=000001, name=Ucode Buffer
pc=0x602796FC, size=000115040, count=000008, name=Fair Queueing
pc=0x6022CEF4, size=000065580, count=000001, name=Virtual Exec
pc=0x6027A55C, size=000054004, count=000023, name=*Software IDB*
pc=0x60266090, size=000049196, count=000001, name=Virtual Exec
pc=0x602C4E7C, size=000047560, count=000082, name=Process
pc=0x603A89A4, size=000037296, count=000042, name=IPC Port
pc=0x602402F4, size=000028756, count=000007, name=TTY data
pc=0x6039D0CC, size=000028204, count=000001, name=Init
pc=0x60276660, size=000020924, count=000021, name=Packet Elements
pc=0x6070A29C, size=000020448, count=000001, name=Init
pc=0x6070A18C, size=000020444, count=000001, name=Init
pc=0x603AB578, size=000020044, count=000001, name=IPC Msg Cache
pc=0x60283D38, size=000018920, count=000022, name=Virtual Exec
pc=0x603AB684, size=000016400, count=000100, name=IPC Message
pc=0x60416F18, size=000015168, count=000016, name=IP Input
pc=0x6025079C, size=000014608, count=000212, name=Parser Linkage
pc=0x60059DD8, size=000014508, count=000001, name=Init
pc=0x602B7288, size=000014340, count=000083, name=Process Events
pc=0x60022E5C, size=000013724, count=000028, name=ATMSIG-SHOW
pc=0x60434930, size=000012672, count=000022, name=IDB: IP Routing
pc=0x6042A61C, size=000011428, count=000001, name=DHCPD Message Workspace
.........................................................................
.........................................................................

        Processor Memory

Address  Bytes Prev.    Next     Ref PrevF NextF Alloc PC  What
61418C40 1064  0        61419094 1                602A6670  List Elements
61419094 2864  61418C40 61419BF0 1                602A6670  List Headers
61419BF0 9000  61419094 6141BF44 1                602C979C  Interrupt Stack
6141BF44 44    61419BF0 6141BF9C 1                60B656C0  *Init*
6141BF9C 9000  6141BF44 6141E2F0 1                602C979C  Interrupt Stack
6141E2F0 44    6141BF9C 6141E348 1                60B656C0  *Init*
6141E348 160   6141E2F0 6141E414 1                602C382C  *Init*
.........................................................................
.........................................................................
```

Another possibility, although rare, is the ability to locate a bug or abnormal condition by notifying your Cisco engineer of an abnormal situation resulting from the display of memory information.

Determining Memory Problems with `show buffers`

If you use the `show memory` command and determine that a very small amount of free memory is available, you should also consider using the `show buffers` EXEC command. If you enter this command without arguments, you obtain a display of information about all of your router's buffer pools. In Figure 5-4 note that the entry for `VeryBigBuffers` contains 20 entries for no memory, which indicates that there were 20 failures that occurred because there was no memory available to create a new buffer. This would verify that a low value for free memory displayed as a

Figure 5-4   Using the `show buffers` command to determine if low memory is causing packet drops.

```
Router# show buffers
Buffer elements:
     500 in free list   (500 max allowed)
     12870 hits, 0 misses, 0 created

Public buffer pools:
Small buffers, 104 bytes (total  20, permanent  20):
     20 in free list ( 5  min, 30 max allowed)
     18937 hits, 0 misses, 0 trims, 0 created
     0 failures (0 no memory)
Middle buffers, 600 bytes (total 100, permanent 100):
     80 in free list (10 min, 200 max allowed)
     9257 hits, 0 misses, 0 trims, 0 created
     0 failures (0 no memory)
Big buffers, 1524 bytes (total 120, permanent 120):
     100 in free list (5 min, 300 max allowed)
     113 hits, 0 misses, 0 trims, 0 created
     0 failures (0 no memory)
VeryBig buffers, 4520 bytes (total 10, permanent 10):
     10 in free list (0 min, 300 max allowed)
     47 hits, 20 misses, 0 trims, 0 created
     20 failures (20 no memory)
Large buffers, 5024 bytes (total 10, permanent 10):
     10 in free list (0 min, 30 max allowed)
     0 hits, 0 misses, 0 trims, 0 created
     0 failures (0 no memory)
Huge buffers, 18024 bytes (total 0, permanent 0):
     0 in free list (0 min, 13 max allowed)
     0 hits, 0 misses, 0 trims, 0 created
     0 failures (0 no memory)
```

result of the show memory command is causing a problem, in this case packet drops. Since the fields in the display resulting from the show buffers command can provide you with valuable information about the use of buffer pools, let's focus on the key fields shown in Figure 5-4.

BUFFER ELEMENTS

A buffer element is a small structure used as a placeholder for buffers in internal operating system queues. Thus, a buffer element can be considered a pointer. That pointer is used for situations where a buffer needs to be on more than one queue. The field labeled "free list" indicates the number of unallocated buffer elements, while the field labeled "max allowed" indicates the maximum number of buffers available for allocation. In the second line under the buffer elements entry in Figure 5-4 the field labeled "hits" indicates the count of successful attempts to allocate a buffer when needed. The field labeled "misses" then indicates the count of allocation attempts that required a growth in the buffer pool to allocate a buffer. The third field, "created," indicates the count of new buffers created to satisfy buffer allocation attempts when the available buffers in the pool were already allocated.

PUBLIC BUFFER POOLS

The second section of the display in Figure 5-4 shows the listing of information for six types of public buffer pools, with their size ranging from 104 to 18,024 bytes. For each type of buffer its length, in bytes, is first displayed, followed by two fields, labeled "total" and "permanent." The field labeled "total" indicates the total number of a particular type of buffer, while the field labeled "permanent" indicates the number of such buffers that are permanent.

The second line for each type of buffer has three fields, labeled "free list," "min," and "max allowed." The field labeled "free list" indicates the number of available and unallocated buffers for a particular type of public pool. The field labeled "min" indicates the minimum number of free or unallocated buffers in the particular buffer pool. The third field, "max allowed," indicates the maximum number of free or unallocated buffers in a particular pool.

Continuing our exploration of the display, the third line in each public buffer pool's entry contains the fields labeled "hits," "misses," "trims," and "created." Since we previously described three of these four fields during our examination of buffer elements, let's look at the field labeled "trims," which is only applicable to public buffer pools. The Trims field contains a count of buffers released to the system because they were not being used. Finally, the fourth line for each type of public buffer pool has two fields, labeled "failures" and "no memory." The field labeled "failures" indicates the total number of allocation requests that failed because no buffer was available for allocation. Although each such failure results in the loss of a datagram, the loss does not necessarily result from a lack of memory. Such failures primarily occur at a CPU interrupt level and can indicate that too much processing was occurring to obtain a free buffer at a particular point in time. In comparison, the field labeled "no memory" indicates the number of failures that occurred because no memory was available to create a new buffer. Although the number of failures and no memory is shown as being equal for the ...VeryBig Buffers entry in Figure 5-4, as previously noted these entries do not always have to match one another.

USING THE buffers COMMAND

Once you examine the use of a router's buffer pools, it is possible to use the buffers global configuration command to adjust the initial buffer pool settings and to define limits at which temporary buffers are created and destroyed. Of course, if you have already determined you have a memory problem, the buffers command is more useful if you resolved the problem. An exception to this is the situation where your router has a large number of permanent buffers that are rarely used. Since large and huge buffers require 5024 and 18,024 bytes, respectively, it is possible that a prior adjustment for a certain operating environment that was temporary in nature could be changed and free up enough resources to alleviate a router upgrade.

If your operating environment favors one size of datagrams over other sizes, it might be beneficial to adjust your router's buffers. For example, in a voice over IP environment datagrams are normally under 80 bytes. Thus, if you expect a significant amount of voice over IP traffic, it might be advisable to adjust the maximum number of free or unallocated small buffers.

The format of the buffers global configuration command is shown here:

```
buffers {small|middle|big|verybig|large|huge type type
     number}{permanent|max-free|min-free|initial} number
```

As previously noted, small, middle, big, very big, large, and huge are different types of buffer pools with different lengths in bytes. From Figure 5-4 you can determine the length of each type of public buffer pool. Type indicates the interface type of the buffer pool, whose value cannot be *fiber-distributed data interface* (FDDI). The number indicates the interface number of the interface buffer pool. A permanent entry defines the number of permanent buffers that the system should attempt to allocate. Max-free and Min-free are the maximum and minimum number of free or unallocated buffers for a specific public buffer pool. Initial indicates the number of additional temporary buffers that should be allocated when the system is reloaded while the second field, labeled number, indicates the number of buffers to allocate.

As a general rule, you should observe the state of router buffers with the show buffers all command. If you note a depleted or near-depleted buffer pool, you should then focus your effort on increasing that pool. To illustrate a potential use of the buffers command, let's assume that because we noted that we ran out of very big buffers, we decided to increase the maximum number of such buffers from 300 to 400. To do so, we would enter the following command:

```
buffers verybig max-free 400
```

USING THE show processes COMMAND

Another helpful command you can use to determine information about the use of a router is the show processes EXEC command. The format of this command is shown here:

```
show processes {cpu|memory}
```

where the keyword cpu displays detailed CPU utilization information while the keyword memory displays memory utilization information attributable to different processes. Figure 5-5 illustrates the resulting display

Figure 5-5 Using the show processes cpu command.

```
Router# show processes ?
  cpu      Show CPU use per process
  memory   Show memory use per process
  |        Output modifiers
  <cr>

Router# show processes cpu
CPU utilization for five seconds: 7%/7%; one minute: 8%; five minutes: 6%
 PID  Runtime(ms)  Invoked  uSecs   5Sec    1Min    5Min  TTY Process
   1           52  1369347      0   0.00%   0.00%   0.00%   0 Load Meter
   2         1864   114105     16   0.00%   0.00%   0.00%   0 CEF Scanner
   3      1390960   695378   2000   0.00%   0.00%   0.00%   0 Check heaps
   4          852     2451    347   0.00%   0.00%   0.00%   0 PoolManager
   5            0        2      0   0.00%   0.00%   0.00%   0 Timers
   6         9008    32413    277   0.00%   0.00%   0.00%   0 SerialBackgroun
   7            0        1      0   0.00%   0.00%   0.00%   0 OIR Handler
   8            0        1      0   0.00%   0.00%   0.00%   0 IPC Zone Manager
   9         2144  6846238      0   0.00%   0.00%   0.00%   0 IPC Periodic Tim
  10      1467848 55552149     26   0.00%   0.01%   0.00%   0 IPC Seat Manager
  11        92896   578645    160   0.00%   0.00%   0.00%   0 ARP Input
  12        25192  1382705     18   0.00%   0.00%   0.00%   0 HC Counter Timer
  13            0       73      0   0.00%   0.00%   0.00%   0 DDR Timers
  14            0        2      0   0.00%   0.00%   0.00%   0 Dialer  event
  15            0        1      0   0.00%   0.00%   0.00%   0 Entity MIB  API
  16            0        1      0   0.00%   0.00%   0.00%   0 SERIAL A'detect
```

Figure 5-5 *(Continued)*

PID	Runtime(ms)	Invoked	uSecs	5Sec	1Min	5Min	TTY	Process
17	0	1	0	0.00%	0.00%	0.00%	0	Microcode Loader
18	0	38	0	0.00%	0.00%	0.00%	0	Critical Bkgnd
19	142972	1129348	126	0.00%	0.00%	0.00%	0	Net Background
20	4	781087	0	0.00%	0.00%	0.00%	0	Logger
21	3392	6846238	0	0.00%	0.00%	0.00%	0	TTY Background
22	7780	6846237	1	0.00%	0.00%	0.00%	0	Per-Second Jobs
PID	Runtime(ms)	Invoked	uSecs	5Sec	1Min	5Min	TTY	Process
23	0	1	0	0.00%	0.00%	0.00%	0	IP Crashinfo Inp
24	0	1	0	0.00%	0.00%	0.00%	0	DSX3MIB 11 handl
25	9792	6846242	1	0.00%	0.00%	0.00%	0	RSP Background
26	12040	228209	52	0.00%	0.00%	0.00%	0	Slave Time
27	0	1	0	0.00%	0.00%	0.00%	0	Slave IPC OIR
28	1884	22861	82	0.16%	0.81%	0.34%	2	Virtual Exec
29	176	1938481	0	0.00%	0.00%	0.00%	0	Chassis Daemon
30	3048	114105	26	0.00%	0.00%	0.00%	0	RSP Chassis Back
31	0	1	0	0.00%	0.00%	0.00%	0	MIP Mailbox
32	0	1	0	0.00%	0.00%	0.00%	0	vcq_proc
33	0	1	0	0.00%	0.00%	0.00%	0	CT3 Mailbox
34	0	1	0	0.00%	0.00%	0.00%	0	CE3 Mailbox
35	1750232	80880192	21	0.00%	0.00%	0.00%	0	IPC CBus process
36	0	2	0	0.00%	0.00%	0.00%	0	ATM OAM Input
37	0	2	0	0.00%	0.00%	0.00%	0	ATM OAM TIMER
38	1637828	41249959	39	0.00%	0.03%	0.01%	0	IP Input
39	219028	1446965	151	0.00%	0.00%	0.00%	0	CDP Protocol
40	0	1	0	0.00%	0.00%	0.00%	0	PPP IP Add Route
41	0	11399	0	0.00%	0.00%	0.00%	0	MOP Protocols
42	0	1	0	0.00%	0.00%	0.00%	0	X.25 Encaps Mana
43	0	1	0	0.00%	0.00%	0.00%	0	MPC Router Proce
44	0	2	0	0.00%	0.00%	0.00%	0	SSCOP Input
PID	Runtime(ms)	Invoked	uSecs	5Sec	1Min	5Min	TTY	Process
45	0	2	0	0.00%	0.00%	0.00%	0	SSCOP Output
46	4224	114107	37	0.00%	0.00%	0.00%	0	SSCOP Timer
47	232692	378265	615	0.00%	0.00%	0.00%	0	IP Background
48	0	2	0	0.00%	0.00%	0.00%	0	ILMI Input
49	0	1	0	0.00%	0.00%	0.00%	0	SNMP Timers
50	0	2	0	0.00%	0.00%	0.00%	0	ILMI Request
51	0	2	0	0.00%	0.00%	0.00%	0	ILMI Response
52	0	1	0	0.00%	0.00%	0.00%	0	ILMI Timer Proce
53	4	2	2000	0.00%	0.00%	0.00%	0	ATM PVC Discover
54	84376	114105	736	0.00%	0.00%	0.00%	0	Adj Manager
55	9496	6983195	1	0.00%	0.00%	0.00%	0	CEF process
56	0	3394	0	0.00%	0.00%	0.00%	0	TCP Timer
57	72	415	173	0.00%	0.00%	0.00%	0	TCP Protocols
58	0	1	0	0.00%	0.00%	0.00%	0	Probe Input
59	4288	136140	31	0.00%	0.00%	0.00%	0	RARP Input
60	0	1	0	0.00%	0.00%	0.00%	0	Socket Timers
61	64688	267855	241	0.00%	0.00%	0.00%	0	DHCPD Receive
62	5240	114105	45	0.00%	0.00%	0.00%	0	IP Cache Ager
63	0	1	0	0.00%	0.00%	0.00%	0	PAD InCall
64	0	2	0	0.00%	0.00%	0.00%	0	X.25 Background
65	0	1	0	0.00%	0.00%	0.00%	0	ISDN Timer
66	0	1	0	0.00%	0.00%	0.00%	0	Time Range Proce
PID	Runtime(ms)	Invoked	uSecs	5Sec	1Min	5Min	TTY	Process
67	12	246671	0	0.00%	0.00%	0.00%	0	RIP Send

(Continued)

Figure 5-5 *(Continued)*

PID								
68	0	1	0	0.00%	0.00%	0.00%	0	SYSMGT
Events								
69	0	1	0	0.00%	0.00%	0.00%	0	ISDNMIB Backgrou
70	0	1	0	0.00%	0.00%	0.00%	0	CallMIB Backgrou
71	0	1	0	0.00%	0.00%	0.00%	0	SNMP ConfCopyPro
72	60	13693440	0	0.00%	0.00%	0.00%	0	cbus utilization
73	1033464	58127301	17	0.00%	0.00%	0.00%	0	Net Input
74	180	1369349	0	0.00%	0.00%	0.00%	0	Compute load avg
75	491256	114105	4305	0.00%	0.00%	0.00%	0	Per-minute Jobs
76	56852	1286935	44	0.00%	0.00%	0.00%	0	RIP Router
77	166112	115020	1444	0.00%	0.00%	0.00%	0	IP-RT Background
78	0	1	0	0.00%	0.00%	0.00%	0	IP NAT Ager
79	0	57057	0	0.00%	0.00%	0.00%	0	DHCPD Timer
80	15952	1939770	8	0.00%	0.00%	0.00%	0	DHCPD Database
82	451960	374930	1205	0.00%	0.00%	0.00%	0	IP SNMP
83	64	264	242	0.00%	0.00%	0.00%	0	SNMP Traps

from the use of the show processes cpu command while Figure 5-6 shows the resulting display obtained from the show processes memory command. Let's first look at Figure 5-5 and decipher the information the show processes cpu command provides.

The first column labeled PID is the Process Identification or ProcessID. Note that processes are displayed in numeric order. The Runtime (ms) column indicates the CPU time each process has used. This time is denoted in milliseconds. While many processes are beyond your control, other processes are controllable and you can examine the Runtime column entries for some processes that you might wish to consider disabling if they are not necessary or as an interim measure until your organization receives a more powerful router. For example, if your router is at the edge of a network, you could disable RIP and employ static routing. From viewing the PID 76 entry, this would reduce the CPU utilization by 58,852 ms, not very much perhaps but certainly a start. If your organization did not need to run *simple network management protocol* (SNMP) or CDP[GF3], additional savings could result.

If you have a high level of CPU utilization, many times the process labeled "ip input," shown as PID 38 in Figure 5-5, can be the culprit. Unfortunately, ip input is a series of ip processes, including redirects, directed broadcasts, and proxy ARP. Thus, you should consider adding the following commands to each of your interfaces unless there is a compelling reason not to:

```
no ip redirects
no ip directed-broadcasts
no ip proxy-arp
```

Figure 5-6 Using the show processes memory command.

```
Router# show processes memory
Total: 46035904, Used: 6221392, Free: 39814512
PID
TTY  Allocated    Freed     Holding   Getbufs    Retbufs Process
  0   0     75844      1252   4413468        0          0 *Init*
  0   0       856   2835676       856        0          0 *Sched*
  0   0  79288512  73858752    344732  1452212          0 *Dead*
  1   0       268       268      3796        0          0 Load Meter
  2   0       228         0      7024        0          0 CEF Scanner
  3   0         0         0      6796        0          0 Check heaps
  4   0  14304760   1044352    298348  9611196    1420800 Pool Manager
  5   0       268       268      6796        0          0 Timers
  6   0       268       268      6796        0          0 Serial Backgroun
  7   0        96         0      3892        0          0 OIR Handler
  8   0        96         0      6892        0          0 IPC Zone Manager
  9   0         0         0      6796        0          0 IPC Periodic Tim
 10   0 954906872 954865848     34936        0          0 IPC Seat Manager
 11   0     11548   1051984     10404        0          0 ARP Input
 12   0         0         0      6796        0          0 HC Counter Timer
 13   0       308       308      6796        0          0 DDR Timers
 14   0       268       268     12796        0          0 Dialer event
 15   0        96         0      6892        0          0 Entity MIB API
 16   0        96         0      6892        0          0 SERIAL A'detect
 17   0      1032         0      7828        0          0 Microcode Loader
 18   0     17148         0     23944        0          0 Critical Bkgnd
 19   0 698773736 698751620     13332        0          0 Net Background
PID TTY Allocated     Freed   Holding   Getbufs    Retbufs Process
 20   0        96         0     12892        0          0 Logger
 21   0     26036      1804      6796        0          0 TTY Background
 22   0         0      7244      6796        0          0 Per-Second Jobs
 23   0       244         0      7040        0          0 IP Crashinfo Inp
 24   0        96         0      6892        0          0 DSX3MIB 11 handl
 25   0         0         0      6796        0          0 RSP Background
 26   0  33931108  33931108      3796        0          0 Slave Time
 27   0        96         0      6892        0          0 Slave IPC OIR
 28   2    278988    277804     14044        0          0 Virtual Exec
 29   0         0         0      3796        0          0 Chassis Daemon
 30   0         0         0      6796        0          0 RSP Chassis Back
 31   0        96         0      6892        0          0 MIP Mailbox
 32   0        96         0      6892        0          0 vcq_proc
 33   0        96         0      6892        0          0 CT3 Mailbox
 34   0        96         0      6892        0          0 CE3 Mailbox
 35   0        96         0      6892        0          0 IPC CBus process
 36   0       512       268     13040        0          0 ATM OAM Input
 37   0       268       268     12796        0          0 ATM OAM TIMER
 38   0   6439404     91200     35508   163620          0 IP Input
 39   0  63270028  63124332     13696   100800          0 CDP Protocol
 40   0       244         0      7040        0          0 PPP IP Add Route
 41   0       512       268      7040        0          0 MOP Protocols
PID TTY Allocated     Freed   Holding   Getbufs    Retbufs Process
 42   0       192         0      6988        0          0 X.25 Encaps Mana
 43   0        96         0      6892        0          0 MPC Router Proce
 44   0       364       268      6892        0          0 SSCOP Input
```

(Continued)

Figure 5-6 (*Continued*)

PID	TTY	Allocated	Freed	Holding	Getbufs	Retbufs	Process
45	0	364	268	6892	0	0	SSCOP Output
46	0	268	268	6796	0	0	SSCOP Timer
47	0	556	6672	9872	0	0	IP Background
48	0	364	268	12892	0	0	ILMI Input
49	0	0	0	6796	0	0	SNMP Timers
50	0	364	268	6892	0	0	ILMI Request
51	0	364	268	6892	0	0	ILMI Response
52	0	0	0	6796	0	0	ILMI Timer Proce
53	0	5796	684	17908	0	0	ATM PVC Discover
54	0	512	268	7040	0	0	Adj Manager
55	0	363796	11152	355228	0	0	CEF process
56	0	0	114000	12796	0	0	TCP Timer
57	0	2828656	0	14256	0	0	TCP Protocols
58	0	244	0	7040	0	0	Probe Input
59	0	96	0	6892	0	0	RARP Input
60	0	0	0	6796	0	0	Socket Timers
61	0	117271632	117242768	22068	0	0	DHCPD Receive
62	0	0	4949404	6796	0	0	IP Cache Ager
63	0	244	0	7040	0	0	PAD InCall
PID	TTY	Allocated	Freed	Holding	Getbufs	Retbufs	Process
64	0	364	268	12892	0	0	X.25 Background
65	0	0	0	6796	0	0	ISDN Timer
66	0	0	0	6796	0	0	Time Range Proce
67	0	96	40721820	6892	0	0	RIP Send
68	0	1324	0	8120	0	0	SYSMGT Events
69	0	0	0	6796	0	0	ISDNMIB Backgrou
70	0	0	0	6796	0	0	CallMIB Backgrou
71	0	96	0	12892	0	0	SNMP ConfCopyPro
72	0	0	0	6796	0	0	cbus utilization
73	0	192	0	6988	0	0	Net Input
74	0	268	268	6796	0	0	Compute load avg
75	0	53159756	5015652	63268	51343680	60054132	Per-minute Jobs
76	0	40785136	49600	20408	0	0	RIP Router
77	0	96	5956	6892	0	0	IP-RT Background
78	0	0	0	6796	0	0	IP NAT Ager
79	0	0	0	6796	0	0	DHCPD Timer
80	0	152	0	6948	0	0	DHCPD Database
82	0	1632547388	1632546336	13848	0	0	IP SNMP
83	0	756224	756128	12892	0	0	SNMP Traps
				6217792 Total			

Thus, a careful examination of the utilization of different processes and the necessity for those processes is a viable area to explore.

Continuing our examination of the entries in Figure 5-5, the column labeled "Invoked" indicates the number of times the process was invoked. The column labeled "uSecs" indicates the microseconds (s) of CPU time for each process invocation. The next three columns, labeled "5 Sec," "1 Min," and "5 Min," indicate CPU utilization by task in hundreds of seconds for the past 5 s, 1 min, and last 5 min, respectively. The column labeled TTY indicates the terminal that controls the process. Finally, the column labeled "Process" identifies the process.

Note that as a result of the show processes cpu command, above the actual table headings in Figure 5-5 the first display line provides a summary of CPU utilization for different periods of time. This is a most useful metric to determine the ability of the processor to keep up with the workload. Although a relatively low level of CPU utilization is shown, this is not always the case and you should periodically view this metric.

Using the show processes memory Command

We noted previously that we could display information about the use of memory through the use of the show process memory command. If we examine the use of that command and the resulting display shown in Figure 5-6 we note a tabular format similar to the display resulting from the use of the show processes cpu display. The first line above the table summarizes the state of router memory, indicating total, used, and free memory. The table that follows is listed by Process ID. It indicates the terminal that controls the process (TTY), the bytes of memory allocated by each process (Allocated), the bytes of memory freed by the process (Freed), the bytes of memory currently allocated to the process (Holding), the number of times the process requested a packet buffer (Getbufs), the number of times the packet relinquished a packet buffer (Retbufs), and the name of the process. If your router is short on free memory, you can use the results from the show processes memory command as a temporary measure to identify and disable optional processes that you can live without for a short period of time until FedEx delivers the memory you requested. Thus, you should consider using both the show processes cpu and the show processes memory commands on a periodic basis to observe the use of router CPU and memory.

Router Performance Features

Now that we understand the display of memory, CPU, and buffer pool information, we conclude this chapter by examining the enabling and disabling of certain router features that can affect its performance. The first feature we consider is the setting of entries in the ARP cache. To alleviate potential confusion, it should be noted that we are referring to entries in memory that facilitate the address resolution process and not the use of the ARP interface command which controls the interface-specific handling of IP address resolution.

Considering ARP Table Entries

In an IP environment stations have two addresses. The Mac address represents the network adapter card 6-byte hex number burnt into ROM. This address is used by layer 2 protocols, such as Ethernet and Token Ring to enable frame delivery. At the network layer, each station configured to support IP has a layer 3 IP address.

When a packet arrives at a router for forwarding, the operating system must determine the appropriate 48-bit Mac address associated with the destination IP address contained in the packet in order to deliver the packet. This is because LAN delivery is based on placing the IP datagram within a layer 2 frame which requires a layer 2 Mac destination address. The process required to obtain the required layer 2 address is referred to as an address resolution process which is based on the use of the address resolution protocol (ARP).

When a router is first powered-on, it has no knowledge of Mac addresses located via a particular interface other than the Mac address of its interface. Thus, when a packet arrives for delivery at a particular interface, the router broadcasts an ARP frame. As a result, this frame is received by all stations on the network. Since the destination IP address is known, it is included in the ARP frame. Each station on the network copies the frame off the network to determine if it is configured with the IP address contained in the frame. The station with the IP address responds with an ARP reply that contains its layer 2 Mac address. The router uses this address to form a frame. In addition, it places the IP address and its associated Mac layer 2 address that was just discovered into memory. Those entries, as well as a time value that governs the period of time an entry stays in cache, form the ARP cache.

To enhance the flow of data through an interface, you can consider the use of two commands: the arp command and the arp timeout command.

THE arp COMMAND

The arp command can be used to specify a static ARP cache entry. Doing so eliminates periodic broadcasts since the ARP entry permanently stays in the cache. The format of the arp command is shown here:

```
arp ip-address MAC-address type
```

In the preceding format the keyword type is replaced by the frame encapsulation method. For Ethernet the frame type is commonly arpa, while it is always snap for FDDI and token-ring interfaces.

The following example illustrates the placement of a static or permanent entry into the ARP cache.

```
arp 198.78.46.8 0800.07B3.1A3C arpa
```

In examining this example, note that the Mac address is entered in hex using dots (.) or periods as a separator for each group of 4-hex digits. By default, there are no permanent entries installed in the ARP cache.

Through the creation of permanent ARP cache entries, you can cut down the level of broadcasts occurring on a network. Although ARP broadcasts only periodically occur because the default time-out for learned entries is 4 h, if you are operating a heavily utilized low-speed LAN, every action you can take to enhance performance will be welcomed by your user community. Now that we understand how to place permanent entries into cache, let's examine an alternative method for reducing ARP broadcasts. This method involves adjusting the time learned entries will reside in cache.

THE arp timeout COMMAND

You can set the length of time an ARP entry is retained in cache. To do so, you use the arp timeout interface command whose format is shown here:

```
arp timeout seconds
```

The default time-out value for ARP entries is 4 h, which is expressed as 14,400 s. A value of 0 s sets no time-out, with the result that no ARP entries are ever cleared. Since you can make all ARP entries permanent with one arp timeout command, you may wish to consider its use instead of selectively using the arp global configuration command that must be used for each entry you wish to be made permanent.

You can use several commands to obtain additional information about the condition of the ARP cache. The show arp EXEC command can be used to display the contents of the ARP cache, while the show ip arp EXEC command can be used to show IP entries. You can remove all non-static entries from the ARP cache via the clear arp-cache privileged EXEC command.

To illustrate the use of the show ip arp, consider Figure 5-7. Note that the first column has the fixed entry Internet as we are limiting our display of ARP cache entries to those with an IP network address. One trick that does not enhance router performance but can save you time and effort is to use this command when you need to know the Mac address of a number of workstations on a network. If they were recently active, the router has an entry in its ARP cache for each station and the use of one router command to generate a display of IP addresses and their associated Mac addresses could save you valuable time.

TCP Header Compression

Similar to the rationale for the compression of files, compression of the headers of TCP/IP packets can reduce the size of such packets. Since transmission time is proportional to packet length, the enabling of TCP header compression can significantly enhance the data transfer capability of relatively low-speed serial lines. In fact, Cisco routers only support TCP header compression on serial lines using high-level data link control (HDLC) encapsulation.

Figure 5-7   Using the show arp command to view the contents of the ARP cache.

```
Router# show ip arp
Protocol  Address           Age (min)    Hardware Addr   Type    Interface
Internet  205.171.62.192       157        0800.3110.a3b6  ARPA    Ethernet1
Internet  205.171.62.245        52        0800.310e.28f8  ARPA    Ethernet1
Internet  205.171.1.140        112        0000.0c01.2812  ARPA    Ethernet0
Internet  205.171.62.160       123        0800.310e.4dab  ARPA    Ethernet1
Internet  205.171.1.111         28        0800.3107.8866  ARPA    Ethernet0
Internet  205.171.1.117        122        0000.0c00.f346  ARPA    Ethernet0
Internet  205.171.1.115         22        0000.0c01.0509  ARPA    Ethernet0
Internet  205.171.1.77          45        0800.310e.57ce  ARPA    Ethernet0
Internet  198.78.36.29         215        aa00.0400.0234  ARPA    Ethernet2
Internet  198.78.36.17         107        2424.c01f.0711  ARPA    Ethernet2
Internet  198.78.36.18         144        0000.0c01.2817  ARPA    Ethernet2
Internet  198.78.36.21         161        2424.c01f.0715  ARPA    Ethernet2
```

The actual method used to compress TCP headers is specified in RFC 1144. Since the headers of TCP/IP packets have a relatively high degree of overhead when transmitting interactive query/response packets that contain small amounts of information, TCP header compression can significantly enhance the throughput of such traffic. Since the fixed header length has a lower amount of packet overhead when you transfer long files, the degree of enhancement is not as noticeable in this environment. Although TCP header compression always results in some transmission enhancement, it may not be advisable if the interface processor has a high level of utilization since compression requires processing and the loss of processing may outweigh the slight gain if traffic primarily consists of lengthy packets.

ENABLING TCP HEADER COMPRESSION

You can enable TCP header compression by using the ip tcp header-compression interface command whose format is shown here:

```
ip tcp header-compression [passive]
```

If you do not use the keyword passive, the router compresses all traffic. If you use the optional passive keyword, outbound packets are compressed only if inbound TCP packets on the same interface are compressed.

While the use of TCP header compression may appear to be a no-brainer, in actuality you should carefully think about its use because compression requires the temporary storage of a packet, which means various router fast switching methods that switch packets on-the-fly must be disabled. In addition, as its name implies, TCP header compression is only applicable for compressing the TCP header and has no effect on other protocol headers such as UDP and ICMP. Thus, you need to carefully consider the characteristics of your network traffic prior to using this command.

OBSERVING THE EFFECT OF COMPRESSION

If you decide to try TCP header compression, you can use the `show ip tcp header-compression` command to display statistics about the effect of this feature. To do so, you enter the following command:

```
show ip tcp header-compression
```

Figure 5-8 illustrates an example of the `show ip tcp header-compression` command. Note that the resulting display first subdivides its summary statistics according to the transmission direction, with information about received packets listed first. The first two fields display the total number of TCP packets received and the total number of TCP packets compressed. The field labeled "errors" is a counter for unknown packets. The next line contains three fields labeled "dropped," "buffer copies," and "buffer failures." The number dropped denotes the number of packets dropped because of invalid compression. The entries for buffer copies indicates the number of packets received that had to be moved into bigger buffers for decompression, while the buffer failures count denotes the number of packets dropped because of a lack of buffers.

For the transmission side of the serial interface, the entries for Sent provide summary statistics as well as the key metric of concern, which is the level of efficiency resulting from compressing transmitted data. For the Sent side the first two fields indicate the total number of TCP packets transmitted and the total number of TCP packets compressed. On the following line the bytes saved and bytes sent field values indicate the number of bytes that did not have to be transmitted due to compression and the total number of bytes actually transmitted. If you divide the bytes

Figure 5-8   Using the `show ip tcp header-compression` command to observe the effect of compression.

```
Router# show ip tcp header-compression
TCP/IP header compression statistics:
  Interface Serial1: (passive, compressing)
    Rcvd:          3870 total, 2481 compressed, 0 errors
                   0 dropped, 1 buffer copies, 0 buffer failures
    Sent:          3984 total, 2894 compressed,
                   124875 bytes saved, 728142 bytes sent
                   1.17 efficiency improvement factor
    Connect:     16 slots, 1463 long searches, 2 misses, 99% hit ratio
                 Five minute miss rate 0 misses/sec, 0 max misses/sec
```

saved by the bytes sent and add the resulting value to 1, you obtain the efficiency improvement factor which is shown as 1.17 in Figure 5-8.

The third series of entries about header compression occurs under the field area labeled "Connect." The value for slots indicates the size of the cache. The value for long searches indicates the number of times compression software had to perform extra processing using the RFC algorithm to find a match in its table entries. The value for the field labeled "Misses" indicates the number of times a compression match could not be made. By default, when you enable tcp header compression, the compression cache supports 16 connections on the serial interface. If the number of misses is high, it indicates that you should increase the number of compression header connections. To do so, you use the ip tcp compression-connections command whose format is shown here:

```
ip tcp compression-connections number
```

where the keyword number denotes the number of header compression connections to be supported by the cache. That number can vary from 3 to 256.

Returning to Figure 5-8, the Hit ratio field entry indicates the percentage of times software found a match and was able to compress the header. The last line in the display indicates the current 5-min miss rate and the maximum value of the previous field. Prior to concluding this chapter with a discussion of router switching modes, let's examine one additional TCP-related action.

TCP Connection Attempt Time

By default, Cisco's IO software waits for a period of up to 30 s in an attempt to establish a TCP connection. Unfortunately, this amount of time may not be sufficient for networks that support dial-up asynchronous communications since it will affect your ability to telnet from one router to another when you attempt to control a distant router via telnet. You can change the amount of time IOS will wait to attempt to establish a TCP connection by using the ip tcp synwait-time command whose format is shown here:

```
ip tcp synwait-time seconds
```

where the keyword seconds represents the new connection attempt time. Note that because the connection attempt time is a host parameter, it does not affect traffic flowing through the router. Instead, it affects traffic originating at the router. Now that we understand the rationale and method associated with increasing the TCP connection attempt time, we conclude this chapter by turning our attention to the manner by which we can enable different router switching methods.

Switching Mode

The primary purpose of a router is to switch or route data from one interface to another so that packets can flow to their intended destination. To accomplish this, a router removes the layer 2 header of packets received from a LAN prior to placing the packet into RAM. As the packet is placed into RAM, the router's CPU examines its routing table to determine the interface or port where the packet should be output and the manner by which the packet should be encapsulated.

PROCESS SWITCHING

The previously described switching method is referred to as a router's *process switching* mode because each packet must be processed by the CPU, which consults the router's routing table to determine where to send the packet. Process switching is the default method of switching performed by certain types of Cisco routers. Thus, you normally do not have to do anything to enable process switching unless you enabled a different type of switching. Then you would disable that switching method to enable process switching.

As we will note later in this chapter, several other methods can be used to switch packets. The availability of those switching modes commonly depends on router platform as well as the availability of certain types of processor boards installed in the router. Although process switching is the oldest type of router switching, it is also the slowest type of switching since it requires the CPU to interrupt whatever it is doing to consult its routing table for each packet to be processed.

In addition to process switching, most modern Cisco routers support several additional types of switching. Those switching methods can include fast switching, autonomous switching, NetFlow, Optimum, and Cisco Express Forwarding (CEF). Although the other switching methods just mentioned generally provide additional efficiencies in the order mentioned, certain variations based on other tasks a router is performing affect its overall level of performance. For example, if your router is configured with extensive access lists, optimum switching may not be as efficient as NetFlow switching. To better understand the performance of different switching methods, let's look at how the other switching methods enhance router performance. In doing so, let's first review the fast switching method.

FAST SWITCHING

In fast switching the router builds a memory cache containing information about destination IP addresses and the next hop interface or port that must be used to route data toward its destination. The router constructs this cache by saving information previously obtained from the routing table. The first packet in a series of packets flowing to a common destination causes the CPU to consult the routing table. However, once the information is obtained from the table concerning the next hop interface for the particular destination, this information is inserted into the fast switching cache and the routing table is not consulted for new packets sent to this destination.

Since most communications applications result in the flow of a sequence of packets to a common destination, the slight additional time required to construct the fast cache entry is more than compensated for because the router can access a fast memory cache for subsequent packets. Thus, the overall effect is that the router can switch packets at a much faster rate than under process switching. In addition, fast switching results in a substantial reduction in the load on the router's CPU.

To enable fast switching, you use the ip route-cache interface command whose format is shown here:

```
ip router-cache {cbus}
```

The reason you use the command ip route-cache for enabling fast switching is due to the association of the term fast switching with the storage of IP destination addresses in cache. When fast switching is enabled, destination IP addresses are stored in high-speed cache memory which alleviates many time-consuming table lookup operations.

AUTONOMOUS SWITCHING

The use of the keyword cbus in the ip route cache command results in both fast and IP autonomous switching, with the latter enabling the ciscoBus to switch packets independently without having to interrupt the system CPU. The use of IP autonomous switching is only applicable to Cisco 7000 series routers that have a switch processor control card and are running microcode version 1.4 or later, or AGST systems with high-speed network controller cards. Since autonomous switching enables the ciscoBus to switch packets without interrupting the system processor, it provides a faster packet processing capability.

Silicon Switching Engine

If your organization operates a Cisco 7000 series router with a *silicon switch processor* (SSP), you can use the *silicon switching engine* (SSE) on the SSP to perform switching independently of the system processor. To do so, you use the ip route-cache interface command with the keyword sse as shown here:

```
ip route-cache sse
```

Until IOS release 10.3, when extended access lists were configured on a router with SSE fast switching enabled, IP traffic was fast switched instead of SSE switched. On more modern versions of IOS, the use of SSE is applicable for both standard and extended IP access list checking.

You can enable both fast switching and autonomous switching with the following command:

```
ip route-cache cbus
```

If you wish to disable both fast switching and autonomous switching on an interface, you enter the following command:

```
no ip route-cache
```

If you only desired to disable autonomous switching on an interface, you enter the following command:

```
no ip route-cache cbus
```

OPTIMUM SWITCHING

Similar to fast switching, optimum switching is based on the creation of a memory cache of information that facilitates the expedient routing of packets. The optimum switching cache includes the destination IP address; an age field to allow periodic purging of entries; an interface field that identifies the output port to the destination; and a next-hop IP address length field, and Mac address field, with the length field indicating the length, in hex, of the Mac address.

Optimum switching is enabled by default for IP on Ethernet, FDDI, and serial interfaces on Cisco 7500 products with a *route switch processor* (RSP) main system processor. On serial interfaces optimum switching is limited to supporting HDLC encapsulation. If you want to use fast switching or process switching, you must disable optimum switching. In order to do so, you enter the following interface configuration command:

```
no ip route-cache optimum
```

Optimum switching functions similarly to fast switching but its table utilization provides an enhanced switching capability. However, the level of performance of both fast and optimum switching is degraded if you previously configured one or more extensive access lists that are applied to interfaces through which packets must flow. Perhaps as a mechanism to alleviate this constraint, Cisco introduced NetFlow switching.

NETFLOW SWITCHING

NetFlow switching is currently supported on Cisco 7200 and 7500 series routers as well as 7000 series products with RSP. Under this switching technique, the first packet in a flow is processed conventionally, with the contents of the packet compared to any entries in an applicable access list prior to the transfer of the packet through the router. Once conventional processing of the first packet in a flow is accomplished, all subsequent packets are processed on a connection-oriented basis as part of the flow. This means that access list processing is bypassed for subsequent packets in the flow, which can considerably enhance the packet processing rate of the router.

Under NetFlow switching, a flow is identified via the commonality of seven metrics, including source and destination IP addresses, source and destination port numbers, protocol type, the value of the Type of Service field, and the input interface on which the packet arrived.

The creation of a flow cache commences by the processing of the first packet in a flow through either fast or optimum switching. This results in each flow being associated with an incoming and outgoing interface port number as well as any applicable security access permission and encryption policy. Once the first packet is processed, NetFlow switching creates a flow cache that contains information required to switch and bypass access list checking for subsequent packets in the flow.

When you configure NetFlow on an interface, you cannot use another switching mode on that interface. To enable NetFlow, you use the `ip route-cache flow` interface command for an applicable interface. When you perform this action, a default cache capable of holding 64-K flow cache entries is created. Since each cache entry requires approximately 64 bytes of storage, this means 4 MB of DRAM are required.

You can adjust the number of entries in the NetFlow cache by using the `ip flow-cache entries` global command whose format is shown here:

```
ip flow-cache entries number
```

where the keyword `number` is a value from 1024 to 524,288, with the default being 65,536. Although you may wish to consider adjusting the number of entries, Cisco literature highly suggests otherwise, as doing so can result in unspecified network problems.

Data Export
In addition to providing an enhanced packet processing capability over fast switching, especially when complex access lists are applied to an interface, NetFlow switching captures a considerable set of statistical information, including IP address information, protocol, port, and type of service data. This information can be extremely useful for network analysis as well as for chargeback. In fact, you can configure NetFlow to export flow information to a designated workstation. In terms of the export of flow information, NetFlow supports two data formats: version 1 which was the initial release and version 5 which includes the addition of *border gateway protocol* (BGP), *autonomous system* (AS) information, and flow sequence numbers. Perhaps one of the great mysteries of life is the fact that Cisco never released NetFlow versions 2 through 4, resulting in the

Table 5-2 Common NetFlow Record Fields

Bytes	Field Description
0-3	Source IP address
4-7	Destination IP address
8-11	Next hop router's IP address
12-15	I/O interface's SNMP index
16-19	Packets in the flow
20-23	Total number of layer 3 bytes in the flow's packets
24-27	SysUptime at start of flow
28-31	SysUptime when last packet of flow received
32-35	TCP/UDP source and destination port number

two distinct data formats referenced as version 1 and version 5. Each version depends upon UDP as a delivery mechanism, with the datagram consisting of a header and one or more flow records. To give you an indication of the type of information that can be obtained from either flow record format, Table 5-2 lists the first 9 of the 12 fields common to both record formats.

In examining the entries in Table 5-2 note that because both a cumulative packet count and duration of a flow are maintained, it becomes possible to bill users based on connection duration or packet count. In addition, because port numbers are captured, it is also possible to bill based on application. For organizations that might require a more complex billing structure the metrics captured by NetFlow enable a wide variety of billing algorithms to be developed.

To export NetFlow switching information, you follow a three-step process. First, you configure your router to export NetFlow cache entries to a specific workstation using the `ip flow-export destination` command whose format is shown here:

```
ip flow-export destination {hostname|ip address} udp-port
```

Once this is done, you use the `ip flow-export version` command to define the version of the NetFlow collector operator on the destination workstation. The latter is a Cisco product which collects and manipulates NetFlow statistics. The format of this command is shown here:

```
ip flow-export version {1|5 [origin-as][peer-as]}
```

Note that the default version is version 1, so you only need to specify version 5. Also note that you must specify an origin or peer autonomous system (AS).

The third step is to configure the source interface used by NetFlow to indicate the source of the exported NetFlow data. To do so, you use the `ip flow-export source` command whose format is shown here.

```
ip flow-export source interface
```

where the keyword `interface` is the interface type to be used as the source interface.

CISCO EXPRESS FORWARDING (CEF)

Introduced during 1998, Cisco Express Forwarding (CEF) is a relatively new switching architecture. Under CEF, all available routing information is used to construct an IP *forwarding information base* (FIB). The FIB is used to make switching decisions, including the routing of the first packet destined to a new location. In comparison, previously developed switching architectures use the first packet in a flow to construct an IP destination cache for use by subsequent packets that have the same destination.

Under CEF, it is possible for line cards to perform express forwarding between port adapters. This can result in CEF becoming less CPU-intensive than fast or optimum switching, allowing additional CPU processing power to be devoted to other functions.

CEF is currently supported by Cisco 7000 series routers equipped with route switch processor (RSP) 7000 modules and by Cisco 7200, 7500, and 12000 series routers. Although you can use CEF in any part of a network, its primary function is to provide a high level of performance for backbone switching. Since the recommended minimum memory requirements for platforms supporting full Internet routing information is 128 MB for each route processor and 32 MB for each line card, CEF can be expensive to implement and is best used at the core of a private network.

Components

CEF has two main components: a FIB and adjacent tables. The FIB maintains both a mirror image of the forwarding information contained in IP routing tables and next hop address information based on the contents of the IP routing table. Whenever a routing or topology change occurs in a network, both the IP routing table and the FIB are updated.

The second component of CEF is adjacency tables. Here the term adjacency indicates that a node is considered adjacent to another node if the nodes can directly reach each other with a single hop across a link. The adjacency table maintains layer 2 next hop addresses for each entry in the FIB, with an adjacency discovery method used to populate the table.

Depending on the presence of line cards, you can consider running CEF in either a centralized or distributed mode. Under a centralized mode of operation, both the CEF FIB and adjacency tables reside on the processor module that contains the CPU, referred to as the *route processor*. In the centralized mode of operation the route processor performs express forwarding. Under the distributed mode of operation, line cards maintain an identical copy of the FIB and adjacency tables and use data in the tables to perform express forwarding between port adapters, which significantly reduces CPU processing.

Unlike fast and optimum switching that support only one entry in cache for a given destination, CEF records all possible paths in its FIB. This allows packet load balancing to be supported over a series of paths. In comparison, no load balancing is possible with the other two switching methods.

One of the key advantages of CEF is its ability to work with NetFlow. In doing so, CEF uses its FIB instead of the NetFlow switching cache for layer 2 and layer 3 information, permitting faster switching while retaining the ability to obtain detailed traffic information.

Configuration

The actual method required to configure Cisco Express Forwarding for operation is relatively simple, requiring the use of one of two commands depending on whether you are implementing centralized or distributed CEF. To enable centralized CEF, you enter the following global configuration command:

```
ip cef switch
```

To enable distributed CEF operation, you enter the following global configuration command:

```
ip cef distributed switch
```

Note that for certain Cisco products, such as their 12000 series routers, distributed CEF is enabled by default. Thus, that product does not support a command to enable distributed CEF.

Once you enable centralized or distributed CEF globally, all interfaces that support CEF on the platform are enabled. If you want to turn off either version of CEF, you use the no version of the previously listed command. You can also disable either version of CEF on a particular interface by using the following interface command:

```
no ip route-cache cef
```

Although the general configuration of CEF for operation is a relatively straightforward process, you may wish to implement several optional tasks under this switching method, including configuring load balancing, network accounting, and distributed tunnel switching.

Load Balancing

You can configure load balancing for CEF on either a per-destination or per-packet basis. For either method this function allows you to optimize network resources by distributing traffic over multiple links to a destination. By default, per-destination load balancing is enabled when you enable CEF. Thus, you do not have to enable this method of load balancing.

The use of per-destination load sharing results in a router transferring packets with the same source-destination address pair on the same path. Thus, this technique becomes more efficient as the number of source-destination pairs increases. The second method of load balancing is performed on a per-packet basis. Under this technique, the router uses a round-robin method to determine which path each packet should take. While per-packet load balancing can provide a better average use of multiple circuits connecting two routers under certain situations, it can introduce the reordering of packets. Since UDP does not have a sequence number in the header, this would be harmful to applications that depend upon that protocol for transport. To enable per-packet load balancing, you use the following interface command:

```
ip load-sharing per-packet
```

Accounting

To facilitate end users desiring to examine CEF patterns, you can configure accounting as well as view accounting information. In terms of the former, you can enable two types of accounting. The first type involves the collection of packets and bytes forwarded to a destination or prefix. To invoke this method of accounting, you use the following global configuration command:

```
ip cef accounting per-prefix
```

The second type of network accounting involves the collection of the number of packets express forwarded through a destination. To invoke this method of accounting, you use the following global configuration command:

```
ip cef accounting non-recursive
```

Once you enable network accounting, you can directly display the captured statistics. To do so, you enter the following EXEC command:

```
show ip cef
```

CHAPTER 6

Testing, Troubleshooting, and Design Principles

We noted previously that there is a relationship between testing and troubleshooting tools and network design principles. This chapter probes deeper and examines that relationship.

Two important testing and troubleshooting tools are built into all TCP protocol stacks: Ping and Traceroute application programs. While you can use those applications from a workstation, when you supplement their use with those applications from a router, you can obtain valuable information for checking infrastructure. This, in turn, can facilitate correct restructure of a network or verification of certain types of service level agreements. Thus, initially this chapter reviews the general use of Ping and Traceroute, followed by an examination of those TCP/IP applications from a router that, in conjunction with other traffic measurements, can be used to answer a variety of important network-related questions including:

- Is the performance level of one or more routers delaying the flow of network traffic?
- Are we obtaining the level of performance associated with a communications carrier's *service level agreement* (SLA)?
- Should we consider altering the path between certain networks?

The Ping Utility Program

Two stories are usually associated with the name of this TCP/IP utility program. One story relates the fact that because a ping operation results in the transmission of a packet to a destination where it is echoed back to the originator, it functions like radar. Since the term used to denote a radar echo is *ping*, this supposedly resulted in the name of the application. A second story reports that the name of this application program is an acronym for Packet Internetwork Groper. Regardless of which story is correct, this program is a valuable tool for checking the status of an interface, verifying that a TCP protocol stack is operating, and determining the round-trip delay between the host issuing the ping and the destination address used when the program is invoked.

Overview

The Ping utility program generates a series of *Internet control message protocol* (ICMP) echo-request packets to a specified destination address. Assuming the destination address is reachable and operational and has an operating TCP/IP protocol stack, it will respond to the source with a series of ICMP echo-reply packets. The response informs the originator that the destination is reachable, operational, and has an operating TCP/IP protocol stack. In addition, because the originator uses its clock to record the time packets were transmitted, it uses the time the echo responses are received to compute the round-trip delay from source to destination.

ROUND-TRIP DELAY UTILIZATION

The ability to determine the round-trip delay to a destination can alleviate problems before they occur. For example, if your organization is thinking about implementing a *voice over IP* (VoIP) application, you could use Ping to determine its practicality because a VoIP application is very time dependent, permitting a total one-way delay, or latency, of a 0.25 s (250 ms) before reconstructed voice sounds awkward. The use of Ping provides a measurement of round-trip delay. You divide that delay by 2 to obtain the one-way delay. Then you examine the specification sheet of the product you are considering or contact the vendor to determine the coding and decoding delays. You then add the coding and decoding delays to network latency to determine one-way delay and compare this total one-way delay to 250 ms to determine if it is possible to implement a VoIP application with a reasonable level of assurance that it will provide acceptable results.

SERVICE LEVEL AGREEMENT VERIFICATION

There are several types of service level agreements offered by different communications carriers. Some SLAs are restricted to availability level defined as follows:

$$\text{Availability \%} = \frac{\text{uptime}}{\text{uptime} + \text{downtime}} * 100$$

While availability is certainly an important metric, most communications carriers provide a level of availability that commonly exceeds 99.9 percent. Of more importance to many organizations is the type of service your organization can expect to receive during the 99.9+ percent of the time that service is available. For example, assume your user population is distributed over several time zones and your organization is using the public TCP/IP Internet as a virtual network to interconnect geographically separated locations. If employees commonly use interactive query-response applications and require access to servers located on distant networks, customer satisfaction would not be very high if the network was always available but the routing of short datagrams between networks required several seconds. As a result, a second area where Ping can provide considerable assistance is in verifying an SLA based on latency or delay through a network. Although you could use a workstation to issue a Ping, you can obtain a more accurate indication of latency by issuing the program from a router. The reason is because when you issue the ping from a workstation with a destination address or another network, the packets must first flow to a router for relay off the source network. Because of this, it becomes possible to use ping from both a workstation and a router to determine different latencies. An example of this is illustrated in Figure 6-1.

Latency Determination

Figure 6-1 illustrates the use of a workstation and one router to issue a series of pings. First, although no specific order is required as long as all pings are performed, let's assume workstation X pings router 2. This action is indicated by A in Figure 6-1. If you divide the round-trip delay by 2 (A/2), you obtain the one-way delay through the local router and the network. Next, let's assume you issue a ping from router 1 to the local WAN interface of router 2, as indicated by B. Now, if you divide this round-trip delay by 2 (B/2), you obtain the network delay, which is the metric you want to use when verifying an SLA.

If you subtract the round-trip delay obtained by pinging from the router from the round-trip delay obtained by issuing a ping from the workstation and divide the difference by 2 [(A − B)/2], you obtain a general indication of the local routing delay. The reason this is only a general indication is because the station on the network is contending with other stations for the services of the router. However, over a period of time this action provides a very accurate indication of the delay through the local router.

Continuing our series of ping generations, C in Figure 6-1 illustrates the generation of a Ping from workstation X on the local network to workstation Y on the remote network. Thus, the ping provides a round-trip

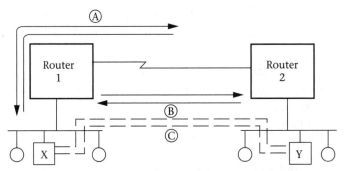

Figure 6-1   Using Ping to determine different latencies. A: workstation x pings to distance router. B: router 1 pings to distant router. C: workstation pings to distant workstation Y. A/2 = network plus delay through one router. B/2 = network delay. A − B/2 = source router delay. C/2 = total one-way delay through the network and two routers. C − B/2 = total router delay.

delay through two routers and the network in both directions. Then, C/2 provides the one-way delay through the network and the local and remote routers. Finally, if we subtract the round-trip delay when the local router pings the distant router (B) from the round-trip delay when workstation X pinged workstation Y (C) and divide by 2, we obtain the total one-way delay through the pair of routers. The ability to compute the latency associated with one or both routers on a point-to-point internetwork can be extremely helpful in resolving finger-pointing problems. For example, many times it is assumed latency problems occur from overloaded servers on a heavily utilized communications facility. While it is certainly true that both represent common latency problem areas, often a heavily utilized router can be contributing to a delay problem. If you can determine the latency associated with the use of one or more routers, you become better prepared to isolate latency problems and initiate corrective measures. Although Figure 6-1 illustrates a relatively simple two-hop network, it is also possible to determine the latency associated with other routers on a path from source to destination if your organization operates the routers or you have a good working relationship with the communications carrier. To determine the latency through a series of routers on a path from source to destination, you can consider using two similar methods. First, ping the ingress side of an intermediate router. Next, if you have an extra unused port, place the port into a loopback mode and ping its interface. The difference in the two round-trip delays divided by 2 should provide you with a reasonable measurement of latency through the router. A second method would involve pinging the ingress and egress interfaces without performing a loopback. While you expect the subtraction of the ingress round-trip delay from the egress delay and the division by 2 to produce a similar latency, a few times this produced a slightly lower value. Without the details of how traffic flows to a loopbacked interface, it appears that pings to the loopbacked interface are slightly delayed. In any event, the results obtained with either method will be very close to one another and let you determine the latency through intermediate routers along a path. Later in this chapter when we cover the use of the Traceroute program, we will note how use of the path provides the hop addresses through a network.

Now that we understand the potential use of ping, let's look at its general method of implementation prior to examining its use on specific platforms.

GENERAL IMPLEMENTATION

A common ping format or command syntax is shown here:

```
Ping[-q][-v][-R][-c count][-i delay][-s size](hostname|ip-address)
```

where -q denotes quiet output, that is, nothing is displayed except summary lines at the beginning and end of program execution; -v denotes verbose output, which results in a listing of ICMP packets that are received; -R indicates the Record route option resulting in the display of the route buffer on returned packets; -c count specifies the number of ICMP echo request packets to be transmitted; i wait specifies the number of seconds the application waits between each packet; -s size specifies the number of data bytes to be transmitted; hostname is the host name of the destination or target system; and ip address is the IP address of the destination or target system.

In examining the preceding general ping format, note that the use of the -s option permits you to specify the number of data bytes to be transmitted. The default value is 56 bytes. Because there is an 8-byte header, this default value results in the default transmission of a 64-byte packet. Also note that although you can enter either the host name or IP address of a destination, the use of the former can result in an additional delay associated with the first round-trip computation. This additional delay occurs if the host name was not previously resolved into an IP address. Then, the first ping to a new host name requires the use of the *domain name service* (DNS) to obtain the IP address since all routing is based upon the use of IP addresses. Thus, if you use a host name in a ping operation, you should consider doing it twice and discarding the first result, in effect eliminating any possible DNS learning time affecting the round-trip delay computation. Now that we understand the general syntax, or format, of ping, let's review its use on specific platforms.

The Windows Ping Program

Microsoft provides a common implementation of the Ping program across different versions of its Windows operating system. Figure 6-2 illustrates the Help menu generated by entering the program name without any options. Note that by using one or more options, you can configure Ping to operate continuously (-t), resolve addresses to hostnames (-a), specify the number of echo request packets to be transmitted instead of the default value of four (-n count), and control other options as indicated in the display. Since you more than likely want an average round-trip delay over a period of time, you can either use the -t or the -n options, piping the output to a file for later analysis.

PIPING OUTPUT FOR ANALYSIS

To illustrate both the use of Ping and the ability to redirect or pipe its output onto a file for later analysis, consider Figure 6-3. The top portion

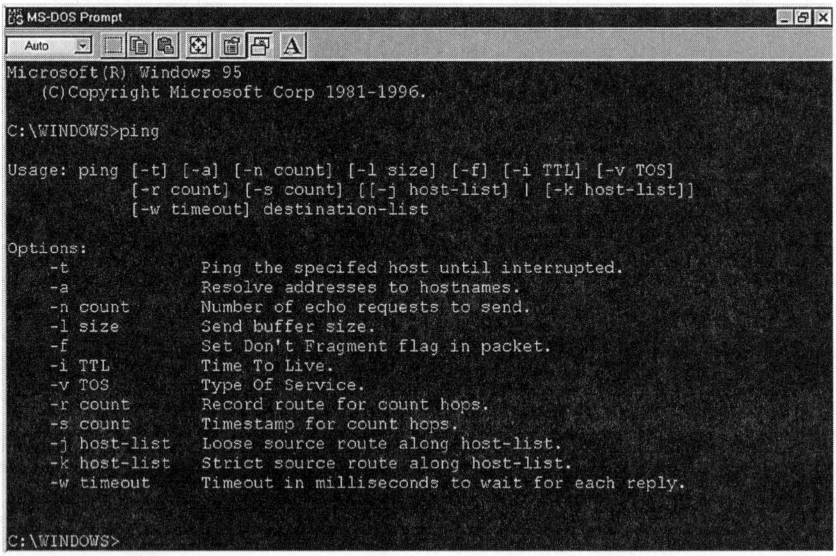

Figure 6-2 Under Windows, entering ping without any options results in the display of a help screen for different program options.

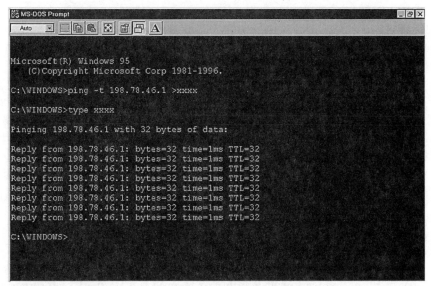

Figure 6-3   Using ping to generate a file of results.

of Figure 6-3 illustrates the use of the -t option in the ping command when this author pinged a local router whose address is 198.78.46.1. Note that a greater than sign (>) follows the IP address, followed in turn by four Xs (XXXX). As a result, the output of Ping is piped onto the file named XXXX. Since the -t option was included in the command line, the program will generate a continuous series of pings, storing each result in the file named XXXX. Since there is only a limited amount of space on a display to illustrate piping, the author quickly issued a CTRL+BREAK operation to terminate the operation and return to the command prompt level. Next, the author used the DOS TYPE command to display the contents of the file XXXX that is shown in the lower portion of Figure 6-3.

Although each of the round-trip delay times shown from the listing of the contents of the file XXXX have the same value of 1 ms, this is not always the case. By creating a file it becomes very easy to import the file into a spreadsheet. However, in doing so you cannot take an average of time=xms, so you should use the Find and Replace option included in most spreadsheet programs to first eliminate time= and then remove ms to obtain a column of millisecond values. Then you can sum the millisecond values in the applicable column and divide by the number of entries to compute the average response time.

PING CONTROL

To overcome potential problems associated with the use of ping, a few words are in order about how different organizations view pinging. Some organizations such as Yale University, permit pings to flow through their router, and their Web servers respond to ping requests. An example of this is shown in the top portion of Figure 6-4. Note that although we pinged *www.yale.edu*, the response came from *elsinore.cis.yale.edu*, which is an alias name for Yale's Web server. Also note that the use of Ping without a -t or -n option results in a default transmission of four echo requests for which we received four echo responses. In examining the replies note the round-trip delay time ranged from a low of 31 ms to a high of 78 ms, which is a considerable degree of variance. Thus, you more than likely would want to periodically use Ping throughout the day to determine an average round-trip delay based on different levels of activity that occur during the day as well as on a broader base of responses than the four shown at the top of Figure 6-4.

Since Harvard and Yale are considered by some persons to be the Ben & Jerry of higher education, it is only fair to ping the Harvard Web server. This action is shown in the middle portion of Figure 6-4. Note that although ping was able to determine the alias host name and IP address of the Harvard Web server, the actual set of pings resulted in the generation of four Destination net unreachable messages.

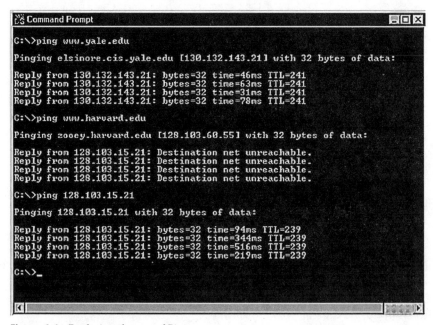

Figure 6-4 Exploring the use of Ping.

A destination unreachable message is issued by a router when it cannot reach the destination network in an IP datagram. Thus, it is highly likely that the router whose WAN interface IP address is 128.103.15.21 is filtering ICMP echo requests since Harvard may have experienced Ping attacks. Under this attack scheme, one or more persons in a computer laboratory go from workstation to workstation invoking the Ping program so that it continuously pings a common IP address. Since the destination has to respond to pings, this affects its ability to do productive work and chews up bandwidth and is a rationale for blocking pings. A second reason to block pings is because a potential hacker can discover active devices on a network as a first step toward exploiting potential security holes. Regardless of the reason for blocking pings, if you need to determine timing or latency information, you basically have three options. If the hardware is under the control of your organization, you may be able to temporarily remove the barrier to pings. If you are attempting to support a new application between two or more organizations and pings are blocked by one or more of the other organizations, it may be a bit difficult to coordinate their temporary unblocking. For either situation in an era where organizations are rightly becoming paranoid about all security issues, you may wish to try a third approach to the problem. That third approach is to note the address of the router that generated the `Destination net unreachable` message and ping its interface. This action is shown in the lower portion of Figure 6-4.

In examining the four responses to this ping action, note the range of round-trip delays varied from a low of 95 ms to a high of 516 ms. Since the one-way maximum delay from the workstation to the remote router is 516/2 or 258 ms, we would not want one out of every four packets transporting a VoIP application to have a delay resulting in a considerable amount of distortion for reconstructed voice. However, prior to throwing our hands upward in exasperation, we should ensure that the 516 ms was not an exception. To do so, we perform an operation similar to that previously shown in Figure 6-3 where we continuously operate Ping over a period of time and pipe its output to a file. Now that we understand the use of Ping under Windows, let's look at how this command is supported on Cisco routers.

Router Ping Operation

Cisco routers support two ping modes of operation, referred to as user and privileged. The user version of Ping is for employees that have nonprivileged access to a router. The general format of the Cisco user and privileged versions of Ping is shown here:

```
ping [protocol]{host|address}
```

where you can enter a specific protocol keyword or ignore the field to accept the default of IP.

TABLE 6-1   Ping Test Characters Displayed

Character	Meaning
!	Each exclamation point indicates the receipt of an echo-reply
.	Each period indicates the network server timed out while waiting for a reply
U	Destination unreachable
P	Protocol unreachable
Q	Source quench
M	Count not fragment
?	Unknown packet type received

USER VERSION

The user version of Ping is intended for IP users that do not have privileged access to a router. The operation of this version of Ping results in the transmission of a sequence of five 100-byte ICMP echo messages. When the router generates the previously mentioned sequence of ICMP echoes, it displays a sequence of characters used to define the result of each ping operation. Table 6-1 lists the ping display characters that Cisco references as test characters since their meaning conveys the result of the test.

To illustrate the operation of the user mode version of Ping, let's reverse an earlier ping operation and use the router to ping a workstation on the network. An example of this is shown in Figure 6-5. In this example note that Cisco supports the use of a CTRL-X multikey operation as an escape sequence to break an in-progress ping operation. Also note that after displaying a line of information about the operation being performed, you

Figure 6-5   Operating the router user version of Ping.

```
Router> ping 198.78.46.8
Type escape sequence to abort.
Sending 5, 100-byte ICMP Echos to 198.78.46.8, timeout is 2 seconds:
!!!!!
Success rate is 100 percent, round-trip min/avg/max = 1/1/1 ms
```

see a line with five exclamation points, indicating that a reply was received for each of the five ICMP echoes. Finally, the last line in Figure 6-5 provides a summary of the operation, including the success rate associated with the sequence of pings generated and the minimum, average, and maximum round-trip delays associated with the default sequence of five ICMP echoes. Thus, the Cisco user version of Ping automatically computes the average round-trip delay. However, this mode of the `ping` command is limited to a nonverbose form and does not permit you to change any default settings of the program nor does it allow you to display information about received packets that you can obtain from the use of the privileged version of Ping.

From a testing perspective, you can ping the broadcast address of 255.255.255.255 to ascertain the state of all active devices. For example, assume your router is connected to the 198.78.46.0 network and stations .8 and .20 are active. The following display is the ping display when you use the broadcast address in the operation.

```
Router>ping 255.255.255.255
     Type escape sequence to abort.
     Sending 5, 100-byte ICMP Echoes to 255.255.255.255, timeout is 2
        seconds
     Reply to request 0 from 198.78.45.8 (1 ms)
     Reply to request 0 from 198.78.45.20 (1 ms)
     Reply to request 1 from 198.78.45.8 (1 ms)
     Reply to request 1 from 198.78.45.20 (1 ms)
     Reply to request 2 from 198.78.45.8 (1 ms)
     Reply to request 2 from 198.78.45.20 (1 ms)
     Reply to request 3 from 198.78.45.8 (1 ms)
     Reply to request 3 from 198.78.45.20 (1 ms)
     Reply to request 4 from 198.78.45.8 (1 ms)
     Reply to request 4 from 198.78.45.20 (1 ms)
```

PRIVILEGE VERSION

The second version of Ping is the router privileged version. To use this version of Ping, you must be in the router's privileged mode of operation which is signified by a pound sign (#) prompt. Similar to the user version of Ping, the privileged version has the same general format, uses the same test characters to indicate the results of each ping operation, and can be used to ping the broadcast address of 255.255.255.255. The key difference between the two modes of Ping is the fact that you can use the latter either as a command by including a host or IP address in the command line and accepting its default settings or by entering the command without any options, with the latter resulting in the entering of Ping's extended command mode. When you enter Ping's extended command mode, the router will display a series of prompts, many with default values indicated in brackets. You can cycle through each option, pressing a RETURN to accept the option or entering an alternate value.

Figure 6-6   Using Ping's privileged extended command mode.

```
Router# ping
Protocol [ip]:
Target IP address: 205.131.176.11
Repeat count [5]:
Datagram size [100]:
Timeout in seconds [2]:
Extended commands [n]: y
Source address: 198.78.46.8
Type of service [0]:
Set DF bit in IP header? [no]:
Data pattern [0xABCD]:
Loose, Strict, Record, Timestamp, Verbose[none]:
Sweep range of sizes [n]:
Type escape sequence to abort.
Sending 5, 100-byte ICMP Echos to 205.131.176.11, timeout is 2 seconds:
!!!!!
Success rate is 100 percent, round-trip min/avg/max = 1/2/3 ms
```

Ping's Privileged Extended Command Mode

Figure 6-6 is an example of Ping's privileged extended command mode. In this example we accepted the default protocol, entered the target IP address of 198.78.46.8, and accepted the default values for the repeat count, datagram size, and time-out in seconds.

The next option shown in Figure 6-6, Extended commands, lets you specify whether or not a series of additional prompts will be displayed. Although the default is n for no, we entered y to display the additional options. Concerning those options, the source address specifies the IP address that appears in the Ping packet as the source address. The type of service identifies the setting of the Service Type field in the IP header and has a default value of 0. The next prompt, labeled Set of bit in IP header? lets packets that encounter a node in its path configured for a smaller MTU than the packet's MTU to be dropped. To do so, you accept the default of no.

The next option, labeled Data pattern [0xABCD], lets you vary a data pattern from the default mix of hex characters. If you want to test repeaters on a local loop, you could set a data pattern of all 0's. You could also consider setting the pattern to alternating 1's and 0's [0xAAA] to test CSUs for correctly encoding and decoding alternating sequences. The reason for using hex A's is because their binary value is 1010, which provides an alternating sequence of 1's and 0's. After the data pattern the prompt Loose, Strict, Record, Timestamp, Verbose appears, with its default value set to none. This prompt indicates the Internet header options you can select. The Loose option is more formally defined as *loose source and record route* (LSRR) in RFC 791, which describes each header option. The LSRR option lets the source of a datagram provide routing information used by gateways during the datagram forwarding process as well as for the recording of route information. The reason the term *loose* is used is because the gateway or host IP is allowed to use any route of any number of other intermediate gateways to reach the next address in the route.

The second option, Strict, represents the *strict source and record route* (SSRR) option. Under this option, the source of an IP datagram can supply routing information used by gateways for forwarding the datagram to its destination and record route information similar to the LSRR option. However, this option results in a strict source route because the gateway or host IP must transmit the datagram to the next address in the source route. Thus, the SSRR option requires use of a specified route.

The third option, labeled Record, is an abbreviation of the RFC 791 *record route IP datagram* option. This option results in the recording of the route of the datagram. In comparison, the Timestamp option adds a 32-bit time stamp in milliseconds to each address while the selection of the Verbose option results in an extended display. You are automatically in a verbose mode if you select any of the previously mentioned options. However, if you select verbose after a preceding option, it works as a toggle switch.

In the example of the use of Ping's privileged extended command mode shown in Figure 6-6, we did not select any of the previously mentioned IP header options. In addition, we selected the default size of echo packets to be transmitted, which is denoted by Sweep range of sizes. You can use this option to vary the size of echo packets transmitted. For diagnostic testing this option can be useful for determining the minimum size of MTUs configured on nodes along a path to the destination address. Thus, by varying certain extended ping options you can obtain a considerable amount of information in addition to determining the round-trip delay from source to destination.

Using the Record Route Option

One of the more valuable options supported by Ping is its Record Route option. When you select this option, the IP datagram option field will be used as per RFC 791 to record route information.

Figure 6-7 illustrates the use of Ping with the Record Route option (r) selected in the command's extended command mode. Note that because there is a limit to the size of the option field within an IP datagram, the use of the Record Route option is limited to recording a maximum of nine IP addresses. Also note that while the number of hops to be recorded has a default of 9, that value is its minimum. Once you respond to each option and the Sending message is displayed as shown in the lower portion of Figure 6-7, the following line that begins with Packet has IP

Figure 6-7 Using the Ping privileged extended command Record Route option.

```
Router# ping
Protocol [ip]:
Target IP address: 205.131.175.11
Repeat count [5]:
Datagram size [100]:
Timeout in seconds [2]:
Extended commands [n]: y
Source address:
Type of service [0]:
Set DF bit in IP header? [no]:
Data pattern [0xABCD]:
Loose, Strict, Record, Timestamp, Verbose[none]: r
Number of hops [ 9 ]:
Loose, Strict, Record, Timestamp, Verbose[RV]:
Sweep range of sizes [n]:
Type escape sequence to abort.
Sending 5, 100-byte ICMP Echos to 205.131.175.11, timeout is 2 seconds:
Packet has IP options: Total option bytes= 39, padded length=40
Record route: <*> 0.0.0.0 0.0.0.0 0.0.0.0 0.0.0.0
    0.0.0.0 0.0.0.0 0.0.0.0 0.0.0.0 0.0.0.0
```

options indicates that, as a result of your selection of the Record Route option, IP header options were enabled on the outgoing echo packets. This line also indicates the number of option bytes and padded bytes in the header of the packets. Finally, the pair of lines that begin with the label Record route includes a sequence of dotted decimal numbers whose values are initially set to 0's. If you count the 0's you will note there are 36, which correspond to nine IP addresses, the latter being the maximum number of hops as well as the default number of hops selected in the thirteenth line in Figure 6-7.

Figure 6-8 illustrates the results of the use of the extended Ping. Note that because we accepted the default repeat count of five, the beginning of each output display sequence has a numeral that corresponds to one of the five echo requests. However, the numbering begins at 0 and terminates at 4. Also note that following the packet series identifier is the round-trip response time recorded for the packet. Thus, 0 in 6 ms indicates that packet 0 has a 6-ms round-trip delay. After displaying the fact that the packet has options and information about the number of bytes in the option field, the following line that begins with the label Record route indicates there were four nodes in the route of each packet, including the router at source address 206.133.175.1, two intermediate nodes at IP addresses 206.133.175.17 and 205.131.175.1, and the destination IP address of 205.131.175.11. The next line for each displayed response includes the address of the four nodes in the return path of each echo-

Figure 6-8 Viewing the results of a privileged extended ping using a `Record Route` option.

```
0 in 6 ms. Received packet has options
 Total option bytes= 40, padded length=40
 Record route: 206.133.175.1 206.133.175.17 205.131.175.1  205.131.175.11
     205.131.175.11 205.131.175.1 206.133.175.17 206.133.175.1 <*> 0.0.0.0
 End of list
1 in 8 ms. Received packet has options
 Total option bytes= 40, padded length=40
 Record route: 206.133.175.1 206.133.175.17 205.131.175.1 205.131.175.11
     205.131.175.11 205.131.175.1 206.133.175.17 206.133.175.1 <*> 0.0.0.0
 End of list
2 in 5 ms. Received packet has options
 Total option bytes= 40, padded length=40
 Record route: 206.133.175.1 206.133.175.17 205.131.175.1 205.131.175.11
     205.131.175.11 205.131.175.1 206.133.175.17 206.133.175.1 <*> 0.0.0.0
 End of list
3 in 6 ms. Received packet has options
 Total option bytes= 40, padded length=40
 Record route: 206.133.175.1 206.133.175.17 205.131.175.1 205.131.175.11
      205.131.175.11 205.131.175.1 206.133.175.17 206.133.175.1 <*> 0.0.0.0
 End of list
4 in 5 ms. Received packet has options
 Total option bytes= 40, padded length=40
 Record route: 206.133.175.1 206.133.175.17 205.131.175.1 205.131.175.11
     205.131.175.11 205.131.175.1 206.133.175.17 206.133.175.1 <*> 0.0.0.0
 End of list
Success rate is 100 percent, round-trip min/avg/max = 5/6/8 ms
```

response packet. Although each return route is the same as the outbound route in this example, this is not always the case. If the two differ, you note this by a different set of reversed IP addresses.

The conclusion of the receipt of the last echo reply results in a summary line of information. As noted at the bottom of Figure 6-8, that line indicates all five echo-requests received a response since the success rate is indicated as 100 percent. Also note that the minimum, average, and maximum round-trip delays are displayed. Thus, if you use the privileged extended ping command, you can obtain the average round-trip delay without having to resort to a file for analysis.

The Traceroute Utility Program

A second common TCP/IP tool you can use as a supplement to Ping is Traceroute. As its name implies, Traceroute lets you trace the route packets take from the local host issuing the command to the destination remote host.

Overview

Several variations of Traceroute are available, including the name under which the program operates. Although many UNIX systems use Traceroute as the program name, as we shortly note in this section the Windows version uses the name Tracert, while the Cisco router command name is `trace`.

GENERAL FORMAT

The general format of the `traceroute` command is shown here:

```
traceroute [-t count][-q count][-w count][-P
count]{host_name|IP_address}
```

where `-t` indicates the maximum allowable *time-to-live* (TTL) value, measured as the number of hops allowed prior to the program terminating, with the default TTL value being 30; `-q` indicates the number of UDP packets transmitted with each time-to-live setting, with the default being 3; `-w` indicates the amount of time, in seconds, the program waits for an answer from a particular router prior to moving on to the next transmission, with the default wait time being 5 s and an asterisk (*) printed instead of a round-trip delay denoting a time-out; and `-p` represents the invalid port number at the remote host which terminates the operation, with the default port number used by Traceroute being 33434 and some implementations not permitting this port number to be varied.

Operation

Traceroute's default mode of operation results in the program generating three sequences of *user datagram protocol* (UDP) datagrams using an invalid port address for the destination and setting the IP TTL field value initially to 1. Since routers are programmed to decrement the TTL field value by 1 and discard datagrams whose field value is 0 to prevent packets from endlessly wandering the Internet, the first router in the path tosses the datagram into the great bit bucket in the sky. In addition, the router responds to the datagram originator with an ICMP *time exceeded message* (TEM), which indicates that the datagram expired. The host operating traceroute denotes the response to each sequence of datagrams to display information about the first router in the path to the destination as well as the round-trip delay to that device. Next, the Traceroute program increments its TTL value by 1 to 2 and transmits another sequence of three UDP messages, with an IP header TTL field value of 2. This action results in the second router in the path to the destination returning ICMP TEMs. This process continues, with the TTL value incrementing until the destination is reached or the maximum TTL value is reached. When the UDP datagrams finally reach the destination, the use of an invalid port number results in the return of a sequence of ICMP destination unreachable messages. This action informs the program that its operation is complete.

Utilization

Unlike Ping, which has a limited amount of space in the use of an IP header options field for recording a route, Traceroute theoretically has no route discovery limits. Although its default setting restricts its use to 30 hops, you can easily change that value through the use of the program's -t option, which under some implementations requires the use of a different switch variable.

By using traceroute, it becomes possible to identify bottlenecks along the path between source and destination. This, in turn, assists you in working with a service provider to consider other routing options if your organization is operating, or wishes to consider using, time-dependent applications. In addition, it also becomes possible for the service provider or the network manager operating a private IP-based network to consider upgrading or replacing an existing router to alleviate an actual or potential bottleneck. Thus, with traceroute, you can locate bottlenecks and consider several options for expediting the flow of data between two networks.

The Windows Tracert Program

Under Microsoft Windows, the Traceroute program is implemented under the name tracert. Figure 6-9 shows the Help screen that appears when you enter the name of the program without parameters.

```
Command Prompt                                                       _ □ ×
Microsoft(R) Windows NT(TM)
(C) Copyright 1985-1996 Microsoft Corp.

C:\>tracert

Usage: tracert [-d] [-h maximum_hops] [-j host-list] [-w timeout] target_name

Options:
    -d                      Do not resolve addresses to hostnames.
    -h maximum_hops         Maximum number of hops to search for target.
    -j host-list            Loose source route along host-list.
    -w timeout              Wait timeout milliseconds for each reply.

C:\>_
```

Figure 6-9   Microsoft Tracert program options.

In Figure 6-9 note that the Microsoft version of Traceroute is similar to its version of Ping in that they both operate under the Command Prompt box. Also note that the Microsoft version of Traceroute is limited to the support of four options. The -d option requires the use of an IP address in the target name and results in the tabular display of router addresses without displaying descriptions returned from each router. The -h option lets you override the default setting of 30 hops. The -j option represents the use of the IP header option field to record routers and the term *loose* functions in the same manner as previously described for the use of Ping.

The fourth and last option, -w, lets you set a time-out, in milliseconds, for waiting for each reply before the program displays an asterisk (*) and issues the next UDP message.

The best way to become familiar with a program and its capabilities is by its use, so let's do that now. Since we previously noted that we could not ping the Web server at Harvard but were able to obtain its IP address as well as the IP address of a router that indicated the destination network was unreachable (see Figure 6-4), we have two addresses we could consider using in a traceroute command. Those addresses are the resolved address of the Web server (128.103.60.55) and the address of the router (128.103.15.21) that informed us that the destination network was unreachable. Since we have two IP addresses to use, let's use both.

Figure 6-10 illustrates the use of tracert with the previously resolved Harvard Web server IP address. Note that as the UDP datagram sequences are transmitted with varying TTL values, the responses from most routers include a description of the device. For example, for hop 2 the right-most

Figure 6-10   Attempting to trace the route to the Harvard Web server.

column indicates that the router is located in Atlanta and is operated by BBNPlanet, which many years ago was acquired by GTE. Thus, although the description does not inform you of the type of router operated by the ISP or its age, a bit of knowledge about the history of mergers and acquisitions may assist you in determining if your Internet service provider is operating the latest in router technology.

Continuing our examination of the resulting tracert display shows that datagrams are hopping around at certain network hubs such as Atlanta, Georgia; Vienna, Virginia; and New York City. This suggests that if latency was a very critical issue it might be possible to work with your ISP to obtain an alternate route that might avoid one or more potential or actual bottlenecks.

Returning to our use of the IP address of the Harvard Web server, note that the eighteenth hop entry in Figure 6-9 reports that the destination network is not reachable. Since the router issues an ICMP message to report this situation and includes its IP address, we could also use that address for another tracert operation. Let's do so now.

Figure 6-11 illustrates the use of tracert to trace the route to the Harvard router. In comparing the routes displayed to essentially the same location, you will note a slight difference between the results shown in Figures 6-10 and 6-11. Although the first three hops are the same for both uses of the Tracert program, the routing through the BBNPlanet office in Vienna, Virginia, is slightly different, as is the routing through New York City. Thus, another potential use of a Traceroute program is to verify certain ISP commitments such as a fixed routing between networks in addition to guarantees concerning latency.

```
⌂ Command Prompt                                                      ▬ ▢ ▢

C:\>tracert 128.103.15.21

Tracing route to camrtr1.harvard.edu [128.103.15.21]
over a maximum of 30 hops:

  1    <10 ms     <10 ms     <10 ms   205.131.175.2
  2    <10 ms      16 ms      16 ms   s11-0-0-2.atlanta1-cr3.bbnplanet.net [4.0.156.5
  3     15 ms     <10 ms      16 ms   p2-1.atlanta1-nbr1.bbnplanet.net [4.0.5.114]
  4     16 ms      31 ms      16 ms   p3-3.vienna1-nbr3.bbnplanet.net [4.0.5.141]
  5     47 ms      31 ms      16 ms   p1-0.vienna1-nbr2.bbnplanet.net [4.0.5.45]
  6     63 ms      78 ms      15 ms   p2-1.nyc4-nbr2.bbnplanet.net [4.0.3.126]
  7     63 ms      47 ms      31 ms   p10-0-0.nyc4-br2.bbnplanet.net [4.0.5.30]
  8     16 ms      46 ms      32 ms   h11-0-0.nyc1-br2.bbnplanet.net [4.0.2.177]
  9     47 ms      31 ms      31 ms   f1-0.nyc1-cr1.bbnplanet.net [4.0.40.21]
 10     15 ms      32 ms      31 ms   gr1-h20.n54ny.ip.att.net [192.205.31.241]
 11     15 ms      32 ms      31 ms   gbr2-p10.n54ny.ip.att.net [12.123.1.54]
 12     47 ms      47 ms      31 ms   gbr1-p50.cb1ma.ip.att.net [12.122.2.14]
 13     31 ms      47 ms      31 ms   ar3-a300s1.cb1ma.ip.att.net [12.127.5.37]
 14     31 ms      47 ms      31 ms   12.126.99.6
 15     63 ms     219 ms     234 ms   192.5.66.18
 16     31 ms      47 ms      32 ms   camrtr1.harvard.edu [128.103.15.21]

Trace complete.

◄                                                                        ►
```

Figure 6-11   Using the tracert -d option.

Since data transmission over the Internet is a random process, you can expect the flow of datagrams to encounter different delays. This is verified by examining the round-trip delays shown in Figures 6-10 and 6-11. If you examine Figure 6-10, you note that the highest delay occurred at hop 10 for two out of three datagrams. In comparison, an examination of Figure 6-11 indicates that the longest delay occurred at hop 15, also for two out of three datagrams. Thus, the route from the author's workstation to Harvard is a random route, with delays based on the state of traffic flowing to or through a particular node when the program issued its sequence of datagrams.

In concluding our examination of the Microsoft version of Traceroute, Figure 6-12 illustrates the use of the program's -d option. As previously noted, the use of the -d switch option not only does not resolve an IP address to a host name, but results in an abbreviated display of node addresses discovered along the route.

One of the advantages of the use of the -d switch option is the fact that it facilitates piping the output of the program into a file. If you use the double greater than sign (>>) in your piping operation, you could append each use of the program's output to the same file, enabling you to create a script to periodically run the Traceroute program and save the results for analysis via a spreadsheet program. Now that we understand the use of the Microsoft Windows version of Traceroute, let's look at Cisco's implementation of this utility program.

```
Command Prompt

C:\>tracert -d 128.103.15.21

Tracing route to 128.103.15.21 over a maximum of 30 hops

  1    <10 ms    <10 ms    <10 ms   205.131.175.2
  2     31 ms     31 ms     31 ms   4.0.156.5
  3    <10 ms     31 ms     16 ms   4.0.5.114
  4     31 ms     16 ms     31 ms   4.0.5.141
  5     32 ms     31 ms     31 ms   4.0.5.45
  6     31 ms     31 ms     31 ms   4.0.3.126
  7     31 ms     31 ms     31 ms   4.0.5.30
  8     47 ms     31 ms     31 ms   4.0.2.177
  9     46 ms     63 ms     31 ms   4.0.40.21
 10     15 ms     78 ms     63 ms   192.205.31.241
 11     16 ms     31 ms     31 ms   12.123.1.54
 12     47 ms     31 ms     62 ms   12.122.2.14
 13     31 ms     31 ms     47 ms   12.127.5.37
 14     31 ms     63 ms     62 ms   12.126.99.6
 15     32 ms     31 ms     31 ms   192.5.66.10
 16     47 ms     94 ms     78 ms   128.103.15.21

Trace complete.

C:\>
```

Figure 6-12 Using Microsoft's tracert program to trace the route to Harvard University's router.

Router trace Command

Similar to Ping, Cisco routers support two versions of Traceroute, both of which are IP commands named trace. The first version is for use under EXEC, and is referred to as a user mode command. The second version of trace operates under the privileged mode and is referred to as privileged trace. Both versions have the same general format, which is the name of the command (and the protocol IP), followed by the host name or IP address of the destination. Similar to the privileged version of Ping, the privileged version of trace supports both regular and extended mode operation, with the latter resulting from the entry of the command name without an address, providing prompts that allow you to vary some of the command options. A good way to become familiar with a command is from its use, so let's do so, first reviewing the user version of trace.

USER VERSION

Under the Cisco version of Traceroute, the trace command results in the display of an asterisk whenever the timer expires prior to a response to a UDP datagram being received. Similar to Ping, you can interrupt an existing trace command by using the CTRL-X multikey sequence.

Figure 6-13 illustrates the use of trace from a router to the Harvard University router. Note that in the resulting display we encountered four time-outs denoted by asterisks. Because of an inconsistent manner by

Figure 6-13   Operating the IP trace command in user mode.

```
Router> trace ip www.harvard.com
Type escape sequence to abort.

Tracing the route to camrtr1.harvard.edu (128.103.15.21)
      1 s11-0-0-2.atlanta1-cr3.bbnplanet.net (4.0.156.5) 47 msec 78 msec 31
        msec
      2 p2-1.atlanta1-nbr1.bbnplanet.net (4.0.5.114) 63 msec 31 msec 78
        msec
      3 p3-3.vienna1-nbr3.bbnplanet.net (4.0.5.141) 46 msec 32 msec 15 msec
      4 p1-0.vienna1-nbr2.bbnplanet.net (4.0.5.45) 16 msec 31 msec 47 msec
      5 p2-1.nyc4-nbr2.bbnplanet.net (4.0.3.126) 31 msec 31 msec 47 msec
      6 p10-0-0.nyc4-br2.bbnplanet.net (4.0.5.30) 31 msec 15 msec 47 msec
      7 h11-0-0.nyc1-br2.bbnplanet.net (4.0.2.177) 31 msec 47 msec 47 msec
      8 f1-0.nyc1-cr1.bbnplanet.net (4.0.40.21) 31 msec 47 msec 31 msec
      9 gr1-h20.n54ny.ip.att.net (192.205.31.241) 32 msec 47 msec 46 msec
     10 gbr2-p10.n54ny.ip.att.net (12.123.1.54) 47 msec 47 msec 31 msec
     11 gbr1-p50.cb1ma.ip.att.net (12.122.2.14) 47 msec 47 msec *
     12 ar3-a300s1.cb1ma.ip.att.net (12.127.5.37) 94 msec * 94 msec
     13 (12.126.99.6) 78 msec 94 msec 94 msec
     14 (192.5.66.10) 125 msec 63 msec *
     15 camrtr1.harvard.edu (128.103.15.21) 78 msec 78 msec *
```

TABLE 6-2 Trace Operation Description Characters.

Character	Description
*	The probe operation timed out
?	Unknown packet type received
Q	Source quench
P	Protocol unreachable
N	Network unreachable
U	Port unreachable
H	Host unreachable

which some routers support the use of TTL, you may encounter a series of TTL time-outs denoted by asterisks that are not really time-outs in the conventional sense of the term. This is because some routers generate an ICMP TTL exceeded message and then reuse the TTL of the received datagram. Since the TTL was 0, the ICMP packets that are forwarded result in the generation of another series of TTL exceeded messages that are either discarded by the following router in the path or again forwarded in error. Thus, occasionally you might view a series of TTL values with asterisks that result from the incorrect handling of an ICMP TTL exceeded situation. However, if there are enough hops in the path to the destination, the TTL values eventually increment a sufficient amount to put the probe datagrams through with TTL values that elicit a correct response.

Although no special trace characters are displayed in Figure 6-13, under certain conditions, different characters are used as an abbreviation for certain predefined trace conditions. Table 6-2 lists the characters that can be displayed in a trace output. This list is applicable to both user and privileged trace modes of operation.

PRIVILEGED TRACE MODE

The key difference between user and privileged trace modes is that the latter permits you to view and alter default trace options. To do so, you first enter the privileged EXEC mode of operation and type the trace command without any options.

Figure 6-14 illustrates the use of the extended version of the privileged trace command. Note that when you enter the command without a host name or IP address, you are automatically placed in an extended dialog

Figure 6-14   Using the extended version of the privileged `trace` command.

```
Router# trace
Protocol [ip]:
Target IP address: 128.103.15.21
Source address:
Numeric display [n]:
Timeout in seconds [3]:
Probe count [3]:
Minimum Time to Live [1]:
Maximum Time to Live [30]:
Port Number [33434]:
Loose, Strict, Record, Timestamp, Verbose[none]:
Type escape sequence to abort.
Tracing the route to camrtr1.harvard.edu (128.103.15.21)
  1 s11-0-0-2.atlanta1-cr3.bbnplanet.net (4.0.156.5) 45 msec 89 msec 33 msec
  2 p2-1.atlanta1-nbr1.bbnplanet.net (4.0.5.114) 53 msec 71 msec 74 msec
  3 p3-3.vienna1-nbr3.bbnplanet.net (4.0.5.141) 26 msec 67 msec 28 msec
  4 p1-0.vienna1-nbr2.bbnplanet.net (4.0.5.45) 18 msec 40 msec 38 msec
  5 p2-1.nyc4-nbr2.bbnplanet.net (4.0.3.126) 33 msec 35 msec 51 msec
  6 p10-0-0.nyc4-br2.bbnplanet.net (4.0.5.30) 32 msec 24 msec 44 msec
  7 h11-0-0.nyc1-br2.bbnplanet.net (4.0.2.177) 34 msec 43 msec 48 msec
  8 f1-0.nyc1-cr1.bbnplanet.net (4.0.40.21) 32 msec 46 msec 32 msec
  9 gr1-h20.n54ny.ip.att.net (192.205.31.241) 32 msec 46 msec 46 msec
 10 gbr2-p10.n54ny.ip.att.net (12.123.1.54) 45 msec 45 msec 32 msec
 11 gbr1-p50.cb1ma.ip.att.net (12.122.2.14) 46 msec 46 msec *
 12 ar3-a300s1.cb1ma.ip.att.net (12.127.5.37) 98 msec * 97 msec
 13 (12.126.99.6) 87 msec 99 msec * msec
 14 (192.5.66.10) 118 msec 83 msec *
 15 camrtr1.harvard.edu (128.103.15.21) 88 msec * 78 msec
```

mode of the command, with prompts generated that describe various options as well as, when applicable, default values for certain options. As we view the extended `trace` operation shown in Figure 6-14, let's also examine the dialog to describe several options worth considering when your organization needs to carefully consider the viability of certain types of service level agreements.

Once you enter the router's privileged mode and type the command `trace` without options or parameters, you are automatically placed in a dialog mode, with each option displayed on a separate line awaiting your action. The first dialog line denotes the protocol, which by default is IP and which is accepted by pressing the RETURN key.

The second dialog box line requests the target IP address. That address can be either a host name or an IP address. In Figure 6-14 we entered the router IP address at Harvard which we previously discovered during a prior operation.

The third line, which is the prompt `Source Address`, permits you to specify one of the interface addresses of your router to use as a source address for the sequence of probes. If you leave this field blank, the router selects the interface that it feels is the best source address to use, if you have multiple WAN interfaces from the router toward the target destination, you may wish to first specify one address and then specify the other interface addresses in separate extended trace sequences. Note that this action lets you obtain both the route and round-trip response times via different interfaces, which can be an important consideration when your organization has multiple access lines into a network. In some situations it is possible that the servicing of different access lines result in different levels of service. Thus, if your organization operates multiple access lines, you should check each when verifying SLAs.

The fourth dialog line displays the prompt Numeric display. This prompt permits both a symbolic and numeric display, which is the default. If you change the default to y, it results in the suppression of any symbols in the resulting display.

The next two dialog lines let you vary the time-out and number of datagrams transmitted at each TTL value. The default time-out period is 3 s and the default probe count is 3. The following dialog line labeled Minimum Time to Live provides you with a most interesting capability that is missing from other implementations of Traceroute this author has used. That is, by varying the minimum TTL value from its default of 1, you can suppress the display response from hops you are not concerned about. For example, accepting the default value of 1 results in the first hop, responding to the first sequence of datagrams. If you were not concerned about the first hop, you might set the minimum TTL value to 2, which results in the first hop decrementing the TTL value in the 1 and passing the datagrams. Similarly, if you were not interested a group of routers, you could adjust the minimum TTL value accordingly. While the ability to set a minimum TTL permits you to suppress the display of known hops the next prompt, Maximum Time to Live, allows you to select a maximum TTL value. Since the default is 30 hops, it should be sufficient for most situations. However, because the command terminates when the maximum value is reached or the destination is obtained, whichever comes first, it is possible you may need to adjust the default to successfully reach a destination. While 30 hops appears to be a sufficient default, if you are routed through some hubs where your datagrams must flow through four, five, or even six devices, it is quite possible that you can reach the 30-hop maximum and need to adjust this metric in order to reach your intended destination.

The next line, labeled Port Number, permits you to adjust the destination port used in the UDP probe messages. The default value is 33434, which is the default value used in other implementations of Traceroute.

The next dialog line, labeled Loose, Strict, Record, Timestamp, Verbose, permits you to use IP header options in the same manner as previously described for the extended Ping privileged command. As a reminder, the Loose option corresponds to Loose Source Routing while the Strict option corresponds to Strict Source Routing. Both options permit you to specify a list of nodes to be traversed when sending datagrams to a specific destination. However, the Loose Source Routing option allows other nodes in addition to those specified to be traversed, while the Strict Source Routing option means only those specified nodes can be traversed when datagrams are transmitted to a specific destination. The Record option lets you leave room in the IP options field for a specific number of hops. Similarly, the Timestamp option permits you to specify the number of time stamps to leave room for. Finally, the Verbose mode will be selected either by selecting any of the other options or by selecting Verbose. When this option is invoked, the execution of the command results in the display of the contents of the option field in any inbound packets. By selecting Verbose, you can toggle this option off.

Design Principles

In the prior sections we examined the use of Ping and Traceroute utility programs to verify a service level agreement as well as for network testing and troubleshooting. This chapter concludes with an examination of several aspects of network design and indicates how those utility programs can assist in periodically examining the flow of data through a network as well as serve to help determine if an adjustment to the network should be considered.

Topology Considerations

The basic function of a router is to relay packets received on one interface to another interface toward their ultimate destination. The ability to perform routing depends on the topology or structure of the network as well as the manner by which routers are configured. The topology is highly dependent upon organizational locations to be interconnected as well as their data transfer requirements. Thus, there is no one best way to structure routers into a network because of the differences in the locations where organizations have offices as well as their operational requirements, including reliability and redundancy. As a result, we focus primarily on general design techniques in this section, commencing with a relatively simple interconnection of two geographically separated locations.

TWO-LOCATION NETWORK

The top portion of Figure 6-15 illustrates the use of a pair of routers to connect two geographically separated LANs. In this example we assume

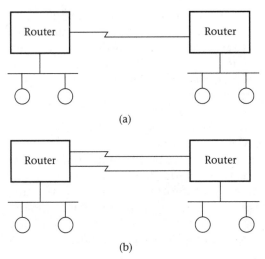

(a)

(b)

Figure 6-15 A basic two-location network. (*a*) Single transmission path; (*b*) multiple transmission paths. ○ = LAN workstations.

there is no requirement for a high degree of reliability and only one digital transmission facility is used to connect the two routers. Since this is a simple two-point network, static routes could be configured for each router.

The lower portion of Figure 6-15 illustrates the use of dual transmission facilities. The use of dual transmission facilities could be due to either a higher level of traffic between the two locations than can be handled by one circuit or the need for redundancy. Concerning the latter, if your organization is installing a pair of circuits between geographically separated locations for redundancy, be sure to request diversity routing from your communications carrier so your communications carrier will route each circuit through different central offices and to different higher-order transmission groups to ensure no common points of failure. In this operating environment you could either use one transmission line for true backup or use load balancing across both transmission lines which would result in one line functioning as a backup for the other. Since you would want a routing protocol to allow the selection of an operational line if the second one should fail, you would not use static routing in this environment.

If the configurations illustrated in Figure 6-15 represent access lines or local loops into a public packet network, you could use both Ping and Traceroute to verify any SLA as well as a troubleshooting mechanism. Now that we understand a simple two-point network configuration, let's examine the use of the so-called hub-and-spoke network configuration.

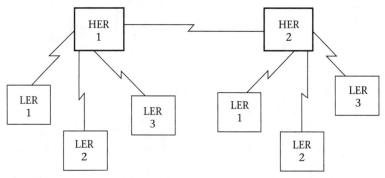

Figure 6-16 A hub-and-spoke network results in one or more high-end routers serving low-end routers located within a common geographical area. HER = high-end router; LER = low-end router.

HUB-AND-SPOKE NETWORK

A hub-and-spoke network is a design configuration in which branch offices are commonly connected directly to a regional office. The hub, or regional office location, commonly uses a high-end router with a sufficient number of interfaces to service the regional office locations that, from a topological perspective, resemble spokes. Hence the term hub-and-spoke network.

Figure 6-16 illustrates an example of a simple hub-and-spoke network. In this example two regional offices function as hubs, with low-end routers serving as the spokes for each hub.

Since a spoke always sends traffic to a hub, it is possible to configure each spoke with a static routing entry. Then, each spoke can use the hub that services its location as a default gateway. This technique eliminates routing table updates between a hub and its spoke.

The primary reason for using a hub-and-spoke network design is economics. For most small- and medium-size organizations it is often difficult to justify the creation of a full or partial mesh structured network. However, if your organization requires certain branch locations to have a better level of redundancy or the ability to continue operations on an alternate path if the primary connection should fail, you would then consider redesigning the network. One common method to do so involves the creation of multiple exit points for one or more spokes. Figure 6-17 illustrates an example of a two-hub hub-and-spoke network in which two spokes are configured with multiple exit points.

A decision to configure multiple exit points for one or more low-end routers at a spoke can be based on the need for additional reliability or traffic considerations. In terms of the former, you could simply add an additional circuit between a spike and its serving hub. However, if a need arises for multiple exits due to traffic considerations, a number of possible

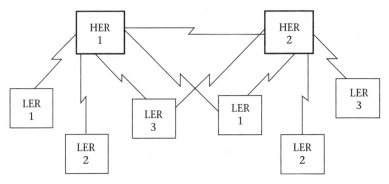

Figure 6-17 Using spokes with multiple exit points (HER = high-end router; LER = low-end router).

exit strategies arise. For example, assume the connection between HER1 and LER3 is experiencing heavy traffic and, as a result, an increase in latency. Depending upon the source-destination traffic relationship, you could consider installing a second exit to an LER within the LERs directly serviced by HER1 or HER2, installing another circuit to HER1, or creating an exit to HER2.

When attempting to determine which exit strategy to pursue, statistics concerning the flow of packets and bytes only provide a portion of information that may be required to make an informed decision. This is because it is possible that although a hub-to-spoke link is lightly utilized, traffic through the hub serving a spoke may be heavy. Then, adding an exit for LER3 via LER2 might not be a wise decision, even if the transmission line from HER1 to LER2 was lightly utilized.

To assist your effort in determining the appropriate connection of exit points, you can consider using both Ping and Traceroute to examine the flow of traffic through alternate locations. For example, if you were examining the possibility of connecting LER3 to LER2 to provide an alternate exit point for outbound and inbound traffic, prior to doing so you could examine the flow of traffic through HER1 to LER2. If you noted potential congestion or delay times that exceed that required for a specific application, you might consider routing the exit to another device.

In Figure 6-16 the second LER3 exit is shown routed to HER2. While this could result from the fact that more traffic is directed to the spokes served by HER2, it could also result from the discovery that the high-speed transmission line connecting the two high-end routers has sufficient bandwidth to support alternate routing. Thus, although it may appear peculiar, it could be possible for traffic routed from LER3 to LER2 to arrive quicker by being routed via HER2 to HER1 and then to LER2. By the use of Ping and Traceroute, you can often note such peculiarities and take advantage of nonobvious methods for rearranging the structure of a network.

CHAPTER 7

Observing Metrics over Time

Previous chapters examined a variety of techniques for displaying the state of various router methods. We noted that many router counters are limited to storing data for a 5-min period. Even for those counters that store cumulative values, their display requires you to periodically extract data from different counters and plot such data over a period of time to note trends and compare current metric values to a baseline. Thus, any method that lets you plot different router metrics over time is a welcomed addition to tools used by network managers and LAN administrators and is the focus of this chapter.

Today many tools exist to extract performance metrics from different communications devices, including Cisco routers. These tools range in scope from network management products that can cost thousands of dollars to freeware and shareware programs. Each of these tools is based on the use of the *simple network management protocol* (SNMP). Thus, the first part of this chapter provides an overview of the operation of SNMP by examining the relationship between an SNMP agent and management platform as well as the structure of the global naming tree which locates elements in a database of network management information referred to as a *management information base* (MIB). Once this is accomplished, we review the operation and utilization of a program that displays various types of network traffic via Web pages. Referred to as the *Multirouter traffic grapher* (MRTG), this program was originally written for operation under UNIX but now also operates under different versions of Microsoft Windows. MRTG consists of a Perl script that uses SNMP to read defined traffic counters of your routers or any other SNMP device and creates graphs that represent various metrics on a monitored network connection.

In examining the operation and utilization of MRTG we note the location where the program can be obtained. In addition, we examine its setup and configuration, including obtaining the required version of Perl needed to run MRTG scripts. Although there are many professional software products that use SNMP, a quick search of the Web shows that many organizations adopted MRTG because of its capability and simplicity. While the program is relatively easy to use, the current version of available documentation requires a bit of elaboration, which is provided here as we discuss the use of this networking tool in the second portion of this chapter.

Simple Network Management Protocol (SNMP)

SNMP is a TCP/IP transport-level application that uses the *user datagram protocol* (UDP). SNMP resembles a reverse client-server architecture, with the server represented by a manager that issues commands and the client represented by an agent which responds to commands.

Components

The three major components of SNMP include a manager, agent, and MIB. The *manager* permits query of devices that operate SNMP agents. Depending on how the agent is configured, the manager may be able to extract information and/or control how the device operates by setting one or more parameters. The *agent* is software or firmware on a communications device that maintains a database of information and controls access to that database. The *MIB* is a database maintained by the agent. Figure 7-1 illustrates the general relationship between the three major SNMP components.

In Figure 7-1 note that an SNMP manager can manage multiple agents, each with its own MIB. Although most SNMP management stations primarily issue commands to agents and receive responses, it is also possible for agents to communicate unsolicited information. To do so, an agent is configured to issue a trap when a metric reaches a predefined value.

SNMP Versions

Currently, three versions of SNMP are available. Version 1, which emerged as a defined standard in 1988, is still the primary version of SNMP used. Version 1 uses community names that are text strings, such as public, to control access to agents. As a result, its level of protection against unwanted access is severely limited. In fact, although SNMP allows updating of information in agents, including changing the settings of a device,

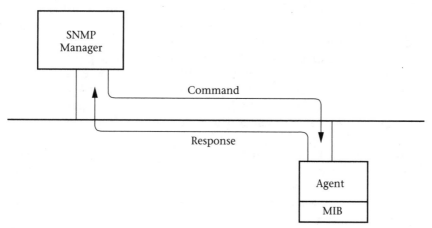

Figure 7-1 The major components of SNMP include a manager, one or more agents, and MIBs maintained by each agent.

most communications equipment manufacturers that developed SNMP-compatible products elected to prevent configuration changes via SNMP due to the weakness of community names.

Version 2 was originally developed with the intention of adding security to version 1. However, because of conflicts of opinion between key members of standards-making organizations over methods for enhancing security, no agreement on a common security method was reached. Thus, the addition of security to SNMP was deferred and the primary improvement to version 2 was the ability of network managers to communicate with one another. Only a few vendors actually implemented version 2 products and its use is rather limited.

In 1999 a third version of SNMP, SNMPv3, was standardized. SNMPv3 adds security and also provides backward compatibility with the original version of SNMP. Today the original version of SNMP represents, by far, the most common implementation of SNMP and can be expected to remain so for the foreseeable future.

The Management Information Base (MIB)

As previously mentioned, the MIB is a database. Each managed device maintains an MIB that contains statistics, counters, and other information. MIB entries have four items of information: an object identifier, a syntax, an access field, and a status field. The *object identifier* consists of text information used to name the MIB object. That name is associated with a sequence of nonnegative integers, which identifies the object within an inverted tree. As we shortly note, the structure of the inverted tree is standardized and permits identification of standardized objects and proprietary objects used by different vendors to provide information about different products from a common SNMP management platform. The *syntax* identifies the data type for the object, such as an integer, array, counter, or a type of address. The *access field* defines the type of operation that can be performed, such as not accessible, which means entries cannot be read or written, read, write and read/write. The *status field* defines the status of the object, such as whether it is mandatory, optional, will soon be made obsolete, or is obsolete. This field is primarily of interest to an implementer.

Two additional fields within an MIB entry are description and reference fields. The *description field*, if included, consists of ASCII text that describes the MIB entry while the *reference field* provides a reference to the MIB, typically in terms of a *request for comment* (RFC). The general format of an MIB entry is shown here:

```
name of entry OBJECT-TYPE
       SYNTAX
       ACCESS
       STATUS
       DESCRIPTION
       REFERENCE
```

ADDRESS CONSIDERATIONS

When you use a management platform to attempt to access and retrieve an MIB, you need to specify two addresses: (1) the IP address of the agent that maintains the MIB and (2) the location of the MIB object in the inverted tree structure. Since an understanding of this tree structure and the addressing methods used to locate objects in the tree is critical for the use of most network management programs, let's look at the structure of information in that inverted tree.

RATIONALE FOR A TREE STRUCTURE

Tree structures are a commonly used method for providing access to information. The reason for the use of a tree structure is because the path from the root via one or more branches to a leaf node provides a unique method for addressing information stored at the end of the path.

The most common use of a tree structure inverts the tree, resulting in the placement of the root at the top. From the root, one or more branches flows downward and separates into subbranches. This subdivision can, theoretically, continue indefinitely, with a major restriction being the number of characters, digits, or another type of identifier used to define a path downward through the inverted tree.

The directory structure employed in computer-based systems is the most commonly used inverted tree structure. Here the root of the tree is the top of the directory, while subdirectories represent branches under the root. Although the directory structure provides, theoretically, an infinite number of subdirectories, most operating systems limit a directory path to 255 characters which is a constraint on the ability to nest directories.

THE GLOBAL NAMING TREE

As a result of the need for standardizing assignment of unique identifiers to different types of resources, the *International Standards Organization* (ISO) and the *International Telecommunications Union–Telecommunications Standardization Sector* (ITU–TSS) cooperated to develop jointly a tree-based structure. This structure, which is commonly referred to as a *global naming tree*, permits assignment of unique identifiers to different types of objects. Objects in the global naming tree can represent any type of information. Since this book is on router performance, and objects related to this area fall under network management information, the primary focus is on the use of the global naming tree with respect to this area.

Overview

Figure 7-2 illustrates the general structure of the global naming tree, with special emphasis placed on the network management portion of the tree. At the top of the tree, directly under the root, are three top-level nodes. The top-level nodes indicate the organization that administers the subtree under the node. The three top-level nodes currently allow the ITU, ISO, and the ISO and ITU jointly to administer distinct portions of the global naming tree.

In examining the nodes in Figure 7-2, note that each node in the tree has a label and a numeric identifier. By tracing the path through the tree to a specific object identifier, we encounter a series of labels and numeric identifiers. We can group the labels or numeric identifiers into a sequence to represent a unique path to a specific object. Later we discuss the use of object identifiers created by using a string of integers separated by dots to access both standardized and vendor-specific metrics. Returning to Figure 7-2, the third node (ORG), which is located under the ISO node, delegates authority to other organizations. One of those organizations is the U.S. Department of Defense (DoD), which is the sixth node under the ORG node. For simplicity the other nodes under ORG are not shown in Figure 7-2 as we are focusing primarily on network management information.

If you remember the basic evolution history of the Internet, you also remember that the U.S. DoD initially funded the *Advanced Research Projects Agency network* (ARPAnet), which is considered the predecessor to the Internet. Thus, the first node under the DoD node is shown as the Internet node. The Internet node and the subtree located under it, which is the remaining portion of Figure 7-2, is owned by the *Internet Activities Board* (IAB) and administered by the *Internet Assigned Numbers Authority*

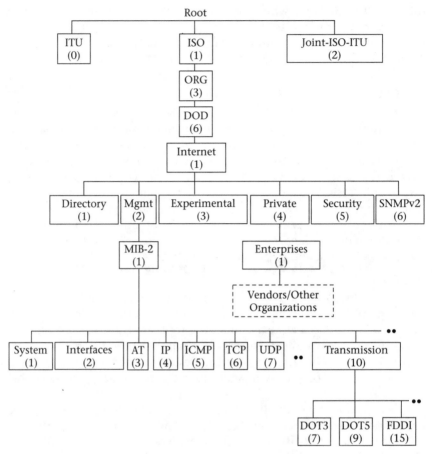

Figure 7-2   The network management portion of the global naming tree.

(IANA). The IANA maintains a document of assigned numbers, which tracks the complete set of parameters used in the TCP/IP protocol suite, including addresses in the Internet subtree that identify SNMP and *remote monitoring* (RMON) objects. If you carefully examine Figure 7-2, you will note the node identified by dashed lines and labeled Vendors/Other Organizations. Through this node, organizations that wish to develop extensions to SNMP and RMON standard objects, such as router CPU utilization, can be assigned distinct identifiers within the Internet subtree that can be used for defining different product objects.

The Internet Subtree
The Internet subtree shown in the middle to lower portion of Figure 7-2 provides two nodes of direct interest. Those nodes are Mgmt and Private. The Mgmt tree holds all standardized network management variables and

is that portion of the global naming tree with which most network management systems are designed to work. Those extensions result in the creation of a private MIB. To do so, an organization first applies for and is assigned a node under the private/enterprises path that is their defined location within the global naming tree. Within that subtree an organization is free to define its own structure for product MIB object definitions required to manage a specific product or group of products. The Cisco private MIB is identified by the object identifier 1.3.6.1.4.1.9 or *iso.org.dod.internet.private.enterprise.cisco.* Later in this section, we examine Cisco's private MIB.

Although it is almost impossible for any one network management product to be aware of every vendor-specific set of objects located under the private/enterprise node, the use of path identifiers and the assignment of object descriptors to numeric locations provides a discovery capability. That is, it becomes possible for network managers and LAN administrators to use different programs to *walk through* the global naming tree structure. In doing so, they can locate a private MIB for a specific vendor or vendor product and continue down the path to possibly view or alter information. This walk through the global naming tree provides persons with a capability they might not otherwise obtain by relying on the standard features of a network management system. In addition, because of the capability of many vendor-specific network management systems to support the retrieval of MIB information based upon the entry of object identifiers, it becomes possible to use one vendor's product with another vendor's equipment.

The MIB-2 Subtree

Continuing our exploration of the global naming tree, under the Mgmt node you will note the node labeled MIB-2. This node contains a series of groups that are organized into specific subtrees based upon a common management function. This grouping simplifies network management operations. Depending on the operating characteristics of a device, it may or may not support one or more of the groups shown under the MIB-2 node. The reason MIB-2 is shown is because the original MIB for managing a TCP/IP network was superseded by a newer version referred to as MIB-2. Note that the path to the system group is 1.3.6.1.2.1.1. For an understanding of the structure of information within MIB-2, let's examine the entries in a few groups.

The System Group

The system group contains seven object identifiers that provide administrative information about a managed device. While implementation of the system group is mandatory for SNMP devices, it does not mean that information about one or more of the seven objects within the system group will be available for retrieval because some objects, such as sysDescr,

Table 7-1   The MIB-2 System Group

Object Identifier	Location	Description
sysDescr	1.3.6.1.2.1.1.1	A test description about the device.
sysObjectID	1.3.6.1.2.1.1.2	An identifier assigned to the device by its vendor.
sysUpTime	1.3.6.1.2.1.1.3	The time, in hundredths of a second, since the system was last reinitialized.
sysContact	1.3.6.1.2.1.1.4	The person responsible for the device.
sysName	1.3.6.1.2.1.1.5	An administratively assigned name.
sysLocation	1.3.6.1.2.1.1.6	The physical location of the device.
sysServices	1.3.6.1.2.1.1.7	A coded number that indicates the layer in the ISO model at which the device performs services.

which provides a text description about the device, may or may not be configured by a network manager or LAN administrator. Table 7-1 lists the seven object identifiers in the system group, including their location in the global naming tree and a description of the identifier.

The Interfaces Group
Since a managed device can have several interfaces, the interfaces group provides information on both the number of interfaces present on the device and a table of data for each interface. Each interface table consists of approximately 20 entries, including a text string containing information about the interface, a code that indicates the type of interface, the size of the largest datagram that can be transmitted and received via the interface, its bandwidth, Mac address, operational status, and several counters. Examples of counters include the time since the interface was last initialized, the number of octets, unicast packets, nonunicast packets, and various types of erroneous packets transmitted and received via the interface.

Two of the more valuable and frequently used interface MIB objects are labeled ifInOctets and ifOutOctets, and they provide the number of bytes transmitted and received on an interface. The location of each object identifier in the global naming tree is 1.3.6.1.2.1.2.2.1.10 and 1.3.6.1.2.1.2.2.1.16, respectively. The appendix contains a list and description of MIB-2 groups and the objects in each group that you can use as a reference guide for determining the applicable positions in the global naming tree if you wish to extract one or more objects by using a network management system or plot MIB-2 statistics over time by using the MRTG program. Although the appendix lists the object identifiers in each MIB-2 group, a few words about some of the other groups are warranted.

Other MIB-2 Groups

The AT group includes object identifiers used in a layer 3 to layer 2 address translation process. This group contains tables that store network address to physical address equivalencies, in effect being an ARP table although it can also hold other mappings.

The IP group contains information about the IP headers in datagrams as well as datagram statistics. Examples of IP group object identifiers include the default Time-to-Live field value of IP datagrams originated by the device, the total number of datagrams received, datagrams discarded as a result of errors in their IP headers, and datagrams discarded because of invalid IP addresses. In addition, the IP group object identifiers also provide statistics on datagrams forwarded as well as on several types of error conditions and the state and quantity of IP fragments. Another valuable set of object identifiers in the IP group is an IP routing table, which contains an entry for each route known by the managed device.

The ICMP group provides statistics on ICMP messages, including a count of the number of ICMP messages transmitted and received and specific types of ICMP messages such as ICMP destination unreachable, ICMP time exceeded, ICMP parameter problem, ICMP source quench, ICMP redirect, ICMP echo request, and ICMP echo reply messages.

The TCP group provides detailed information about TCP connections such as the retransmission time-out, the number of connections that can be supported, and various TCP connection transitions. In addition, the TCP object group maintains statistics covering transmitted and received segments and different types of erroneous segments. The UDP group provides a similar series of statistics for UDP datagrams.

One group that requires some additional explanation is the Transmission group. This group does not have any object identifiers directly within its node. Instead, it is a node position in the global naming tree under which groups applicable to different transmission technologies are placed. Three examples of transmission technologies are shown in Figure 7-2 under the transmission node: DOT3, DOT5, and FDDI. The DOT3 and DOT5 nodes refer to local area networks standardized by the IEEE as 802.3 and 802.5. Those standards are better known as Ethernet and Token Ring.

Assigning Identifiers and Managing Objects

As indicated earlier, each object in a device to be managed is represented by a unique address within the global naming tree. Although it is possible to identify an object via linking text labels with underscores or dots, the most commonly used method to express an object identifier is by using a string of integers separated by dots to form a path to the object. For example, the path to the system group shown in Figure 7-2 would be 1.3.6.1.2.1.1, while the first object located in the group would have the position 1.3.6.1.2.1.1.1 in the global naming tree. Since some devices, such as a bridge or router, can have at least two interfaces, you must specify a particular interface when you need to retrieve information from a particular interface. In doing so, you append a digit to the identifier path to denote the specific interface from which you wish to retrieve information. Other objects represent a one-of-a-kind value, such as the description or location of a device. To provide consistency, an index is added at the end of an identifier. Thus, if the object is a one-of-a-kind object, you add a 0 to its path. For example, because the first object in the system group, sysDescr, is a one-of-a-kind object, its path identifier becomes 1.3.6.1.2.1.1.1.0. Although the omission of the trailing 0 is a common error when users of a network management system use path addresses to retrieve object values, some systems automatically internally add the unique one-of-a-kind 0 to an object identifier location. Now that we understand the structure of the global naming tree and the numeric paths to locate specific object identifiers, let's look at Cisco's private MIB by focusing primarily on a few router object identifiers.

Cisco System's Private MIB

Since this chapter's focus is on obtaining metric information over time, it is important to understand how MIB object identifiers can be retrieved. In addition, since this book provides information on the performance of Cisco routers, the ability to extract router-relevant MIB information can facilitate our task. Over the years, Cisco, like other communications product vendors, developed a comprehensive series of private MIBs.

This section examines Cisco's private MIB for their *Internetwork Operations System* (IOS). However, prior to doing so, it is important to note that public and private object identifiers should be considered for the use of MRTG or any SNMP platform. In the public arena MIB-2 provides a rich set of information concerning the TCP/IP protocol suite. However, because that suite does not deal with the internal operation of a device, such as CPU utilization or the state of its various buffers, you must also consider working with private MIBs for a full picture of the operational capabilities and level of performance of a communications device.

Overview

The entry point or top object identifier for the Cisco private MIB is located at 1.3.6.1.4.1.9 in the global naming tree. This top-level Cisco node is directly under the enterprise group and, as indicated in Figure 7-2, from tracing a path from the root of the global naming tree has the text identifier *iso.org.dod.internet.private.enterprise.cisco.*

The Cisco MIB is subdivided into three main areas: local variables that do not change and were intended to be supported in subsequent releases of system software, temporary variables whose meanings or values can change in subsequent releases of IOS, and management variables. Due to changes in the evolution of SNMP, the local variables subtree is now restricted to MIB objects defined prior to IOS Release 10.2, which was based upon the *structure of management information* (SMI) supported by SNMPv1. Beginning with IOS Release 10.2, Cisco MIBs are defined using SNMPv2 and are placed under the ciscoMgmt tree. According to Cisco, MIBs currently defined in the local subtree are being replaced with new objects defined in the ciscoMgmt subtree.

Structure

Figure 7-3 illustrates the general structure of Cisco's private MIB. Note that the local variables are located under node 2 under the Cisco private MIB node while temporary variables are located under node 3. Under the local variables and temporary variables nodes are different groups that represent object identifiers that are related and fit into a particular category. For example, the system group is identified as node 1 under the local variable group. Within that group, the first local system group variable is the *read-only memory identifier* (romId). This object identifier is a one-of-a-kind variable. Thus, its location in the global naming tree becomes

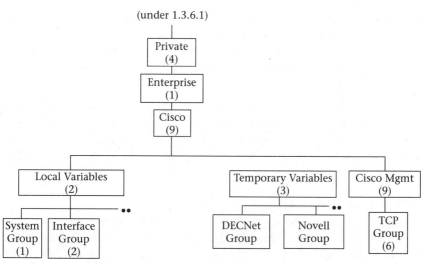

Figure 7-3 The Cisco private MIB structure.

1.3.6.1.4.1.9.2.1.1.0, with the appended 0 used to indicate that it is a one-of-a-kind variable.

LOCAL VARIABLES

The local variables node contains groups of object identifiers that are applicable to all Cisco devices. Originally, 10 groups were located under the local variable node (1.3.6.1.4.1.9.2); however, some groups are no longer supported in new devices. The following subsections summarize presently supported groups, including their location under the local variables node and a brief description of each group.

System Group (.1)

The system group provides information about systemwide parameters for Cisco products such as the software version in use, host name, domain name, buffer size, configuration files, and environmental statistics. Some of the object identifiers within the system group provide significant information on router performance. As noted later in this section, system group object identifiers provide information about CPU utilization and the state of different categories of buffer memory.

Interface Group (.2)

The object identifiers in this interface group provide information about device interfaces such as the status of the line, traffic statistics, average speed of input and output packets, and error information.

Internet Protocol Group (.4)

The Internet protocol (IP) group contains object identifiers that provide information about how an interface obtained its address, ICMP messages, and datagram statistics.

Terminal Services Group (.9)

The object identifiers in the terminal services group provide information about terminal services, including the number of physical lines, line status, line type, type of flow control, and type of modem used on a line.

Flash Group (.10)

As its name implies, the Flash group contains object identifiers that pertain to Flash memory, which is used to store, boot, and write system software images, including Flash memory size and its contents. The Flash group in local variables after IOS version 10.3 was deprecated by the Cisco Flash group located in ciscoMgmt.

TEMPORARY VARIABLES

As discussed earlier, the temporary variable node contains groups whose variables are subject to change. Although most of the groups in this node are for vendor-specific protocols (.1 for DECnet, .3 for AppleTalk, .5 for

VINES, etc.), one group can be used to ascertain hardware information about your router and it deserves mentioning. That group is the Chassis group (.6), which includes object identifiers that provide information about the number of slots in the chassis, the types of cards used by the device, and the hardware version of the cards.

ciscoMgmt VARIABLES

The ciscoMgmt node contains 12 groups. Some of those groups are directly related to router performance in an IP operating environment and include the Cisco Flash group (.10), which in IOS version 10.3 and later versions replaces the group that resided under the local variables subtree, and the Cisco Transmission Control Protocol (TCP) group (.6), which provides more functionality than a counterpart that resided in the local variables subtree. Now that we understand the structure of Cisco's private MIBs, let's examine more closely the variables in the system group located under the local variables subtree. The reason we select this group is because the object identifiers permit us to obtain information concerning CPU utilization and metrics about the state of different types of buffers. Thus, let's review the location of the applicable object identifiers associated with CPU and buffer metrics and examine the information provided by each object identifier.

CPU Utilization

Within the local variables system group are three object identifiers associated with CPU utilization. The location of each CPU-related variable, its label, and a description of its contents is contained in Table 7-2.

In examining the entries in Table 7-2 note that the scheduler is a software module that determines which process or task takes priority over

Table 7-2   CPU Utilization Object Identifiers

Location	Object identifier	Description
1.3.6.1.4.1.9.2.1.56	avgBusyPer	The percentage of CPU usage over the first 5-s period in the scheduler
1.3.6.1.4.1.9.2.1.57	avgBusy1	A cumulative average of the CPU usage over a 1-min period
1.3.6.1.4.1.9.2.1.58	avgBusy5	A cumulative average of the CPU usage over a 5-min period

another and invokes them accordingly. Thus, this object identifier provides you with an indication of how busy the CPU is in scheduling different functions rather than performing actual tasks. Also note that the variables avgBusy1 and avgBusy5 are called by the scheduler every 5 s. Each variable computes the CPU busy time for the past 5-s period as well as a 5-min, exponentially delayed busy time. The average sampling time is given by the following equation:

$$\text{Average} = ((\text{average interval}) \times -t/c) + \text{interval}$$

where $t = 5$ s
$c = 1$ min (avgBusy1) or 5 min (avgBusy5)
$t/c = 0.920$ for avgBusy1, 0.983 for avgBusy5

Of the three object identifiers, most who use a program to periodically extract CPU metrics choose the avgBusy5 object identifier, because many programs can be set to extract information at 5-min intervals, which corresponds nicely to the 5-min period used by avgBusy5 to provide a cumulative average of the percentage of CPU usage. Thus, the object identifier whose position is 1.3.6.1.4.1.9.2.1.58 in the global naming tree is a commonly accessed location in the Cisco private MIB tree hierarchy.

Buffer Information

A large number of object identifiers within the system group can provide information about the state of different memory areas and various memory problems. If you remember our discussion of buffer memory from Chapter 6, Cisco routers support five types of buffers: small, middle, big, large, and huge. Each type of buffer has eight object identifiers, resulting in a total of 40 directly associated with different types of buffers. In addition, two identifiers are associated with buffer problems and five identifiers are associated with buffer elements, as well as an identifier that provides information on free memory. This section examines the previously mentioned object identifiers, commencing with free memory.

FREE MEMORY
The free memory object identifier is located at 1.3.6.1.4.1.9.2.1.8 in the global naming tree. This identifier provides the number of bytes of free memory available in a managed Cisco router and is another popular location for periodic extraction and display.

BUFFER PROBLEMS
Within the system group are two buffer problem object identifiers: bufferFail and bufferNoMem, and they are located at nodes 46 and 47

within the system group. The bufferFail identifier contains the number of allocation requests that could not be honored due to a lack of free buffers. In comparison, the bufferNoMem identifier provides a count of the number of failures due to insufficient memory to create a new buffer.

BUFFER ELEMENTS

Five object identifiers provide information about blocks of memory used in internal operating system queues. These object identifiers are grouped into the category of buffer elements and represent positions 9 through 13 under the system group tree. Table 7-3 lists the location, label, and a brief description of each buffer element.

CONFIGURABLE BUFFER INFORMATION

Each of the five types of buffers supported by Cisco routers can be configured. Thus, it becomes possible to determine if an adjustment to one or more buffers is required by carefully examining the value of object identifiers that provide information about each type of buffer.

There are eight object identifiers associated with each type of buffer. Since the function of each identifier is the same for each type of buffer and only its position in the global naming tree changes, we examine the identifiers as an entity applicable to each type of buffer. However, prior to

Table 7-3   Buffer Element-Related Object Identifiers

Location	Object Identifier	Description
1.3.6.1.4.1.9.2.1.9	bufferElFree	Number of buffer elements not currently allocated and available for use.
1.3.6.1.4.1.9.2.1.10	bufferElMax	Maximum number of buffer elements the device can have.
1.3.6.1.4.1.9.2.1.11	bufferElHit	The number of successful attempts to allocate a buffer element when one was required.
1.3.6.1.4.1.9.2.1.12	bufferElMiss	The number of allocation attempts that failed because no buffer elements were available.
1.3.6.1.4.1.9.2.1.13	bufferElCreate	Number of new buffer elements created for the device.

Table 7-4 Object Identifier Locations Based on Buffer Category in the System Group Located under 1.3.6.1.4.1.9.2.1

Generic Label	Small Sm	Middle Md	Big Bg	Large Lg	Huge Hg
bufferXXSize	.14	.22	.30	.38	.62
bufferXXTotal	.15	.23	.31	.39	.63
bufferXXFree	.16	.24	.32	.40	.64
bufferXXMax	.17	.25	.33	.41	.65
bufferXXHit	.18	.26	.34	.42	.66
bufferXXMiss	.19	.27	.35	.43	.67
bufferXXTrim	.20	.28	.36	.44	.68
bufferXXCreate	.21	.29	.37	.45	.69

doing so, we first identify the location of the object identifiers in the global naming tree via a matrix. Table 7-4 provides a summary of the object identifiers in matrix form. In examining the entries in Table 7-4 note that the term XX in the identifier label would be replaced by the mnemonic listed under one of the five buffer columns. For example, bufferXXTotal becomes the identifier bufferSmTotal for small buffers, bufferLgTotal for large buffers, etc.

Since each of the eight object identifiers for each type of buffer functions in a similar manner, it would be repetitious to review them individually. Instead, let's examine their generic function, which is easily associated with a specific type of buffer by substituting small, middle, big, large, or huge for a particular type. Table 7-5 summarizes the function of the object identifiers associated with each category of buffer.

In addition to the previously described object identifiers, literally hundreds of other identifiers are useful for different applications. A full description of those identifiers would require an entire book, but before visiting the Cisco Web site, a few words concerning the Interface Group table located under the local variables subtree (1.3.6.1.4.1.9.2.2.1.1) is warranted. Through the use of this table, you can monitor a variety of network performance metrics associated with different router interfaces. Table 7-6 summarizes some of the object identifiers that, in this author's opinion,

Table 7-5   Object Identifiers Applicable to Each Buffer Type

Generic Object Identifier	Description
bufferXXSize	Provides the size, in bytes, for a particular type of buffer.
bufferXXTotal	Provides the total number of a particular type of buffer allocated to a managed device.
bufferXXFree	Provides the current available number of a particular type of buffer.
bufferXXMax	Provides the maximum number of a particular type of buffer that can be allocated.
bufferXXHit	Provides the number of allocation attempts that failed due to a lack of a particular type of buffer.
bufferXXMiss	Provides the number of allocation attempts that failed due to a lack of a particular type of buffer.
bufferXXTrim	Provides the number of a particular type of buffer destroyed in the device.
bufferXXCreate	Provides the number of a particular type of buffer created in the device.

can be useful when periodically displayed. Note that this table is maintained for each interface and the variable information you can extract is obtained by specifying an interface number with the object identifier location within the table. Since a private MIB can be expected to change periodically, it is suggested that you access the Cisco Web site (*www.Cisco.com*) and search on such keywords as mib, private mib, and router private mib. By performing this search, you should be able to retrieve not only periodic changes to Cisco's MIBs but also a full set of documents, including the object identifiers for all Cisco private MIBs. When retrieving the latter, it is highly recommended that you download the Adobe Acrobat version of the document because the drawings of different private MIB groups are barely readable if you view or print the HTML version of the document. Now that we understand SNMP, including the global naming tree and Cisco's private MIBs, let's look at the MRTG program.

Table 7-6 Interface Group Object Identifiers That Provide Performance Information

Location under 1.3.6.1.4.1.9.2.2.1.1	Label	Description
.6	locIfInBitsSec	Provides a weighted 5-min exponentially decaying average of the interface input, in bits per second.
.8	locIfOutBitsSec	Provides a weighted 5-min exponentially decaying average of interface output, in bits per second.
.14	locIfInOverrun	Provides the number of times serial receiver hardware was unable to transmit to a hardware buffer because the input rate exceeded the ability of the receiver to handle the data.
.15	locIfInIgnored	Provides the number of input packets ignored because the hardware ran low on internal buffers.
.24	locIfLoad	Provides the loading factor of the interface as a fraction of 255 computed as an exponential average over 5 min.

Working with Multirouter Traffic Grapher (MRTG)

This section examines the use of a popular program to display graphically objects of an MIB. That program is the *multirouter traffic grapher* (MRTG).

Overview

MRTG was developed by Tobias Oetiker who presently works at the Swiss Federal Institute of Technology in Zurich. While working at DeMontfort University in Liecester, United Kingdom, Mr. Oetiker was involved in a networking situation in which one 64-kbps connection to the Internet served approximately 1000 networked computers. Since an upgrade to a higher-speed Internet connection was a year away, it became desirable to provide network users with information about the status of the connection. To do so, Mr. Oetiker developed a Perl language script that used external utilities to perform SNMP queries and create GIF images for display on HTML pages. The resulting script queried the octet counters of the university's Internet gateway router every 5 min and the resulting display allowed members of the university community to observe the performance of the Internet connection. Although this original version of MRTG, as well as later versions of the program, had no effect on the capacity of communications circuits, it did provide information that was useful in convincing appropriate persons that a faster Internet connection was necessary.

The original version of MRTG was placed on the Internet early in 1995. Since that time, its ease of use and functionality has contributed to a rapid growth in its use as well as user feedback that resulted in several revisions to the program. The version that we examine is MRTG.2.8.11; however, according to Mr. Oetiker, development of MRTG-3 was being planned at the time this book was prepared.

License Information

The current version, as well as previous versions, of MRTG are available under the GNU General Public License. Under this license, persons are permitted to share and exchange free software. The GNU Project dates to 1984 and the development of a free UNIX-like operating system is referred to as the GNU system. Since then, the development of GNU software has significantly increased, with Linux, which is more accurately referred to as GNU/Linux, probably representing the most widely known version of GNU software.

Since its development to work under UNIX, MRTG was extended to work under Windows NT as well as Windows 95 and Windows 98. Today, there are several hundred locations, ranging from community colleges and universities to businesses and government agencies that have posted their addresses on an MRTG page. That page, whose address is *http://eestaff.ethz.ch/~oetiker/webtools/mrtg/users.html* also includes links to MRTG companion sites. Those sites provide a variety of MRTG information, including the use of the program to monitor frame-relay PVCs on BayNetworks routers, Lucent Portmasters, and to obtain NT server metrics.

Preparing to Use MRTG

One of the things often overlooked by many persons is that you must configure your router to enable MRTG to extract SNMP information. To do so, you must enable users to access your router and permit access to the SNMP protocol. The first function is accomplished by using an applicable access list, while the second function requires the use of the snmp-server community command.

To illustrate the creation of applicable Cisco router configuration statements required to enable MRTG, or for that matter any SNMP management platform to extract SNMP information from your router, the IP address of each platform must be able to obtain either read-only (RO) or read-write (RW) MIB access permission. In terms of the latter, you use the snmp-server community statement whose format is shown here:

```
snmp-server community community-string [RO|RW][access-list #]
```

where community-string is an alphanumeric string that functions in a manner similar to a password, which when matched by a management station permits access to the agent; RO is used to specify read-only access permitted to MIBs, where RO is the default access method; RW is used to specify read-write access and is permitted to retrieve and modify MIBs; and access-list # is an integer between 1 and 99 that specifies an access list of IP addresses that can use the community string to gain access to the SNMP agent.

In examining the format of the snmp-server community statement note that it only supports access list numbers between 1 and 99. This means the statement is only used within a standard IP access list. The format of a standard IP access list is shown here:

```
access-list access-list# {permit|deny} source[source-mask]
```

where permit allows access if the conditions in a statement are matched; deny denies access if the conditions in a statement are not matched; source is the source IP address of the host transmitting a packet; and source-mask is a 32-bit dotted-decimal address that functions in a reverse manner to a subnet mask, that is, a binary 0 indicates a match and a binary 1 a don't care condition.

To illustrate a few examples of Cisco configuration statements required to provide SNMP access to a router, let's first assume you wish to allow a workstation with the address 198.78.46.8 to have read-only access to the router's SNMP agent. Let's further assume the community name used by the router is the well-known public name. Your configuration statements would be as follows:

```
access-list|permit 198.78.46.8
snmp-server community public RO1
```

Now let's assume that instead of permitting one station on the network with access to the router's SNMP agent, you want all stations to be able to obtain such access. To do so, you enter the following configuration statements:

```
access-list 1 permit 198.78.46.0 0.0.0.255
snmp-server community public RO 1
```

In examining the first statement note that the mask 0.0.0.255 results in a don't care condition being associated with the last position in the IP address. Since 198.78.46.0 is a class C address, hosts 1 through 254 on the 198.178.46.0 network now have read-only access to the router's SNMP agent.

As a third example, let's assume that you want to allow the world to have access to your router's performance measurements. Without justifying the merits of this situation, you could accomplish this in one of two ways. First, you could enter the following two statements, with the keyword any permitting any IP address read-only access to your router's SNMP agent's MIBs as long as they use the community name public:

```
access-list 1 permit any
snmp-server community public RO 1
```

As an alternative, you can do away with the access list and enter the second statement without any access-list number. Now that we understand how to configure a router to permit SNMP access, let's look at the retrieval, setup, and use of MRTG by focusing attention on the Window's version of the program.

Program Acquisition

If you surf to the Web site located at *http://eestaff.ethz.ch/~oetiker/ webtools/mrtg/pub/*, you encounter a directory of MRTG program and program-related files. Figure 7-4 displays the directory during the early part of 2000. In examining Figure 7-4 note that the latest version of MRTG is mrtg-2.8.11, which is shown with a last modified date of 17 Jan 2000. In a Windows environment you would download the ZIP version of the program. In addition to the mrtg-2.8.11.zip file, you should also download fiveminutes.zip, which contains a series of batch files that allow you to control the operation of the program and 95MRTGScheduler.zip, which is a scheduler for Windows 95. You may also wish to consider downloading get1f1.2.zip, a program that can be used to display such useful information as machine reachability, system information, routing table, interface and address table data, and DNS lookup information.

Once you download the appropriate files, you need WinZip, PKZip, or a similar program to extract the files. The MRTG ZIP file contains a large number of individual files with a predefined directory structure. Figure 7-5 is a partial view of the files in the ZIP file. In examining the directory paths

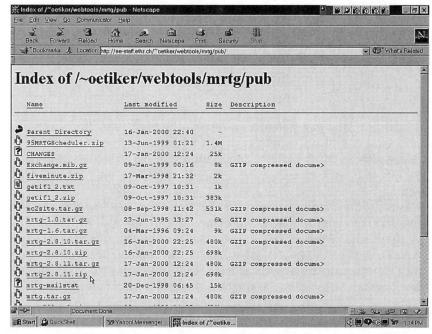

Figure 7-4 Viewing a portion of the directory that contains various versions of MRTG and related programs.

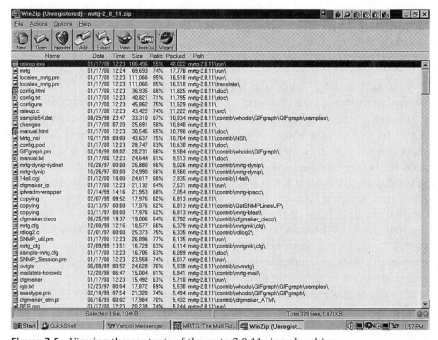

Figure 7-5 Viewing the contents of the mrtg-2.8.11 zipped archive.

listed in the right portion of Figure 7-5 note that the path begins with mrtg-2.8.11. This means that when you extract the files from the program, you should point your unzipping program to the root of a drive to have the files placed under the directory mrtg-2.8.11 that is created during the file extraction process.

Since MRTG uses Perl scripts, you need the latest version of Perl, which was Perl 5.22 when this book was written. You can obtain a copy of Perl from *http://www.ActiveState.com*. If you are running Windows 95, you also need Distributed Component Object Model (DCOM) for Windows 95 to use active Perl; however, this program is not required for Windows 98 or Windows NT. DCOM provides support for communication between COM components, including Active X controls, scripts, and Java applets that can reside on different hosts in a LAN, a WAN, or on the Internet. You can download DCOM for Windows 95 from *http://www.microsoft.com/com/ dcom/dcom95/dcom1.3.asp*. From this location, you can download a self-extracting file where you simply click on the file to install its contents. However, you have to restart your computer for the changes to go into effect. Since you also have to reboot your computer when you install Perl, you might save a boot and wait a while to do so.

Returning to the downloading of active Perl, note that the executable file named APi522e.exe requires approximately 5.37 Mbytes. Thus, the speed of your Internet connection, as well as available storage, should be considered when downloading this file. When you run the program, it self-extracts its contents to the directory C:\PERL. Thus, if your C drive has only a limited amount of available disk space, consider moving files and directories to another drive or place the self-extracting file on a different drive since it extracts its contents to drive C. In terms of storage requirements, once Perl's components are extracted, they use approximately 25 Mbytes of storage.

After Perl is installed, you have to perform two functions to ensure it is operating correctly. First, you will have to add C:\PERL\BIN to the PATH=line in your AUTOEXEC.BAT file. If you do not have a PATH command, as a minimum you should code the following line into your AUTOEXEC.BAT file:

```
PATH=C:\WINDOWS;C:\WINDOWS\COMMAND;C:\PERL\BIN
```

Second, you must restart your computer. However, prior to doing so, let's examine a few other items we need to be aware of. First, in a Windows environment we need to change an entry in the MRTG Perl script file to identify the fact that the operating system is NT (actually by specifying NT we inform the program we are operating in a Microsoft Windows environment) and not the default, which is UNIX. To do so, you must change both the fourth and fifth lines in the file C:\MRTG-2.8.11\RUN\MRTG from:

```
$main::OS='UNIX';
#$main::OS='NT';
```

to

```
#$main::OS='UNIX';
$main::OS='NT';
```

Here the # sign at the beginning of a line tells Perl the line is a comment and its contents should be ignored.

Figure 7-6 shows the top portion of file MRTG located in the subdirectory RUN after you perform the previously mentioned MRTG.zip file extraction. If you are familiar with the Perl language, you will be able to examine how the program operates. However, if you are not conversant in Perl, you only have to understand how to create a configuration file to use MRTG to extract and display router metrics, a topic we cover shortly.

Either before or after creating an MRTG.CFG configuration file, you should copy the graphics files from the directory C:\mrtg-2.8.11\ images\ to the directory c:\mrtg. The latter is a directory you should create and specify in the configuration file as a default working directory where the HTML pages generated by using MRTG will be placed. Under the directory \images\ are eight graphics files, four in GIF format and

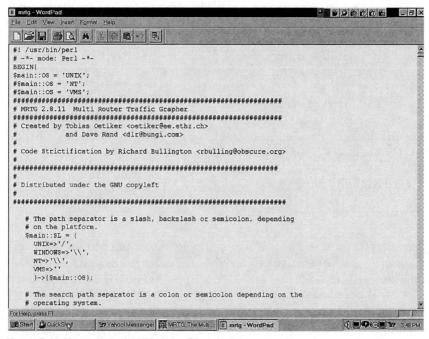

Figure 7-6 Viewing the MRTG script file.

four in PNG format. You can select the contents of the directory and drag them into the new directory or enter the following DOS command:

```
COPY C:\mrtg-2.8.11\images\*.* c:\mrtg
```

Now that we understand the basic items to consider prior to creating a configuration file to use with MRTG, let's look at that file.

The Configuration File

The MRTG.CFG file is the key to accessing and extracting statistics from a router or any SNMP-compatible device. To understand the construction of a configuration file, we discuss and describe a core set of configuration file statements and gradually create an MRTG.CFG configuration file used to extract CPU utilization information from a Cisco router as well as indicate how we can use a configuration maker program included in the MRTG zipped file.

LOCATION AND EXECUTION

In order to avoid guesswork, let's describe two key configuration file-related items: its location and execution. The MRTG.CFG file should be placed in the C:\mrtg-2.8.11\run directory. Once this is accomplished, you can execute the configuration you created by entering the following command:

```
Perl C:\mrtg-2.8.11\run\mrtg
```

FILE STATEMENTS

Included with the MRTG program are several files that provide configuration file format information. This abbreviated description of MRTG statements is included in this book as a guide so readers can get the program up and running, and it is not intended to replace the program's documentation. Thus, readers are referred to the configuration file format documentation for a complete list of MRTG keywords and their use in configuration statements.

The creation of the MRTG.CFG file can be accomplished with a text editor or word processor. However, when you save the file, be sure to save it as a text file.

WorkDir

The WorkDir keyword is used to define the location where MRTG log files and Web pages should be created. To use this keyword, as well as other configuration file keywords, you must follow the keyword by a colon (:) and a space prior to entering any associated keyword parameters. An example of the use of the WorkDir keyword to specify the use of the directory MRTG on drive C is shown here:

```
WorkDir: C:\mrtg
```

Interval
The keyword Interval is used to define the frequency by which the
MRTG program is called. The keyword is followed by the call time, in minutes, with a default value of 5 min used if this statement is not included
in your MRTG.CFG file. The following example illustrates the statement
required to set the call time to 10 min:

```
Interval: 10
```

Target
The Target keyword is a mandatory keyword as it informs the program
about what needs to be monitored. Several formats are supported by the
Target keyword. The basic format is shown here:

```
Target[name]:[-][index:]community@device_address
[:port[:timeout[:retries[:backoff]]]]
```

where name is a name that associates the target being monitored with the
use of other keywords that display the monitored parameters; -permits
incoming and outgoing traffic metrics to be reversed and should be used
if you are located on the wrong side of a link; index is a value that corresponds to the SNMP interface group, for example, a value of 1 corresponds
to the object identifier ifIndex and provides access to the input/output
octet counters for the interface; community is the community name used
by the managed device; device_address is the host name or IP address of
the managed device; port is the UDP port used for contacting the SNMP
agent, with the default port value being 161; timeout is the initial time-
out, in seconds, for SNMP queries, with the default being 2; retries is the
number of times a timed-out request will be retried, with the default being
5; and backoff is the factor by which the time-out is multiplied on each
retry, with the default being 1.

To illustrate an example of the use of the basic Target keyword format,
let's assume you want to generate a traffic graph for the input/output
octet counters for a router located at 205.131.176.2 whose community
name is public. To do so, you enter the following Target statement:

```
Target[macon_i/o]: 1:public@205.131.176.2
```

A second popular format for the Target keyword permits you to specify specific object identifiers. To do so, you use the following format:

```
Target[name]:object_id1&object_id2:community@device_address
```

In the preceding format you need to specify two object identifiers
because MRTG needs to graph two variables. However, it is also possible to

specify the same object identifier twice, as we soon note. To illustrate an example of the use of object identifiers in a `Target` keyword statement, let's assume you want to plot Cisco router CPU utilization. As indicated earlier, the object identifier for CPU utilization is in Cisco's private MIB at location 1.3.6.1.4.1.9.2.1.58 in the global naming tree. Since this is a one-of-a-kind identifier, you would add a 0 suffix to the object identifier. Thus, to read the CPU utilization of a router located at 205.131.176.2 whose community name is public, you would enter the following `Target` keyword statement:

```
Target[macon_cpu]:1.3.6.1.4.1.9.2.1.58.0&1.3.6.1.4.9.2.1.58.
0:public@205.131.176.2
```

RouterUptime

The use of the `RouterUptime` keyword displays the router uptime and router name on a Web page. You would normally use this keyword statement to compute the used bandwidth from several interfaces. The format of this keyword statement is shown here:

```
RouterUptime[name]: community@device_address
```

To illustrate an example of the use of the `RouterUptime` keyword statement, let's again assume we are working with the router at 205.131.175.2. Even though its community name and IP address were specified in the `Target` keyword statement, we must specify its community and address gain with the `RouterUpdate` keyword statement as shown here:

```
RouterUptime[macon_cpu]: public@205.131.176.2
```

MaxBytes

The `MaxBytes` keyword statement allows you to specify monitored traffic in terms of bytes per second. Since the `MaxBytes` value is used in calculating the Y range for unscaled graphs, you set it to a value of 100 if you are monitoring CPU utilization or a similar metric that provides information on a scale from 0 to 100. Since most communications facilities are rated in bits per second, your unscaled graphs can provide data in bytes per second by dividing the operating rate of the transmission facility by 8 and using the result as the `MaxBytes` value. For example, if you were using a T1 line, you would use the following `MaxBytes` statement:

```
MaxBytes[macon_t1]: 193000
```

If you were monitoring a 10-Mbps Ethernet 10BASE-T interface, you would then use the following `MaxBytes` statement:

```
MaxByte[macon_ethernet]: 1250000
```

If you are monitoring two different transmission facilities, you can use MaxBytes1 and MaxBytes2 instead of MaxBytes. You use each keyword in the same manner as the MaxBytes keyword.

Title

The Title keyword allows you to place a title on HTML pages generated for the graphs being created. The format of the Title keyword statement is shown here:

```
Title[name]: text
```

An example of the use of a Title keyword statement is shown here:

```
Title[macon_cpu]: Macon CPU load
```

PageTop

The PageTop keyword statement permits you to add information to the top of a generated HTML page. The format of this keyword statement is shown here:

```
PageTop[name]: <H1>text string</H1>
[optional text string [\n]]...[optional test string]
```

where \n is used to generate line breaks.

An example of the use of the PageTop keyword statement is shown here:

```
PageTop[macon_cpu]: <H1>CPU load %</H1>
```

Unscaled

The default graphing method of MRTG results in data being visible even when it has a much lower value than the MaxBytes values. Through the use of the Unscaled keyword, you can suppress data visibility when the value of data is much lower than the value specified in MaxBytes. The format of the Unscaled keyword statement is shown here:

```
Unscaled[name]: [y[m[w[d]]]]
```

where y, m, w, and d represent year, month, week, and day periods for each graph you do not wish to be sealed. The reason there are four options is because MRGT generates four graphs by default. To illustrate the use of the Unscaled keyword statement, let's assume we want to suppress scaling for year, month, week, and daily graphs. To do so, we enter the following Unscaled keyword statement:

```
Unscaled[macon_cpu]: ymwd
```

Suppress

As previously discussed, by default MRTG generates four graphs, covering [d]aily, [w]eekly, [m]onthly, and [y]early time periods. Through the use of the Suppress keyword statement, you can suppress one or more graphs. The following example illustrates the use of the Suppress keyword statement to suppress monthly and yearly graphs:

```
Suppress[macon_cpu]: my
```

Xsize *and* Ysize

Through the use of the Xsize and Ysize keyword statements, you can change the dimension of graphs generated by MRTG. By default, graphs are 100 by 400 pixels. Through the use of Xsize, you can change the horizontal size of the graph, while Ysize allows you to change the vertical size of the graph. The general format for the two statements is as follows:

```
Xsize[name]: x
Ysize[name]: y
```

where X must be between 20 and 600 while Y must be greater than 20.

To illustrate the use of Xsize and Ysize keywords, let's assume you want to resize the MRTG graphs from their default of 100 by 400 pixels to 380 by 100. To do so, you enter the following keyword statements:

```
Xsize[macon_cpu]: 380
Ysize[macon_cpu]: 100
```

Legend *Keywords*

MRTG supports eight optional Legend-related keyword statements that let you override the text displayed by default. This section briefly examines those keywords. The YLegend keyword allows you to define a label for the *y*-axis of the graph. The following example illustrates the use of the YLegend keyword statement:

```
YLegend[macon_cpu]: CPU Utilization
```

A second Legend-related keyword is ShortLegend. This keyword has a default of b/s that is displayed for the maximum, average, and current plots. Since we are plotting CPU utilization, we would not want to accept the default. Thus, we could use the ShortLegend keyword statement as follows:

```
ShortLegend[macon_cpu]: %
```

In addition to the two previously mentioned Legend-related keywords, six keywords define strings for the color legend. Those keywords begin with Legend and have a one-letter suffix of 1, 2, 3, 4, I, and O.

Options

The Options keyword can set a variety of boolean switches. To do so, you enter the keyword Options followed by the name of one or more

Table 7-7 MRTG Options Switches

Switch	Description
growright	Instead of having the graph grow to the left, this switch flips its direction of growth.
bits	Results in all monitored values being multiplied by 8.
perminute	Results in all monitored values being multiplied by 60.
perhour	Results in all monitored values being multiplied by 3600.
gauge	Causes the values obtained to be considered absolute and not as an incrementing counter.
absolute	Causes the values obtained to be considered absolute values. This option is for counters that are reset after they are read.

switches you wish to invoke, with each switch separated from the next by a comma. Some of the more popular switches are described in Table 7-7.

In examining the entries in Table 7-7 it should be noted that if you do not specify either a gauge or absolute option, MRTG will consider the variable as a counter. When it does so, the program then computes the difference between the current and previous value, dividing the difference by the elapsed time between the two readings to obtain the value to be plotted. Since our sample MRTG.CFG file is being created to display CPU utilization information, we want the object identifier values to be treated as absolute.

To illustrate an example of the use of the Options keyword statement, let's assume we want to flip the direction of the growth of the graph. In addition, since we are monitoring CPU utilization, we want to have each object identifier treated as an absolute value. To do so, we enter the following Options keyword statement:

```
Options[macon_cpu]: gauge, growright
```

Using MRTG

Remembering the old adage that "the proof of the pudding is in the eating," the best way to examine the use of MRTG is by example. Thus, let's create a same MRTG.CFG file and use it to generate a Web page we can view.

Figure 7-7 Sample MRTG.CFG configuration file.

```
WorkDir: D:\mrtg
Target[macon_cpu]:1.3.6.1.4.1.9.2.1.58.0&1.3.6.1.4.1.9.2.1.58.0:suranoc@
205.131.176.1
RouterUptime[macon_cpu]: public@205.131.176.1
MaxBytes[macon_cpu]:100
Title[macon_cpu]: hobart : CPU LOAD
PageTop[macon_cpu]:<H1>CPU Load %</H1>
Unscaled[macon_cpu]:ymwd
ShortLegend[macon_cpu]:%
XSize[macon_cpu]:380
YSize[macon_cpu]:100
YLegend[macon_cpu]:CPU Utilization
Legend1[macon_cpu]:CPU Utilization in % (Load)
Legend2[macon_cpu]:CPU Utilization in % (Load)
Legend3[macon_cpu]:
Legend4[macon_cpu]:
LegendI[macon_cpu]:
LegendO[macon_cpu]:  Usage
Options[macon_cpu]: gauge, growright
```

Figure 7-7 shows the contents of a sample MRTG.CFG configuration file that will be used to create a display of CPU load in percent for daily, weekly, monthly, and yearly periods. If you examine the statements in Figure 7-7, note that they correspond to the configuration keyword statements discussed.

Since I previously mentioned an old adage, we obviously want to execute Perl to run MRTG with the previously created MRTG.CFG file. To do so, we enter the following command, assuming we saved the configuration file in the directory C:\mrtr-2.8.11\run:

```
Perl C:\mrtg-2.8.11\mrtg C:\mrtg-2.8.11\mrtg.cfg
```

Figure 7-8 is the view of the execution of MRTG using the previously created configuration file. What was not mentioned until now, but what requires a few words, is that included with the zipped MRTG file are a series of batch files you can use to repeatedly execute MRTG. Those files are appropriately labeled a.bat, b.bat, and c.bat and are found in the zipped file named fiveminute.zip.

By examining the instructions within the fiveminute.zip file, you can learn that they run at increments of 15 min, which enables you to execute the MRTG every 5 min. When you examine the files within fiveminute.zip, you also note another file named mrtgkick.bat. This file, which is referenced in a.bat, b.bat, and c.bat kicks off the MRTG pro-

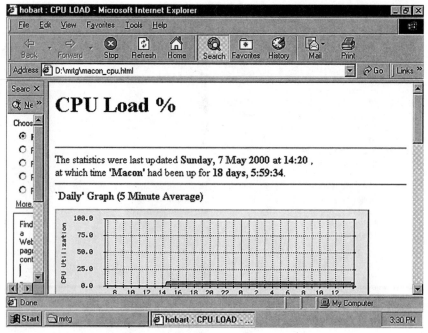

Figure 7-8 Viewing an MRTG HTML page.

gram and includes the location of the Perl program, MRTG, and MRTG.CFG. As a hint to alleviate potential problems, double-check the directory paths to ensure they reference locations where you placed the applicable files.

In examining Figure 7-8 note that only a portion of the four graphs is displayed. The first graph at the top of the HTML display is a daily graph. Note that because we did not include an `Interval` keyword statement in our previously created MRTG.CFG file, the default 5-min period was used.

In concluding our discussion of MRTG the author would be remiss if he did not mention that there are several configmaker (configuration maker or creator) scripts included in the zipped file that can be used to create a configuration file for a particular device. One that should be of particular interest to readers is located under the directory `C:\mrtg-2.8.11>\con-trib`, which can be used to create a configuration file for Cisco routers. This configuration-maker program was created by the author of MRTG, Tobias Oetiker, and is also distributed under the GNU license.

Figure 7-9 shows a portion of the resulting configuration file generated by the use of the configuration-maker file for Cisco routers. Note that the

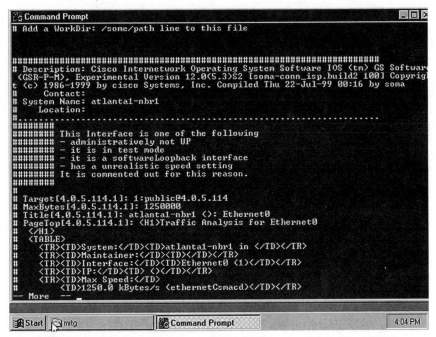

Figure 7-9 Viewing a portion of a configuration file generated for a Cisco router.

first line in the generated configuration file is a comment that tells you to add a working directory (WorkDir) to the configuration file. The full listing of the generated configuration file is shown in Figure 7-10.

In examining the full listing of the router configuration file generated by the use of Cisco configuration maker, note that the initial portion of the file consists of a series of comments because the first interface (Ethernet0) is not operational. The reason can be that the interface is administratively down, in a test mode, in a software loopback mode of operation, or has an inappropriate speed setting.

The second interface is operational and the configuration generator does its job and generates a configuration for the POS1/0 interface. Similarly, the configuration maker generates predefined configuration file statements for the next two interfaces prior to encountering another interface that is not operational. Thus, in addition to allowing you to generate predefined configuration statements you can easily add to for specific user requirements, it also lets you rapidly determine the general state of router interfaces. Although this may not have been the intended goal of the program's author, it is a welcome addition to the use of the Cisco configuration-maker program.

Figure 7-10 Sample result obtained by the Cisco configmaker program.

```
# Add a WorkDir: /some/path line to this file

################################################################
# Description: Cisco Internetwork Operating System Software IOS (tm) GS
    Software (GSR-P-M), Experimental Version 12.0(5.3)S2 [soma-
    conn_isp.build2 100] Copyright (c) 1986-1999 by cisco Systems, Inc.
    Compiled Thu 22-Jul-99 00:16 by soma
#     Contact:
# System Name: atlanta1-nbr1
# Location:
#...............................................................
########
######## This Interface is one of the following
######## - administratively not UP
######## - it is in test mode
######## - it is a softwareLoopback interface
######## - has a unrealistic speed setting
######## It is commented out for this reason.
########
#
# Target[4.0.5.114.1]: 1:public@4.0.5.114
# MaxBytes[4.0.5.114.1]: 1250000
# Title[4.0.5.114.1]: atlanta1-nbr1 (): Ethernet0
# PageTop[4.0.5.114.1]: <H1>Traffic Analysis for Ethernet0
#   </H1>
#   <TABLE>
#     <TR><TD>System:</TD><TD>atlanta1-nbr1 in </TD></TR>
#     <TR><TD>Maintainer:</TD><TD></TD></TR>
#     <TR><TD>Interface:</TD><TD>Ethernet0 (1)</TD></TR>
#     <TR><TD>IP:</TD><TD> ()</TD></TR>
#     <TR><TD>Max Speed:</TD>
#         <TD>1250.0 kBytes/s (ethernetCsmacd)</TD></TR>
#   </TABLE>
#
#------------------------------------------------

Target[p1-0.atlanta1-nbr1.bbnplanet.net]: 2:public@4.0.5.114
MaxBytes[p1-0.atlanta1-nbr1.bbnplanet.net]: 19375000
Title[p1-0.atlanta1-nbr1.bbnplanet.net]: atlanta1-nbr1
  (p1-0.atlanta1-nbr1.bbnplanet.net): POS1/0
PageTop[p1-0.atlanta1-nbr1.bbnplanet.net]: <H1>Traffic Analysis for
  POS1/0
  </H1>
  <TABLE>
    <TR><TD>System:</TD><TD>atlanta1-nbr1 in </TD></TR>
    <TR><TD>Maintainer:</TD><TD></TD></TR>
    <TR><TD>Interface:</TD><TD>POS1/0 (2)</TD></TR>
    <TR><TD>IP:</TD><TD>p1-0.atlanta1-nbr1.bbnplanet.net
(4.0.5.202)</TD></TR>
    <TR><TD>Max Speed:</TD>
        <TD>19.4 MBytes/s (propPointToPointSerial)</TD></TR>
  </TABLE>
#------------------------------------------------
```

Figure 7-10 *(Continued)*

```
Target[p1-1.atlanta1-nbr1.bbnplanet.net]: 3:public@4.0.5.114
MaxBytes[p1-1.atlanta1-nbr1.bbnplanet.net]: 19375000
Title[p1-1.atlanta1-nbr1.bbnplanet.net]: atlanta1-nbr1 (p1-1.atlanta1-
nbr1.bbnplanet.net): POS1/1
PageTop[p1-1.atlanta1-nbr1.bbnplanet.net]: <H1>Traffic Analysis for
POS1/1
 </H1>
 <TABLE>
   <TR><TD>System:</TD><TD>atlanta1-nbr1 in </TD></TR>
   <TR><TD>Maintainer:</TD><TD></TD></TR>
   <TR><TD>Interface:</TD><TD>POS1/1 (3)</TD></TR>
   <TR><TD>IP:</TD><TD>p1-1.atlanta1-nbr1.bbnplanet.net
(4.0.5.206)</TD></TR>
   <TR><TD>Max Speed:</TD>
       <TD>19.4 MBytes/s (propPointToPointSerial)</TD></TR>
   </TABLE>
#-----------------------------------
Target[p1-2.atlanta1-nbr1.bbnplanet.net]: 4:public@4.0.5.114
MaxBytes[p1-2.atlanta1-nbr1.bbnplanet.net]: 19375000
Title[p1-2.atlanta1-nbr1.bbnplanet.net]: atlanta1-nbr1 (p1-2.atlanta1-
nbr1.bbnplanet.net): POS1/2
PageTop[p1-2.atlanta1-nbr1.bbnplanet.net]: <H1>Traffic Analysis for
POS1/2
 </H1>
 <TABLE>
   <TR><TD>System:</TD><TD>atlanta1-nbr1 in </TD></TR>
   <TR><TD>Maintainer:</TD><TD></TD></TR>
   <TR><TD>Interface:</TD><TD>POS1/2 (4)</TD></TR>
   <TR><TD>IP:</TD><TD>p1-2.atlanta1-nbr1.bbnplanet.net
(4.0.5.142)</TD></TR>
   <TR><TD>Max Speed:</TD>
       <TD>19.4 MBytes/s (propPointToPointSerial)</TD></TR>
   </TABLE>
#-----------------------------------
########
######## This Interface is one of the following
######## - administratively not UP
######## - it is in test mode
######## - it is a softwareLoopback interface
######## - has a unrealistic speed setting
######## It is commented out for this reason.
########
#
# Target[4.0.5.114.5]: 5:public@4.0.5.114
# MaxBytes[4.0.5.114.5]: 19375000
# Title[4.0.5.114.5]: atlanta1-nbr1 (): POS1/3
# PageTop[4.0.5.114.5]: <H1>Traffic Analysis for POS1/3
#  </H1>
#  <TABLE>
#    <TR><TD>System:</TD><TD>atlanta1-nbr1 in </TD></TR>
#    <TR><TD>Maintainer:</TD><TD></TD></TR>
#    <TR><TD>Interface:</TD><TD>POS1/3 (5)</TD></TR>
#    <TR><TD>IP:</TD><TD> ()</TD></TR>
```

(Continued)

Figure 7-10 *(Continued)*

```
#     <TR><TD>Max Speed:</TD>
#        <TD>19.4 MBytes/s (propPointToPointSerial)</TD></TR>
#     </TABLE>
#
#————————————————————-
Target[p2-0.atlanta1-nbr1.bbnplanet.net]: 6:public@4.0.5.114
MaxBytes[p2-0.atlanta1-nbr1.bbnplanet.net]: 19375000
Title[p2-0.atlanta1-nbr1.bbnplanet.net]: atlanta1-nbr1
  (p2-0.atlanta1-nbr1.bbnplanet.net): POS2/0
PageTop[p2-0.atlanta1-nbr1.bbnplanet.net]: <H1>Traffic Analysis for
  POS2/0
 </H1>
 <TABLE>
     <TR><TD>System:</TD><TD>atlanta1-nbr1 in </TD></TR>
     <TR><TD>Maintainer:</TD><TD></TD></TR>
     <TR><TD>Interface:</TD><TD>POS2/0 (6)</TD></TR>
     <TR><TD>IP:</TD><TD>p2-0.atlanta1-nbr1.bbnplanet.net
       (4.0.5.122)</TD></TR>
     <TR><TD>Max Speed:</TD>
        <TD>19.4 MBytes/s (propPointToPointSerial)</TD></TR>
 </TABLE>
#————————————————————-
Target[p2-1.atlanta1-nbr1.bbnplanet.net]: 7:public@4.0.5.114
MaxBytes[p2-1.atlanta1-nbr1.bbnplanet.net]: 19375000
Title[p2-1.atlanta1-nbr1.bbnplanet.net]: atlanta1-nbr1
  (p2-1.atlanta1-nbr1.bbnplanet.net): POS2/1
PageTop[p2-1.atlanta1-nbr1.bbnplanet.net]: <H1>Traffic Analysis for
  POS2/1
 </H1>
 <TABLE>
   <TR><TD>System:</TD><TD>atlanta1-nbr1 in </TD></TR>
   <TR><TD>Maintainer:</TD><TD></TD></TR>
   <TR><TD>Interface:</TD><TD>POS2/1 (7)</TD></TR>
   <TR><TD>IP:</TD><TD>p2-1.atlanta1-nbr1.bbnplanet.net
     (4.0.5.114)</TD></TR>
   <TR><TD>Max Speed:</TD>
        <TD>19.4 MBytes/s (propPointToPointSerial)</TD></TR>
 </TABLE>
#————————————————————-
Target[p2-2.atlanta1-nbr1.bbnplanet.net]: 8:public@4.0.5.114
MaxBytes[p2-2.atlanta1-nbr1.bbnplanet.net]: 19375000
Title[p2-2.atlanta1-nbr1.bbnplanet.net]: atlanta1-nbr1
  (p2-2.atlanta1-nbr1.bbnplanet.net): POS2/2
PageTop[p2-2.atlanta1-nbr1.bbnplanet.net]: <H1>Traffic Analysis for
  POS2/2
 </H1>
 <TABLE>
   <TR><TD>System:</TD><TD>atlanta1-nbr1 in </TD></TR>
   <TR><TD>Maintainer:</TD><TD></TD></TR>
   <TR><TD>Interface:</TD><TD>POS2/2 (8)</TD></TR>
   <TR><TD>IP:</TD><TD>p2-2.atlanta1-nbr1.bbnplanet.net
     (4.0.5.226)</TD></TR>
   <TR><TD>Max Speed:</TD>
        <TD>19.4 MBytes/s (propPointToPointSerial)</TD></TR>
 </TABLE>
#————————————————————-
```

Figure 7-10   (*Continued*)

```
Target[p2-3.atlanta1-nbr1.bbnplanet.net]: 9:public@4.0.5.114
MaxBytes[p2-3.atlanta1-nbr1.bbnplanet.net]: 19375000
Title[p2-3.atlanta1-nbr1.bbnplanet.net]: atlanta1-nbr1
  (p2-3.atlanta1-nbr1.bbnplanet.net): POS2/3
PageTop[p2-3.atlanta1-nbr1.bbnplanet.net]: <H1>Traffic Analysis for
  POS2/3
 </H1>
 <TABLE>
   <TR><TD>System:</TD><TD>atlanta1-nbr1 in </TD></TR>
   <TR><TD>Maintainer:</TD><TD></TD></TR>
   <TR><TD>Interface:</TD><TD>POS2/3 (9)</TD></TR>
   <TR><TD>IP:</TD><TD>p2-3.atlanta1-nbr1.bbnplanet.net
     (4.24.5.166)</TD></TR>
   <TR><TD>Max Speed:</TD>
       <TD>19.4 MBytes/s (propPointToPointSerial)</TD></TR>
   </TABLE>
#-----------------------------------
########
######## This Interface is one of the following
######## - administratively not UP
######## - it is in test mode
######## - it is a softwareLoopback interface
######## - has a unrealistic speed setting
######## It is commented out for this reason.
########
#
# Target[4.0.5.114.10]: 10:public@4.0.5.114
# MaxBytes[4.0.5.114.10]: 77750000
# Title[4.0.5.114.10]: atlanta1-nbr1 (No hostname defined for IP
  address): POS3/0
# PageTop[4.0.5.114.10]: <H1>Traffic Analysis for POS3/0
#  </H1>
#  <TABLE>
#    <TR><TD>System:</TD><TD>atlanta1-nbr1 in </TD></TR>
#    <TR><TD>Maintainer:</TD><TD></TD></TR>
#    <TR><TD>Interface:</TD><TD>POS3/0 (10)</TD></TR>
#    <TR><TD>IP:</TD><TD>No hostname defined for IP address
       (4.24.5.222)</TD></TR>
#    <TR><TD>Max Speed:</TD>
#        <TD>77.8 MBytes/s (propPointToPointSerial)</TD></TR>
#    </TABLE>
#
#-----------------------------------
########
######## This Interface is one of the following
######## - administratively not UP
######## - it is in test mode
######## - it is a softwareLoopback interface
######## - has a unrealistic speed setting
######## It is commented out for this reason.
########
#
# Target[4.0.5.114.11]: 11:public@4.0.5.114
# MaxBytes[4.0.5.114.11]: 77750000
```

(*Continued*)

Figure 7-10 (*Continued*)

```
# Title[4.0.5.114.11]: atlanta1-nbr1 (No hostname defined for IP
  address): POS4/0
# PageTop[4.0.5.114.11]: <H1>Traffic Analysis for POS4/0
#  </H1>
#  <TABLE>
#    <TR><TD>System:</TD><TD>atlanta1-nbr1 in </TD></TR>
#    <TR><TD>Maintainer:</TD><TD></TD></TR>
#    <TR><TD>Interface:</TD><TD>POS4/0 (11)</TD></TR>
#    <TR><TD>IP:</TD><TD>No hostname defined for IP address
(4.24.6.146)</TD></TR>
#    <TR><TD>Max Speed:</TD>
#        <TD>77.8 MBytes/s (propPointToPointSerial)</TD></TR>
#  </TABLE>
#
#————————————————————————————-
########
######## This Interface is one of the following
######## - administratively not UP
######## - it is in test mode
######## - it is a softwareLoopback interface
######## - has a unrealistic speed setting
######## It is commented out for this reason.
########
#
# Target[4.0.5.114.12]: 12:public@4.0.5.114
# MaxBytes[4.0.5.114.12]: 536870911
# Title[4.0.5.114.12]: atlanta1-nbr1 (): Null0
# PageTop[4.0.5.114.12]: <H1>Traffic Analysis for Null0
#  </H1>
#  <TABLE>
#    <TR><TD>System:</TD><TD>atlanta1-nbr1 in </TD></TR>
#    <TR><TD>Maintainer:</TD><TD></TD></TR>
#    <TR><TD>Interface:</TD><TD>Null0 (12)</TD></TR>
#    <TR><TD>IP:</TD><TD> ()</TD></TR>
#    <TR><TD>Max Speed:</TD>
#        <TD>536.9 MBytes/s (Other)</TD></TR>
#  </TABLE>
#
#————————————————————————————-
########
######## This Interface is one of the following
######## - administratively not UP
######## - it is in test mode
######## - it is a softwareLoopback interface
######## - has a unrealistic speed setting
######## It is commented out for this reason.
########
#
# Target[10.atlanta1-nbr1.bbnplanet.net]: 13:public@4.0.5.114
# MaxBytes[10.atlanta1-nbr1.bbnplanet.net]: 536870911
# Title[10.atlanta1-nbr1.bbnplanet.net]: atlanta1-nbr1 (10.atlanta1-
nbr1.bbnplanet.net): Loopback0
# PageTop[10.atlanta1-nbr1.bbnplanet.net]: <H1>Traffic Analysis for
Loopback0
```

Figure 7-10   (*Continued*)

```
#   </H1>
#   <TABLE>
#     <TR><TD>System:</TD><TD>atlanta1-nbr1 in </TD></TR>
#     <TR><TD>Maintainer:</TD><TD></TD></TR>
#     <TR><TD>Interface:</TD><TD>Loopback0 (13)</TD></TR>
#     <TR><TD>IP:</TD><TD>10.atlanta1-nbr1.bbnplanet.net
(4.0.4.73)</TD></TR>
#     <TR><TD>Max Speed:</TD>
#         <TD>536.9 MBytes/s (softwareLoopback)</TD></TR>
#   </TABLE>
#
#————————————————————————————--
```

Appendix

The SNMP Management Information Base (MIB-II)

This appendix lists the object identifiers included in the 10 groups which form the SNMP management information base (MIB-II). The groups included in this appendix include

1. System group
2. Interfaces group
3. Address translation group
4. IP group
5. ICMP group
6. TCP group
7. UDP group
8. EGP group
9. Transmission group
10. SNMP group

The System Group

Implementation of the system group is mandatory for all systems. If an agent is not configured to have a value for any of these variables, a string of length 0 is returned.

sysDescr OBJECT-TYPE

Syntax	DisplayString (SIZE (0..255))
Access	read-only
Status	mandatory
Description	A textual description of the entity. This value should include the full name and version identification of the system's hardware type, software operating system, and networking software. It is mandatory that this only contain printable ASCII characters.
::=	{ system 1 }}

sysObjectID OBJECT-TYPE

Syntax	OBJECT IDENTIFIER
Access	read-only
Status	mandatory
Description	The vendor's authoritative identification of the network management subsystem contained in the entity. This value is allocated within the SMI enterprises subtree (1.3.6.1.4.1) and provides an easy and unambiguous means for determining what kind of box is being managed. For example, if vendor Flintstones, Inc. was assigned the subtree 1.3.6.1.4.1.4242, it could assign the identifier 1.3.6.1.4.1.4242.1.1 to its Fred Router.
::=	{ system 2 }

sysUpTime OBJECT-TYPE

Syntax	TimeTicks
Access	read-only
Status	mandatory
Description	The time (in hundredths of a second) since the network management portion of the system was last reinitialized.
::=	{ system 3 }

sysContact OBJECT-TYPE

Syntax	DisplayString (SIZE (0..255))
Access	read-write
Status	mandatory

Description   The textual identification of the contact person for this
                managed node, together with information on how to
                contact this person.

::=   { system 4 }

sysName OBJECT-TYPE

Syntax   DisplayString (SIZE (0..255))

Access   read-write

Status   mandatory

Description   An administratively assigned name for this managed
                node. By convention, this is the node's fully-qualified
                domain name.

::=   { system 5 }

sysLocation OBJECT-TYPE

Syntax   DisplayString (SIZE (0..255))

Access   read-write

Status   mandatory

Description   The physical location of this node (e.g., telephone
                closet, 3d floor).

::=   { system 6 }

sysServices OBJECT-TYPE

Syntax   INTEGER (0..127)

Access   read-only

Status   mandatory

Description   A value which indicates the set of services that this
                entity primarily offers. The value is a sum. This sum
                initially takes the value zero, then, for each layer, L, in
                the range 1 through 7, that this node performs transac-
                tions for, 2 raised to $(L - 1)$ is added to the sum. For
                example, a node which performs primarily routing
                functions would have a value of 4 $(2 \times (3 - 1))$. In
                contrast, a node which is a host offering application
                services would have a value of 72 $[2 \times (4 - 1) + 2 \times (7 - 1)]$. Note that in the context of the Internet suite of
                protocols, values for layer functionality should be cal-
                culated accordingly: 1—physical (for example,
                repeaters); 2—datalink/subnetwork (for example,

bridges); 3—Internet (for example, IP gateways); 4—
end-to-end (for example, IP hosts); and 7—applications
(for example, mail relays). For systems including OSI
protocols, layers 5 and 6 may also be counted.

::=   { system 7 }

Interfaces Group

Implementation of the interfaces group is mandatory for all systems.

ifNumber OBJECT-TYPE

Syntax   INTEGER

Access   read-only

Status   mandatory

Description   The number of network interfaces (regardless of their
                current state) present on this system.

::=   { interfaces 1 }

Interfaces Table

The interfaces table contains information on the entity's interfaces. Each
interface is thought of as being attached to a subnetwork. Note that this
term should not be confused with subnet, which refers to an addressing
partitioning scheme used in the Internet suite of protocols.

ifTable OBJECT-TYPE

Syntax   SEQUENCE OF IfEntry

Access   not-accessible

Status   mandatory

Description   A list of interface entries. The number of entries is
                given by the value of ifNumber.

::=   { interfaces 2 }

ifEntry OBJECT-TYPE

Syntax   IfEntry

Access   not-accessible

Status   mandatory

Description   An interface entry containing objects at the subnet-
                work layer and below for a particular interface.

Index   { ifIndex }

::=   { ifTable 1 }

```
IfEntry ::=
    SEQUENCE
        ifIndex
            INTEGER,
        ifDescr
            DisplayString,
        ifType
            INTEGER,
        ifMtu
            INTEGER,
        ifSpeed
            Gauge,
        ifPhysAddress
            PhysAddress,
        ifAdminStatus
            INTEGER,
        ifOperStatus
            INTEGER,
        ifLastChange
            TimeTicks,
        ifInOctets
            Counter,
        ifInUcastPkts
            Counter,
        ifInNUcastPkts
            Counter,
        ifInDiscards
            Counter,
        ifInErrors
            Counter,
        ifInUnknownProtos
            Counter,
        ifOutOctets
            Counter,
        ifOutUcastPkts
            Counter,
        ifOutNUcastPkts
            Counter,
        ifOutDiscards
            Counter,
        ifOutErrors
            Counter,
        ifOutQLen
            Gauge,
        ifSpecific
            OBJECT IDENTIFIER
}
```

ifIndex OBJECT-TYPE

Syntax   INTEGER

Access   read-only

Status	mandatory
Description	A unique value for each interface. Its value ranges between 1 and the value of ifNumber. The value for each interface must remain constant at least from one reinitialization of the entity's network management system to the next reinitialization.
::=	{ ifEntry 1 }

ifDescr OBJECT-TYPE

Syntax	DisplayString (SIZE (0..255))
Access	read-only
Status	mandatory
Description	A textual string containing information about the interface. This string should include the name of the manufacturer, the product name and the version of the hardware interface.
::=	{ ifEntry 2 }

ifType OBJECT-TYPE

Syntax   INTEGER {

```
                other(1),                        — none of the following
                regular1822(2),
                hdh1822(3),
                ddn-x25(4),
                rfc877-x25(5),
                ethernet-csmacd(6),
                iso88023-csmacd(7),
                iso88024-tokenBus(8),
                iso88025-tokenRing(9),
                iso88026-man(10),
                starLan(11),
                proteon-10Mbit(12),
                proteon-80Mbit(13),
                hyperchannel(14),
                fddi(15),
                lapb(16),
                sdlc(17),
                ds1(18),                         — T-1
                e1(19),                          — european equiv. of T-1
                basicISDN(20),
                primaryISDN(21),                 — proprietary serial
                propPointToPointSerial(22),
                ppp(23),
                softwareLoopback(24),
                eon(25),                         — CLNP over IP [11]
                ethernet-3Mbit(26)
                nsip(27),                        — XNS over IP
```

```
      slip(28),              — generic SLIP
      ultra(29),             — ULTRA technologies
      ds3(30),               — T-3
      sip(31),               — SMDS
      frame-relay(32)
   }
```

Access	read-only
Status	mandatory
Description	The type of interface, distinguished according to the physical/link protocol(s) immediately below the network layer in the protocol stack.
::=	{ ifEntry 3 }

ifMtu OBJECT-TYPE

Syntax	INTEGER
Access	read-only
Status	mandatory
Description	The size of the largest datagram which can be sent/received on the interface, specified in octets. For interfaces that are used for transmitting network datagrams, this is the size of the largest network datagram that can be sent on the interface.
::=	{ ifEntry 4 }

ifSpeed OBJECT-TYPE

Syntax	Gauge
Access	read-only
Status	mandatory
Description	An estimate of the interface's current bandwidth in bits per second. For interfaces which do not vary in bandwidth or for those where no accurate estimation can be made, this object should contain the nominal bandwidth.
::=	{ ifEntry 5 }

ifPhysAddress OBJECT-TYPE

Syntax	PhysAddress
Access	read-only
Status	mandatory

Description   The interface's address at the protocol layer immedi-
                  ately below the network layer in the protocol stack. For
                  interfaces which do not have such an address (for
                  example, a serial line), this object should contain an
                  octet string of zero length.

::=   { ifEntry 6 }

ifAdminStatus OBJECT-TYPE

Syntax   INTEGER {

```
                    up(1),              — ready to pass packets
                    down(2),
                    testing(3)          — in some test mode
                  }
```

Access   read-write

Status   mandatory

Description   The desired state of the interface. The testing(3) state
                  indicates that no operational packets can be passed.

::=   { ifEntry 7 }

ifOperStatus OBJECT-TYPE

Syntax   INTEGER {

```
                    up(1),              — ready to pass packets
                    down(2),
                    testing(3)          — in some test mode
                  }
```

Access   read-only

Status   mandatory

Description   The current operational state of the interface. The test-
                  ing(3) state indicates that no operational packets can
                  be passed.

::=   { ifEntry 8 }

ifLastChange OBJECT-TYPE

Syntax   TimeTicks

Access   read-only

Status   mandatory

Description   The value of sysUpTime at the time the interface
                  entered its current operational state. If the current state

was entered prior to the last reinitialization of the local network management subsystem, then this object contains a zero value.

::=   { ifEntry 9 }

ifInOctets OBJECT-TYPE

Syntax   Counter

Access   read-only

Status   mandatory

Description   The total number of octets received on the interface, including framing characters.

::=   { ifEntry 10 }

ifInUcastPkts OBJECT-TYPE

Syntax   Counter

Access   read-only

Status   mandatory

Description   The number of subnetwork-unicast packets delivered to a higher-layer protocol.

::=   { ifEntry 11 }

ifInNUcastPkts OBJECT-TYPE

Syntax   Counter

Access   read-only

Status   mandatory

Description   The number of nonunicast (that is, subnetwork-broadcast or subnetwork-multicast) packets delivered to a higher-layer protocol.

::=   { ifEntry 12 }

ifInDiscards OBJECT-TYPE

Syntax   Counter

Access   read-only

Status   mandatory

Description   The number of inbound packets which were chosen to be discarded even though no errors had been detected to prevent their being deliverable to a higher-layer protocol. One possible reason for discarding such a packet could be to free up buffer space.

::=   { ifEntry 13 }

ifInErrors OBJECT-TYPE

Syntax   Counter

Access   read-only

Status   mandatory

Description   The number of inbound packets that contained errors preventing them from being deliverable to a higher-layer protocol.

::=   { ifEntry 14 }

ifInUnknownProtos OBJECT-TYPE

Syntax   Counter

Access   read-only

Status   mandatory

Description   The number of packets received via the interface which were discarded because of an unknown or unsupported protocol.

::=   { ifEntry 15 }

ifOutOctets OBJECT-TYPE

Syntax   Counter

Access   read-only

Status   mandatory

Description   The total number of octets transmitted out of the interface, including framing characters.

::=   { ifEntry 16 }

ifOutUcastPkts OBJECT-TYPE

Syntax   Counter

Access   read-only

Status   mandatory

Description   The total number of packets that higher-level protocols requested be transmitted to a subnetwork-unicast

address, including those that were discarded or not
sent.

::=   { ifEntry 17 }

ifOutNUcastPkts OBJECT-TYPE

Syntax	Counter
Access	read-only
Status	mandatory
Description	The total number of packets that higher-level protocols requested be transmitted to a nonunicast (that is, a subnetwork-broadcast or subnetwork-multicast) address, including those that were discarded or not sent.
::=	{ ifEntry 18 }

ifOutDiscards OBJECT-TYPE

Syntax	Counter
Access	read-only
Status	mandatory
Description	The number of outbound packets which were chosen to be discarded even though no errors had been detected to prevent their being transmitted. One possible reason for discarding such a packet could be to free up buffer space.
::=	{ ifEntry 19 }

ifOutErrors OBJECT-TYPE

Syntax	Counter
Access	read-only
Status	mandatory
Description	The number of outbound packets that could not be transmitted because of errors.
::=	{ ifEntry 20 }

ifOutQLen OBJECT-TYPE

Syntax	Gauge
Access	read-only

Status   mandatory

Description   The length of the output packet queue (in packets).

::=   { ifEntry 21 }

ifSpecific OBJECT-TYPE

Syntax   OBJECT IDENTIFIER

Access   read-only

Status   mandatory

Description   A reference to MIB definitions specific to the particular media being used to realize the interface. For example, if the interface is realized by an Ethernet, then the value of this object refers to a document defining objects specific to Ethernet. If this information is not present, its value should be set to the OBJECT IDENTI-FIER { 0 0 }, which is a syntactically valid object identifier, and any conformant implementation of ASN.1 and BER must be able to generate and recognize this value.

::=   { ifEntry 22 }

Address Translation Group

Implementation of the address translation group is mandatory for all systems. Note, however, that this group is deprecated by MIB-II, that is, it is being included solely for compatibility with MIB-I nodes, and will most likely be excluded from MIB-III nodes. From MIB-II and onward, each network protocol group contains its own address translation tables.

The address translation group contains one table which is the union across all interfaces of the translation tables for converting a NetworkAddress (for example, an IP address) into a subnetwork-specific address. For lack of a better term, this document refers to such a subnetwork-specific address as a *physical* address.

Examples of such translation tables are: for broadcast media where ARP is in use, the translation table is equivalent to the ARP cache; or, on an X.25 network where nonalgorithmic translation to X.121 addresses is required, the translation table contains the NetworkAddress to X.121 address equivalences.

atTable OBJECT-TYPE

Syntax   SEQUENCE OF AtEntry

Access   not-accessible

Status	deprecated
Description	The address translation tables contain the NetworkAddress to physical address equivalences. Some interfaces do not use translation tables for determining address equivalences (for example, DDN-X.25 has an algorithmic method); if all interfaces are of this type, then the address translation table is empty, that is, has zero entries.
::=	{ at 1 }

atEntry OBJECT-TYPE

Syntax	AtEntry
Access	not-accessible
Status	deprecated
Description	Each entry contains one NetworkAddress to physical address equivalence.
Index	{ IfIndex, atNetAddress }
::=	{ atTable 1 }

```
AtEntry ::=
    SEQUENCE {
        atIfIndex
            INTEGER,

        atPhysAddress
            PhysAddress,
        atNetAddress
            NetworkAddress
    }
```

atIfIndex OBJECT-TYPE

Syntax	INTEGER
Access	read-write
Status	deprecated
Description	The interface on which this entry's equivalence is effective. The interface identified by a particular value of this index is the same interface as identified by the same value of ifIndex.
::=	{ atEntry 1 }

atPhysAddress OBJECT-TYPE

Syntax	PhysAddress

Access	read-write
Status	deprecated
Description	The media-dependent physical address. Setting this object to a null string (one of zero length) has the effect of invaliding the corresponding entry in the atTable object. That is, it effectively dissasociates the interface identified with said entry from the mapping identified with said entry. It is an implementation-specific matter as to whether the agent removes an invalidated entry from the table. Accordingly, management stations must be prepared to receive tabular information from agents that corresponds to entries not currently in use. Proper interpretation of such entries requires examination of the relevant atPhysAddress object.
::=	{ atEntry 2 }

atNetAddress OBJECT-TYPE

Syntax	NetworkAddress
Access	read-write
Status	deprecated
Description	The NetworkAddress (for example, the IP address) corresponding to the media-dependent physical address.
::=	{ atEntry 3 }

IP Group

Implementation of the IP group is mandatory for all systems.

ipForwarding OBJECT-TYPE

Syntax	INTEGER {

```
            forwarding(1),        - acting as a gateway
            not-forwarding(2)     - NOT acting as a gateway
            }
```

Access	read-write
Status	mandatory
Description	The indication of whether this entity is acting as an IP gateway in respect to the forwarding of datagrams received by, but not addressed to, this entity. IP gate-

ways forward datagrams. IP hosts do not, except those source-routed via the host. Note that for some managed nodes, this object may take on only a subset of the values possible. Accordingly, it is appropriate for an agent to return a badValue response if a management station attempts to change this object to an inappropriate value.

::=   { ip 1 }

ipDefaultTTL OBJECT-TYPE

Syntax	INTEGER
Access	read-write
Status	mandatory
Description	The default value inserted into the Time-To-Live field of the IP header of datagrams originated at this entity, whenever a TTL value is not supplied by the transport layer protocol.

::=   { ip 2 }

ipInReceives OBJECT-TYPE

Syntax	Counter
Access	read-only
Status	mandatory
Description	The total number of input datagrams received from interfaces, including those received in error.

::=   { ip 3 }

ipInHdrErrors OBJECT-TYPE

Syntax	Counter
Access	read-only
Status	mandatory
Description	The number of input datagrams discarded due to errors in their IP headers, including bad checksums, version number mismatch, other format errors, time-to-live exceeded, errors discovered in processing their IP options, etc.

::=   { ip 4 }

ipInAddrErrors OBJECT-TYPE

Syntax	Counter
Access	read-only
Status	mandatory
Description	The number of input datagrams discarded because the IP address in their IP header's destination field was not a valid address to be received at this entity. This count includes invalid addresses (for example, 0.0.0.0) and addresses of unsupported classes (for example, class E). For entities which are not IP gateways and therefore do not forward datagrams, this counter includes datagrams discarded because the destination address was not a local address.
::=	{ ip 5 }

ipForwDatagrams OBJECT-TYPE

Syntax	Counter
Access	read-only
Status	mandatory
Description	The number of input datagrams for which this entity was not their final IP destination, as a result of which an attempt was made to find a route to forward them to that final destination. In entities which do not act as IP gateways, this counter will include only those packets which were source-routed via this entity, and the source-route option processing was successful.
::=	{ ip 6 }

ipInUnknownProtos OBJECT-TYPE

Syntax	Counter
Access	read-only
Status	mandatory
Description	The number of locally addressed datagrams received successfully but discarded because of an unknown or unsupported protocol.
::=	{ ip 7 }

ipInDiscards OBJECT-TYPE

Syntax	Counter

Access	read-only
Status	mandatory
Description	The number of input IP datagrams for which no problems were encountered to prevent their continued processing, but which were discarded (for example, for lack of buffer space). Note that this counter does not include any datagrams discarded while awaiting reassembly.
::=	{ ip 8 }

ipInDelivers OBJECT-TYPE

Syntax	Counter
Access	read-only
Status	mandatory
Description	The total number of input datagrams successfully delivered to IP user protocols (including ICMP).
::=	{ ip 9 }

ipOutRequests OBJECT-TYPE

Syntax	Count
Access	read-only
Status	mandatory
Description	The total number of IP datagrams which local IP user protocols (including ICMP) supplied to IP in requests for transmission. Note that this counter does not include any datagrams counted in ipForwDatagrams.
::=	{ ip 10 }

ipOutDiscards OBJECT-TYPE

Syntax	Counter
Access	read-only
Status	mandatory
Description	The number of output IP datagrams for which no problem was encountered to prevent their transmission to their destination, but which were discarded (for example, for lack of buffer space). Note that this counter would include datagrams counted in ipForwDatagrams if any such packets met this (discretionary) discard criterion.
::=	{ ip 11 }

ipOutNoRoutes OBJECT-TYPE

Syntax	Counter
Access	read-only
Status	mandatory
Description	The number of IP datagrams discarded because no route could be found to transmit them to their destination. Note that this counter includes any packets counted in ipForwDatagrams which meet this no-route criterion. Note that this includes any datagrams which a host cannot route because all of its default gateways are down.
::=	{ ip 12 }

ipReasmTimeout OBJECT-TYPE

Syntax	INTEGER
Access	read-only
Status	mandatory
Description	The maximum number of seconds which received fragments are held while they are awaiting reassembly at this entity.
::=	{ ip 13 }

ipReasmReqds OBJECT-TYPE

Syntax	Counter
Access	read-only
Status	mandatory
Description	The number of IP fragments received which needed to be reassembled at this entity.
::=	{ ip 14 }

ipReasmOKs OBJECT-TYPE

Syntax	Counter
Access	read-only
Status	mandatory
Description	The number of IP datagrams successfully reassembled.
::=	{ ip 15 }

ipReasmFails OBJECT-TYPE

Syntax	Counter
Access	read-only
Status	mandatory
Description	The number of failures detected by the IP reassembly algorithm (for whatever reason: timed out, errors, etc.). Note that this is not necessarily a count of discarded IP fragments since some algorithms (notably the algorithm in RFC 815) can lose track of the number of fragments by combining them as they are received.
::=	{ ip 16 }

ipFragOKs OBJECT-TYPE

Syntax	Counter
Access	read-only
Status	mandatory
Description	The number of IP datagrams that have been successfully fragmented at this entity.
::=	{ ip 17 }

ipFragFails OBJECT-TYPE

Syntax	Counter
Access	read-only
Status	mandatory
Description	The number of IP datagrams that have been discarded because they needed to be fragmented at this entity but could not be, for example, because their Don't Fragment flag was set.
::=	{ ip 18 }

ipFragCreates OBJECT-TYPE

Syntax	Counter
Access	read-only
Status	mandatory
Description	The number of IP datagram fragments that have been generated as a result of fragmentation at this entity.
::=	{ ip 19 }

IP Address Table
The IP address table contains this entity's IP addressing information.

ipAddrTable OBJECT-TYPE

Syntax	SEQUENCE OF IpAddrEntry
Access	not-accessible
Status	mandatory
Description	The table of addressing information relevant to this entity's IP addresses.
::=	{ ip 20 }

ipAddrEntry OBJECT-TYPE

Syntax	IpAddrEntry
Access	not-accessible
Status	mandatory
Description	The addressing information for one of this entity's IP addresses.
Index	{ ipAdEntAddr }
::=	{ ipAddrTable 1 }

IpAddrEntry ::=

```
SEQUENCE {
    ipAdEntAddr
        IpAddress,
    ipAdEntIfIndex
        INTEGER,
    ipAdEntNetMask
        IpAddress,
    ipAdEntBcastAddr
        INTEGER,
    ipAdEntReasmMaxSize
        INTEGER (0..65535)
    }
```

ipAdEntAddr OBJECT-TYPE

Syntax	IpAddress
Access	read-only
Status	mandatory
Description	The IP address to which this entry's addressing information pertains.
::=	{ ipAddrEntry 1 }

ipAdEntIfIndex OBJECT-TYPE

Syntax	INTEGER
Access	read-only
Status	mandatory
Description	The index value which uniquely identifies the interface to which this entry is applicable. The interface identified by a particular value of this index is the same interface as identified by the same value of ifIndex.
::=	{ ipAddrEntry 2 }

ipAdEntNetMask OBJECT-TYPE

Syntax	IpAddress
Access	read-only
Status	mandatory
Description	The subnet mask associated with the IP address of this entry. The value of the mask is an IP address with all the network bits set to 1 and all the host's bits set to 0.
::=	{ ipAddrEntry 3 }

ipAdEntBcastAddr OBJECT-TYPE

Syntax	INTEGER
Access	read-only
Status	mandatory
Description	The value of the least-significant bit in the IP broadcast address used for sending datagrams on the (logical) interface associated with the IP address of this entry. For example, when the Internet standard all-ones broadcast address is used, the value will be 1. This value applies to both the subnet and network broadcast's addresses used by the entity on this (logical) interface.
::=	{ ipAddrEntry 4 }

ipAdEntReasmMaxSize OBJECT-TYPE

Syntax	INTEGER (0..65535)
Access	read-only
Status	mandatory

Description   The size of the largest IP datagram which this entity
                  can reassemble from incoming IP fragmented data-
                  grams received on this interface.

::=   { ipAddrEntry 5 }

IP Routing Table
The IP routing table contains an entry for each route presently known to
this entity.

ipRouteTable OBJECT-TYPE

Syntax   SEQUENCE OF IpRouteEntry

Access   not-accessible

Status   mandatory

Description   This entity's IP Routing table.

::=   { ip 21 }

ipRouteEntry OBJECT-TYPE

Syntax   IpRouteEntry

Access   not-accessible

Status   mandatory

Description   A route to a particular destination.

Index   { ipRouteDest }

::=   { ipRouteTable 1 }

IpRouteEntry ::=

```
SEQUENCE {
    ipRouteDest
        IpAddress,
    ipRouteIfIndex
        INTEGER,
    ipRouteMetric1
        INTEGER,
    ipRouteMetric2
        INTEGER,
    ipRouteMetric3
        INTEGER,
    ipRouteMetric4
        INTEGER,
    ipRouteNextHop
        IpAddress,
    ipRouteType
        INTEGER,
    ipRouteProto
        INTEGER,
    ipRouteAge
```

```
                INTEGER,
         ipRouteMask
                IpAddress,
         ipRouteMetric5
                INTEGER,
         ipRouteInfo
                OBJECT IDENTIFIER
     }
```

ipRouteDest OBJECT-TYPE

Syntax	IpAddress
Access	read-write
Status	mandatory
Description	The destination IP address of this route. An entry with a value of 0.0.0.0 is considered a default route. Multiple routes to a single destination can appear in the table, but access to such multiple entries is dependent on the table-access mechanisms defined by the network management protocol in use.
::=	{ ipRouteEntry 1 }

ipRouteIfIndex OBJECT-TYPE

Syntax	INTEGER
Access	read-write
Status	mandatory
Description	The index value which uniquely identifies the local interface through which the next hop of this route should be reached. The interface identified by a particular value of this index is the same interface as identified by the same value of ifIndex.
::=	{ ipRouteEntry 2 }

ipRouteMetric1 OBJECT-TYPE

Syntax	INTEGER
Access	read-write
Status	mandatory
Description	The primary routing metric for this route. The semantics of this metric are determined by the routing protocol specified in the route's ipRouteProto value. If this metric is not used, its value should be set to −1.
::=	{ ipRouteEntry 3 }

ipRouteMetric2 OBJECT-TYPE

Syntax	INTEGER
Access	read-write
Status	mandatory
Description	An alternate routing metric for this route. The semantics of this metric are determined by the routing protocol specified in the route's ipRouteProto value. If this metric is not used, its value should be set to -1.
::=	{ ipRouteEntry 4 }

ipRouteMetric3 OBJECT-TYPE

Syntax	INTEGER
Access	read-write
Status	mandatory
Description	An alternate routing metric for this route. The semantics of this metric are determined by the routing protocol specified in the route's ipRouteProto value. If this metric is not used, its value should be set to -1.
::=	{ ipRouteEntry 5 }

ipRouteMetric4 OBJECT-TYPE

Syntax	INTEGER
Access	read-write
Status	mandatory
Description	An alternate routing metric for this route. The semantics of this metric are determined by the routing protocol specified in the route's ipRouteProto value. If this metric is not used, its value should be set to -1.
::=	{ ipRouteEntry 6 }

ipRouteNextHop OBJECT-TYPE

Syntax	IpAddress
Access	read-write
Status	mandatory
Description	The IP address of the next hop of this route. (In the case of a route bound to an interface which is realized via a broadcast media, the value of this field is the

agent's IP address on that interface.)

::=   { ipRouteEntry 7 }

ipRouteType OBJECT-TYPE

Syntax   INTEGER {

```
                    other(1),            — none of the following
                    invalid(2),          — an invalidated route
                                         — route to directly
                    direct(3),           — connected (sub-)network
                                         — route to a non-local
                    indirect(4)          — host/network/sub-network
                  }
```

Access   read-write

Status   mandatory

Description   The type of route. Note that the values direct(3) and indirect(4) refer to the notion of direct and indirect routing in the IP architecture. Setting this object to the value invalid(2) has the effect of invalidating the corresponding entry in the ipRouteTable object. That is, it effectively dissasociates the destination identified with said entry from the route identified with said entry. It is an implementation-specific matter as to whether the agent removes an invalidated entry from the table. Accordingly, management stations must be prepared to receive tabular information from agents that corresponds to entries not currently in use. Proper interpretation of such entries requires examination of the relevant ipRouteType object.

::=   { ipRouteEntry 8 }

ipRouteProto OBJECT-TYPE

Syntax   INTEGER {

```
                    other(1),            — none of the following
                                         — non-protocol information,
                                         — e.g., manually configured
                    local(2),               — entries
                                            — set via a network
                    netmgmt(3),             — management protocol
                                            — obtained via ICMP,
                    icmp(4),                — e.g., Redirect
                                         — the remaining values are
                                            — all gateway routing
                                            — protocols
                    egp(5),
                    ggp(6),
```

```
            hello(7),
            rip(8),
            is-is(9),
            es-is(10),
            ciscoIgrp(11),
            bbnSpfIgp(12),
            ospf(13),
            bgp(14)
        }
```

Access	read-only
Status	mandatory
Description	The routing mechanism via which this route was learned. Inclusion of values for gateway routing protocols is not intended to imply that hosts should support those protocols.
::=	{ ipRouteEntry 9 }

ipRouteAge OBJECT-TYPE

Syntax	INTEGER
Access	read-write
Status	mandatory
Description	The number of seconds since this route was last updated or otherwise determined to be correct. Note that no semantics of "too old" can be implied, except through knowledge of the routing protocol by which the route was learned.
::=	{ ipRouteEntry 10 }

ipRouteMask OBJECT-TYPE

Syntax	IpAddress
Access	read-write
Status	mandatory
Description	Indicate the mask to be logical-ANDed with the destination address before being compared to the value in the ipRouteDest field. For those systems that do not support arbitrary subnet masks, an agent constructs the value of the ipRouteMask by determining whether the value of the correspondent ipRouteDest field belongs to a class—A, B, or C network—and then using one of:

Mask	Network
255.0.0.0	class-A
255.255.0.0	class-B
255.255.255.0	class-C

If the value of the ipRouteDest is 0.0.0.0 (a default route), then the mask value is also 0.0.0.0. It should be noted that all IP routing subsystems implicitly use this mechanism.

::=   { ipRouteEntry 11 }

ipRouteMetric5 OBJECT-TYPE

Syntax   INTEGER

Access   read-write

Status   mandatory

Description   An alternate routing metric for this route. The semantics of this metric are determined by the routing protocol specified in the route's ipRouteProto value. If this metric is not used, its value should be set to −1.

::=   { ipRouteEntry 12 }

ipRouteInfo OBJECT-TYPE

Syntax   OBJECT IDENTIFIER

Access   read-only

Status   mandatory

Description   A reference to MIB definitions specific to the particular routing protocol which is responsible for this route, as determined by the value specified in the route's ipRouteProto value. If this information is not present, its value should be set to the OBJECT IDENTIFIER { 0 0 }, which is a syntactically valid object identifier, and any conformant implementation of ASN.1 and BER must be able to generate and recognize this value.

::=   { ipRouteEntry 13 }

IP Address Translation Table

The IP address translation table contains the IpAddress to physical address equivalences. Some interfaces do not use translation tables for determining address equivalences (for example, DDN-X.25 has an algorithmic method); if all interfaces are of this type, then the address translation table is empty, that is, has zero entries.

ipNetToMediaTable OBJECT-TYPE

Syntax	SEQUENCE OF IpNetToMediaEntry
Access	not-accessible
Status	mandatory
Description	The IP address translation table used for mapping from IP addresses to physical addresses.
::=	{ ip 22 }

ipNetToMediaEntry OBJECT-TYPE

Syntax	IpNetToMediaEntry
Access	not-accessible
Status	mandatory
Description	Each entry contains one IpAddress to physical address equivalence.
Index	{ ipNetToMediaIfIndex,
	ipNetToMediaNetAddress }
::=	{ ipNetToMediaTable 1 }

IpNetToMediaEntry ::=

```
SEQUENCE {
    ipNetToMediaIfIndex
        INTEGER,
    ipNetToMediaPhysAddress
        PhysAddress,
    ipNetToMediaNetAddress
        IpAddress,
    ipNetToMediaType
        INTEGER
}
```

ipNetToMediaIfIndex OBJECT-TYPE

Syntax	INTEGER
Access	read-write
Status	mandatory
Description	The interface on which this entry's equivalence is effective. The interface identified by a particular value of this index is the same interface as identified by the

same value of ifIndex.

::=   { ipNetToMediaEntry 1 }

ipNetToMediaPhysAddress OBJECT-TYPE

Syntax   PhysAddress

Access   read-write

Status   mandatory

Description   The media-dependent physical address.

::=   { ipNetToMediaEntry 2 }

ipNetToMediaNetAddress OBJECT-TYPE

Syntax   IpAddress

Access   read-write

Status   mandatory

Description   The IpAddress corresponding to the media- dependent physical address.

::=   { ipNetToMediaEntry 3 }

ipNetToMediaType OBJECT-TYPE

Syntax   INTEGER {

```
other(1),          — none of the following
invalid(2),        — an invalidated mapping
dynamic(3),
static(4)
}
```

Access   read-write

Status   mandatory

Description   The type of mapping. Setting this object to the value invalid(2) has the effect of invalidating the corresponding entry in the ipNetToMediaTable. That is, it effectively dissasociates the interface identified with said entry from the mapping identified with said entry. It is an implementation-specific matter as to whether the agent removes an invalidated entry from the table. Accordingly, management stations must be prepared to receive tabular information from agents that corresponds to entries not currently in use. Proper interpretation of such entries requires examination of the relevant ipNetToMediaType object.

::=   { ipNetToMediaEntry 4 }

Additional IP objects area as follows.

ipRoutingDiscards OBJECT-TYPE

Syntax	Counter
Access	read-only
Status	mandatory
Description	The number of routing entries which were chosen to be discarded even though they are valid. One possible reason for discarding such an entry could be to free up buffer space for other routing entries.
::=	{ ip 23 }

ICMP Group

Implementation of the ICMP group is mandatory for all systems.

icmpInMsgs OBJECT-TYPE

Syntax	Counter
Access	read-only
Status	mandatory
Description	The total number of ICMP messages which the entity received. Note that this counter includes all those counted by icmpInErrors.
::=	{ icmp 1 }

icmpInErrors OBJECT-TYPE

Syntax	Counter
Access	read-only
Status	mandatory
Description	The number of ICMP messages which the entity received but determined as having ICMP-specific errors (bad ICMP checksums, bad length, etc.).
::=	{ icmp 2 }

icmpInDestUnreachs OBJECT-TYPE

Syntax	Counter
Access	read-only

Status	mandatory
Description	The number of ICMP Destination Unreachable messages received.
::=	{ icmp 3 }

icmpInTimeExcds OBJECT-TYPE

Syntax	Counter
Access	read-only
Status	mandatory
Description	The number of ICMP Time Exceeded messages received.
::=	{ icmp 4 }

icmpInParmProbs OBJECT-TYPE

Syntax	Counter
Access	read-only
Status	mandatory
Description	The number of ICMP Parameter Problem messages received.
::=	{ icmp 5 }

icmpInSrcQuenchs OBJECT-TYPE

Syntax	Counter
Access	read-only
Status	mandatory
Description	The number of ICMP Source Quench messages received.
::=	{ icmp 6 }

icmpInRedirects OBJECT-TYPE

Syntax	Counter
Access	read-only
Status	mandatory
Description	The number of ICMP Redirect messages received.
::=	{ icmp 7 }

icmpInEchos OBJECT-TYPE

Syntax	Counter
Access	read-only
Status	mandatory
Description	The number of ICMP Echo (request) messages received.
::=	{ icmp 8 }

icmpInEchoReps OBJECT-TYPE

Syntax	Counter
Access	read-only
Status	mandatory
Description	The number of ICMP Echo Reply messages received.
::=	{ icmp 9 }

icmpInTimestamps OBJECT-TYPE

Syntax	Counter
Access	read-only
Status	mandatory
Description	The number of ICMP Timestamp (request) messages received.
::=	{ icmp 10 }

icmpInTimestampReps OBJECT-TYPE

Syntax	Counter
Access	read-only
Status	mandatory
Description	The number of ICMP Timestamp Reply messages received.
::=	{ icmp 11 }

icmpInAddrMasks OBJECT-TYPE

Syntax	Counter
Access	read-only
Status	mandatory

Description	The number of ICMP Address Mask Request messages received.
::=	{ icmp 12 }

icmpInAddrMaskReps OBJECT-TYPE

Syntax	Counter
Access	read-only
Status	mandatory
Description	The number of ICMP Address Mask Reply messages received.
::=	{ icmp 13 }

icmpOutMsgs OBJECT-TYPE

Syntax	Counter
Access	read-only
Status	mandatory
Description	The total number of ICMP messages which this entity attempted to send. Note that this counter includes all those counted by icmpOutErrors.
::=	{ icmp 14 }

icmpOutErrors OBJECT-TYPE

Syntax	Counter
Access	read-only
Status	mandatory
Description	The number of ICMP messages which this entity did not send due to problems discovered within ICMP such as a lack of buffers. This value should not include errors discovered outside the ICMP layer such as the inability of IP to route the resultant datagram. In some implementations there may be no types of error which contribute to this counter's value.
::=	{ icmp 15 }

icmpOutDestUnreachs OBJECT-TYPE

Syntax	Counter
Access	read-only

Status	mandatory
Description	The number of ICMP Destination Unreachable messages sent.
::=	{ icmp 16 }

icmpOutTimeExcds OBJECT-TYPE

Syntax	Counter
Access	read-only
Status	mandatory
Description	The number of ICMP Time Exceeded messages sent.
::=	{ icmp 17 }

icmpOutParmProbs OBJECT-TYPE

Syntax	Counter
Access	read-only
Status	mandatory
Description	The number of ICMP Parameter Problem messages sent.
::=	{ icmp 18 }

icmpOutSrcQuenchs OBJECT-TYPE

Syntax	Counter
Access	read-only
Status	mandatory
Description	The number of ICMP Source Quench messages sent.
::=	{ icmp 19 }

icmpOutRedirects OBJECT-TYPE

Syntax	Counter
Access	read-only
Status	mandatory
Description	The number of ICMP Redirect messages sent. For a host, this object will always be zero, since hosts do not send redirects.
::=	{ icmp 20 }

icmpOutEchos OBJECT-TYPE

Syntax	Counter
Access	read-only
Status	mandatory
Description	The number of ICMP Echo (request) messages sent.
::=	{ icmp 21 }

icmpOutEchoReps OBJECT-TYPE

Syntax	Counter
Access	read-only
Status	mandatory
Description	The number of ICMP Echo Reply messages sent.
::=	{ icmp 22 }

icmpOutTimestamps OBJECT-TYPE

Syntax	Counter
Access	read-only
Status	mandatory
Description	The number of ICMP Timestamp (request) messages sent.
::=	{ icmp 23 }

icmpOutTimestampReps OBJECT-TYPE

Syntax	Counter
Access	read-only
Status	mandatory
Description	The number of ICMP Timestamp Reply messages sent.
::=	{ icmp 24 }

icmpOutAddrMasks OBJECT-TYPE

Syntax	Counter
Access	read-only
Status	mandatory
Description	The number of ICMP Address Mask Request messages sent.

::=   { icmp 25 }

icmpOutAddrMaskReps OBJECT-TYPE

Syntax	Counter
Access	read-only
Status	mandatory
Description	The number of ICMP Address Mask Reply messages sent.
::=	{ icmp 26 }

TCP Group

Implementation of the TCP group is mandatory for all systems that implement the TCP. Note that instances of object types that represent information about a particular TCP connection are transient; they persist only as long as the connection in question.

tcpRtoAlgorithm OBJECT-TYPE

Syntax	INTEGER {

```
            other(1),      — none of the following
            constant(2),   — a constant rto
            rsre(3),       — MIL-STD-1778, Appendix B
            vanj(4)        — Van Jacobson's algorithm [10]
        }
```

Access	read-only
Status	mandatory
Description	The algorithm used to determine the timeout value used for retransmitting unacknowledged octets.
::=	{ tcp 1 }

tcpRtoMin OBJECT-TYPE

Syntax	INTEGER
Access	read-only
Status	mandatory
Description	The minimum value permitted by a TCP implementation for the retransmission time-out, in milliseconds. More refined semantics for objects of this type depend on the algorithm used to determine the retransmission timeout. In particular, when the time-out algorithm is

rsre(3), an object of this type has the semantics of the LBOUND quantity described in RFC 793.

::=   { tcp 2 }

tcpRtoMax OBJECT-TYPE

Syntax	INTEGER
Access	read-only
Status	mandatory
Description	The maximum value permitted by a TCP implementation for the retransmission time-out, in milliseconds. More refined semantics for objects of this type depend on the algorithm used to determine the retransmission time-out. In particular, when the time-out algorithm is rsre(3), an object of this type has the semantics of the UBOUND quantity described in RFC 793.
::=	{ tcp 3 }

tcpMaxConn OBJECT-TYPE

Syntax	INTEGER
Access	read-only
Status	mandatory
Description	The limit on the total number of TCP connections the entity can support. In entities where the maximum number of connections is dynamic, this object should contain the value −1.
::=	{ tcp 4 }

tcpActiveOpens OBJECT-TYPE

Syntax	Counter
Access	read-only
Status	mandatory
Description	The number of times TCP connections have made a direct transition to the SYN-SENT state from the CLOSED state.
::=	{ tcp 5 }

tcpPassiveOpens OBJECT-TYPE

Syntax	Counter

Access	read-only
Status	mandatory
Description	The number of times TCP connections have made a direct transition to the SYN-RCVD state from the LISTEN state.
::=	{ tcp 6 }

tcpAttemptFails OBJECT-TYPE

Syntax	Counter
Access	read-only
Status	mandatory
Description	The number of times TCP connections have made a direct transition to the CLOSED state from either the SYN-SENT state or the SYN-RCVD state, plus the number of times TCP connections have made a direct transition to the LISTEN state from the SYN-RCVD state.
::=	{ tcp 7 }

tcpEstabResets OBJECT-TYPE

Syntax	Counter
Access	read-only
Status	mandatory
Description	The number of times TCP connections have made a direct transition to the CLOSED state from either the ESTABLISHED state or the CLOSE-WAIT state.
::=	{ tcp 8 }

tcpCurrEstab OBJECT-TYPE

Syntax	Gauge
Access	read-only
Status	mandatory
Description	The number of TCP connections for which the current state is either ESTABLISHED or CLOSE-WAIT.
::=	{ tcp 9 }

tcpInSegs OBJECT-TYPE

Syntax	Counter
Access	read-only

Status	mandatory
Description	The total number of segments received, including those received in error. This count includes segments received on currently established connections.
::=	{ tcp 10 }

tcpOutSegs OBJECT-TYPE

Syntax	Counter
Access	read-only
Status	mandatory
Description	The total number of segments sent, including those on current connections, but excluding those containing only retransmitted octets.
::=	{ tcp 11 }

tcpRetransSegs OBJECT-TYPE

Syntax	Counter
Access	read-only
Status	mandatory
Description	The total number of segments retransmitted, that is, the number of TCP segments transmitted containing one or more previously transmitted octets.
::=	{ tcp 12 }

TCP Connection Table

The TCP connection table contains information about this entity's existing TCP connections.

tcpConnTable OBJECT-TYPE

Syntax	SEQUENCE OF TcpConnEntry
Access	not-accessible
Status	mandatory
Description	A table containing TCP connection-specific information.
::=	{ tcp 13 }

tcpConnEntry OBJECT-TYPE

Syntax	TcpConnEntry

Access	not-accessible
Status	mandatory
Description	Information about a particular current TCP connection. An object of this type is transient, in that it ceases to exist when (or soon after) the connection makes the transition to the CLOSED state.

```
Index   { tcpConnLocalAddress,
          tcpConnLocalPort,
          tcpConnRemAddress,
          tcpConnRemPort }
```

::=	{ tcpConnTable 1 }

TcpConnEntry ::=
```
    SEQUENCE {
        tcpConnState
            INTEGER,
        tcpConnLocalAddress
            IpAddress,
        tcpConnLocalPort
            INTEGER (0..65535),
        tcpConnRemAddress
            IpAddress,
        tcpConnRemPort
            INTEGER (0..65535)
    }
```

tcpConnState OBJECT-TYPE

Syntax	INTEGER {

```
                    closed(1),
                    listen(2),
                    synSent(3),
                    synReceived(4),
                    established(5),
                    finWait1(6),
                    finWait2(7),
                    closeWait(8),
                    lastAck(9),
                    closing(10),
                    timeWait(11),
                    deleteTCB(12)
                }
```

Access	read-write
Status	mandatory
Description	The state of this TCP connection. The only value which may be set by a management station is deleteTCB(12). Accordingly, it is appropriate for an agent to return a badValue response if a management

station attempts to set this object to any other value. If a management station sets this object to the value deleteTCB(12), then this has the effect of deleting the TCB (as defined in RFC 793) of the corresponding connection on the managed node, resulting in immediate termination of the connection. As an implementation-specific option, an RST segment may be sent from the managed node to the other TCP endpoint (note however that RST segments are not sent reliably).

::=   { tcpConnEntry 1 }

tcpConnLocalAddress OBJECT-TYPE

Syntax	IpAddress
Access	read-only
Status	mandatory
Description	The local IP address for this TCP connection. In the case of a connection in the LISTEN state which is willing to accept connections for any IP interface associated with the node, the value 0.0.0.0 is used.
::=	{ tcpConnEntry 2 }

tcpConnLocalPort OBJECT-TYPE

Syntax	INTEGER (0..65535)
Access	read-only
Status	mandatory
Description	The local port number for this TCP connection.
::=	{ tcpConnEntry 3 }

tcpConnRemAddress OBJECT-TYPE

Syntax	IpAddress
Access	read-only
Status	mandatory
Description	The remote IP address for this TCP connection.
::=	{ tcpConnEntry 4 }

tcpConnRemPort OBJECT-TYPE

Syntax	INTEGER (0..65535)
Access	read-only

Status	mandatory
Description	The remote port number for this TCP connection.
::=	{ tcpConnEntry 5 }

Additional TCP objects are as follows:

tcpInErrs OBJECT-TYPE

Syntax	Counter
Access	read-only
Status	mandatory
Description	The total number of segments received in error (e.g., bad TCP checksums).
::=	{ tcp 14 }

tcpOutRsts OBJECT-TYPE

Syntax	Counter
Access	read-only
Status	mandatory
Description	The number of TCP segments sent containing the RST flag.
::=	{ tcp 15 }

UDP Group

Implementation of the UDP group is mandatory for all systems which implement the UDP.

udpInDatagrams OBJECT-TYPE

Syntax	Counter
Access	read-only
Status	mandatory
Description	The total number of UDP datagrams delivered to UDP users.
::=	{ udp 1 }

udpNoPorts OBJECT-TYPE

Syntax	Counter
Access	read-only

Status	mandatory
Description	The total number of received UDP datagrams for which there was no application at the destination port.
::=	{ udp 2 }

udpInErrors OBJECT-TYPE

Syntax	Counter
Access	read-only
Status	mandatory
Description	The number of received UDP datagrams that could not be delivered for reasons other than the lack of an application at the destination port.
::=	{ udp 3 }

udpOutDatagrams OBJECT-TYPE

Syntax	Counter
Access	read-only
Status	mandatory
Description	The total number of UDP datagrams sent from this entity.
::=	{ udp 4 }

UDP Listener Table

The UDP listener table contains information about this entity's UDP end points on which a local application is currently accepting datagrams.

udpTable OBJECT-TYPE

Syntax	SEQUENCE OF UdpEntry
Access	not-accessible
Status	mandatory
Description	A table containing UDP listener information.
::=	{ udp 5 }

udpEntry OBJECT-TYPE

Syntax	UdpEntry
Access	not-accessible
Status	mandatory

Description	Information about a particular current UDP listener.
Index	{ udpLocalAddress, udpLocalPort }
::=	{ udpTable 1 }

UdpEntry ::=

```
SEQUENCE {
    udpLocalAddress
        IpAddress,
    udpLocalPort
        INTEGER (0..65535)
}
```

udpLocalAddress OBJECT-TYPE

Syntax	IpAddress
Access	read-only
Status	mandatory
Description	The local IP address for this UDP listener. In the case of a UDP listener which is willing to accept datagrams for any IP interface associated with the node, the value 0.0.0.0 is used.
::=	{ udpEntry 1 }

udpLocalPort OBJECT-TYPE

Syntax	INTEGER (0..65535)
Access	read-only
Status	mandatory
Description	The local port number for this UDP listener.
::=	{ udpEntry 2 }

EGP Group

Implementation of the EGP group is mandatory for all systems which implement the EGP.

egpInMsgs OBJECT-TYPE

Syntax	Counter
Access	read-only
Status	mandatory
Description	The number of EGP messages received without error.
::=	{ egp 1 }

egpInErrors OBJECT-TYPE

Syntax	Counter
Access	read-only
Status	mandatory
Description	The number of EGP messages received that proved to be in error.
::=	{ egp 2 }

egpOutMsgs OBJECT-TYPE

Syntax	Counter
Access	read-only
Status	mandatory
Description	The total number of locally generated EGP messages.
::=	{ egp 3 }

egpOutErrors OBJECT-TYPE

Syntax	Counter
Access	read-only
Status	mandatory
Description	The number of locally generated EGP messages not sent due to resource limitations within an EGP entity.
::=	{ egp 4 }

EGP Neighbor Table

The EGP neighbor table contains information about this entity's EGP neighbors.

egpNeighTable OBJECT-TYPE

Syntax	SEQUENCE OF EgpNeighEntry
Access	not-accessible
Status	mandatory
Description	The EGP neighbor table.
::=	{ egp 5 }

egpNeighEntry OBJECT-TYPE

Syntax	EgpNeighEntry
Access	not-accessible

Status	mandatory
Description	Information about this entity's relationship with a particular EGP neighbor.
Index	{ egpNeighAddr }
::=	{ egpNeighTable 1 }

EgpNeighEntry ::=

```
SEQUENCE {
     egpNeighState
          INTEGER,
     egpNeighAddr
          IpAddress,
     egpNeighAs
          INTEGER,
     egpNeighInMsgs
          Counter,
     egpNeighInErrs
          Counter,
     egpNeighOutMsgs
          Counter,
     egpNeighOutErrs
          Counter,
     egpNeighInErrMsgs
          Counter,
     egpNeighOutErrMsgs
          Counter,
     egpNeighStateUps
          Counter,
     egpNeighStateDowns
          Counter,
     egpNeighIntervalHello
          INTEGER,
     egpNeighIntervalPoll
          INTEGER,
     egpNeighMode
          INTEGER,
     egpNeighEventTrigger
          INTEGER
     }
```

egpNeighState OBJECT-TYPE

Syntax	INTEGER {

```
               idle(1),
               acquisition(2),
               down(3),
               up(4),
               cease(5)
          }
```

Access	read-only
Status	mandatory

Description	The EGP state of the local system with respect to this entry's EGP neighbor. Each EGP state is represented by a value that is one greater than the numerical value associated with said state in RFC 904.
::=	{ egpNeighEntry 1 }

egpNeighAddr OBJECT-TYPE

Syntax	IpAddress
Access	read-only
Status	mandatory
Description	The IP address of this entry's EGP neighbor.
::=	{ egpNeighEntry 2 }

egpNeighAs OBJECT-TYPE

Syntax	INTEGER
Access	read-only
Status	mandatory
Description	The autonomous system of this EGP peer. Zero should be specified if the autonomous system number of the neighbor is not yet known.
::=	{ egpNeighEntry 3 }

egpNeighInMsgs OBJECT-TYPE

Syntax	Counter
Access	read-only
Status	mandatory
Description	The number of EGP messages received without error from this EGP peer.
::=	{ egpNeighEntry 4 }

egpNeighInErrs OBJECT-TYPE

Syntax	Counter
Access	read-only
Status	mandatory
Description	The number of EGP messages received from this EGP peer that proved to be in error (for example, bad EGP checksum).
::=	{ egpNeighEntry 5 }

egpNeighOutMsgs OBJECT-TYPE

Syntax	Counter
Access	read-only
Status	mandatory
Description	The number of locally generated EGP messages to this EGP peer.
::=	{ egpNeighEntry 6 }

egpNeighOutErrs OBJECT-TYPE

Syntax	Counter
Access	read-only
Status	mandatory
Description	The number of locally generated EGP messages not sent to this EGP peer due to resource limitations within an EGP entity.
::=	{ egpNeighEntry 7 }

egpNeighInErrMsgs OBJECT-TYPE

Syntax	Counter
Access	read-only
Status	mandatory
Description	The number of EGP-defined error messages received from this EGP peer.
::=	{ egpNeighEntry 8 }

egpNeighOutErrMsgs OBJECT-TYPE

Syntax	Counter
Access	read-only
Status	mandatory
Description	The number of EGP-defined error messages sent to this EGP peer.
::=	{ egpNeighEntry 9 }

egpNeighStateUps OBJECT-TYPE

Syntax	Counter
Access	read-only

Status	mandatory
Description	The number of EGP state transitions to the UP state with this EGP peer.
::=	{ egpNeighEntry 10 }

egpNeighStateDowns OBJECT-TYPE

Syntax	Counter
Access	read-only
Status	mandatory
Description	The number of EGP state transitions from the UP state to any other state with this EGP peer.
::=	{ egpNeighEntry 11 }

egpNeighIntervalHello OBJECT-TYPE

Syntax	INTEGER
Access	read-only
Status	mandatory
Description	The interval between EGP Hello command retransmissions (in hundredths of a second). This represents the t1 timer as defined in RFC 904.
::=	{ egpNeighEntry 12 }

egpNeighIntervalPoll OBJECT-TYPE

Syntax	INTEGER
Access	read-only
Status	mandatory
Description	The interval between EGP poll command retransmissions (in hundredths of a second). This represents the t3 timer as defined in RFC 904.
::=	{ egpNeighEntry 13 }

egpNeighMode OBJECT-TYPE

Syntax	INTEGER { active(1), passive(2) }
Access	read-only
Status	mandatory
Description	The polling mode of this EGP entity, either passive or active.
::=	{ egpNeighEntry 14 }

egpNeighEventTrigger OBJECT-TYPE

Syntax	INTEGER { start(1), stop(2) }
Access	read-write
Status	mandatory
Description	A control variable used to trigger operator-initiated Start and Stop events. When read, this variable always returns the most recent value that egpNeighEventTrigger was set to. If it has not been set since the last initialization of the network management subsystem on the node, it returns a value of stop. When set, this variable causes a Start or Stop event on the specified neighbor, as specified on pp. 8–10 of RFC 904. Briefly, a Start event causes an idle peer to begin neighbor acquisition and a nonidle peer to reinitiate neighbor acquisition. A stop event causes a nonidle peer to return to the idle state until a Start event occurs, either via egpNeighEventTrigger or otherwise.
::=	{ egpNeighEntry 15 }

Additional EGP objects are as follows.

egpAs OBJECT-TYPE

Syntax	INTEGER
Access	read-only
Status	mandatory
Description	The autonomous system number of this EGP entity.
::=	{ egp 6 }

Transmission Group

Based on the transmission media underlying each interface on a system, the corresponding portion of the transmission group is mandatory for that system. When Internet-standard definitions for managing transmission media are defined, the transmission group is used to provide a prefix for the names of those objects. Typically, such definitions reside in the experimental portion of the MIB until they are proven, then as a part of the Internet standardization process, the definitions are accordingly elevated and a new object identifier, under the transmission group, is defined. By convention, the name assigned is

```
type OBJECT. IDENTIFIER    ::= { transmission number }
```

where `type` is the symbolic value used for the media in the ifType column of the ifTable object, and `number` is the actual integer value corresponding to the symbol.

SNMP Group

Implementation of the SNMP group is mandatory for all systems which support an SNMP protocol entity. Some of the objects defined here will be zero valued in those SNMP implementations that are optimized to support only those functions specific to either a management agent or a management station. In particular, it should be observed that these objects refer to an SNMP entity, and there may be several SNMP entities residing on a managed node (for example, if the hosting node is acting as a management station).

snmpInPkts OBJECT-TYPE

Syntax	Counter
Access	read-only
Status	mandatory
Description	The total number of messages delivered to the SNMP entity from the transport service.
::=	{ snmp 1 }

snmpOutPkts OBJECT-TYPE

Syntax	Counter
Access	read-only
Status	mandatory
Description	The total number of SNMP messages which were passed from the SNMP protocol entity to the transport service.
::=	{ snmp 2 }

snmpInBadVersions OBJECT-TYPE

Syntax	Counter
Access	read-only
Status	mandatory
Description	The total number of SNMP messages which were delivered to the SNMP protocol entity and were for an unsupported SNMP version.
::=	{ snmp 3 }

snmpInBadCommunityNames OBJECT-TYPE

Syntax	Counter
Access	read-only
Status	mandatory
Description	The total number of SNMP messages delivered to the SNMP protocol entity which used an SNMP community name not known to said entity.
::=	{ snmp 4 }

snmpInBadCommunityUses OBJECT-TYPE

Syntax	Counter
Access	read-only
Status	mandatory
Description	The total number of SNMP messages delivered to the SNMP protocol entity which represented an SNMP operation which was not allowed by the SNMP community named in the message.
::=	{ snmp 5 }

snmpInASNParseErrs OBJECT-TYPE

Syntax	Counter
Access	read-only
Status	mandatory
Description	The total number of ASN.1 or BER errors encountered by the SNMP protocol entity when decoding received SNMP Messages.
::=	{ snmp 6 }

{ snmp 7 }is not used here.

snmpInTooBigs OBJECT-TYPE

Syntax	Counter
Access	read-only
Status	mandatory
Description	The total number of SNMP PDUs which were delivered to the SNMP protocol entity and for which the value of the error-status field is tooBig.
::=	{ snmp 8 }

snmpInNoSuchNames OBJECT-TYPE

Syntax	Counter
Access	read-only
Status	mandatory
Description	The total number of SNMP PDUs which were delivered to the SNMP protocol entity and for which the value of the error-status field is noSuchName.
::=	{ snmp 9 }

snmpInBadValues OBJECT-TYPE

Syntax	Counter
Access	read-only
Status	mandatory
Description	The total number of SNMP PDUs which were delivered to the SNMP protocol entity and for which the value of the error-status field is badValue.
::=	{ snmp 10 }

snmpInReadOnlys OBJECT-TYPE

Syntax	Counter
Access	read-only
Status	mandatory
Description	The total number valid SNMP PDUs which were delivered to the SNMP protocol entity and for which the value of the error-status field is readOnly. It should be noted that it is a protocol error to generate an SNMP PDU which contains the value readOnly in the error-status field, as such this object is provided as a means of detecting incorrect implementations of the SNMP.
::=	{ snmp 11 }

snmpInGenErrs OBJECT-TYPE

Syntax	Counter
Access	read-only
Status	mandatory
Description	The total number of SNMP PDUs which were delivered to the SNMP protocol entity and for which the value of the error-status field is genErr.
::=	{ snmp 12 }

snmpInTotalReqVars OBJECT-TYPE

Syntax	Counter
Access	read-only
Status	mandatory
Description	The total number of MIB objects which have been retrieved successfully by the SNMP protocol entity as the result of receiving valid SNMP Get-Request and Get-Next PDUs.
::=	{ snmp 13 }

snmpInTotalSetVars OBJECT-TYPE

Syntax	Counter
Access	read-only
Status	mandatory
Description	The total number of MIB objects which have been altered successfully by the SNMP protocol entity as the result of receiving valid SNMP Set-Request PDUs.
::=	{ snmp 14 }

snmpInGetRequests OBJECT-TYPE

Syntax	Counter
Access	read-only
Status	mandatory
Description	The total number of SNMP Get-Request PDUs which have been accepted and processed by the SNMP protocol entity.
::=	{ snmp 15 }

snmpInGetNexts OBJECT-TYPE

Syntax	Counter
Access	read-only
Status	mandatory
Description	The total number of SNMP Get-Next PDUs which have been accepted and processed by the SNMP protocol entity.
::=	{ snmp 16 }

snmpInSetRequests OBJECT-TYPE

Syntax   Counter

Access   read-only

Status   mandatory

Description   The total number of SNMP Set-Request PDUs which
                have been accepted and processed by the SNMP proto-
                col entity.

::=   { snmp 17 }

snmpInGetResponses OBJECT-TYPE

Syntax   Counter

Access   read-only

Status   mandatory

Description   The total number of SNMP Get-Response PDUs which
                have been accepted and processed by the SNMP proto-
                col entity.

::=   { snmp 18 }

snmpInTraps OBJECT-TYPE

Syntax   Counter

Access   read-only

Status   mandatory

Description   The total number of SNMP Trap PDUs which have
                been accepted and processed by the SNMP protocol
                entity.

::=   { snmp 19 }

snmpOutTooBigs OBJECT-TYPE

Syntax   Counter

Access   read-only

Status   mandatory

Description   The total number of SNMP PDUs which were generated
                by the SNMP protocol entity and for which the value
                of the error-status field is tooBig.

::=   { snmp 20 }

snmpOutNoSuchNames OBJECT-TYPE

Syntax	Counter
Access	read-only
Status	mandatory
Description	The total number of SNMP PDUs which were generated by the SNMP protocol entity and for which the value of the error-status is noSuchName.
::=	{ snmp 21 }

snmpOutBadValues OBJECT-TYPE

Syntax	Counter
Access	read-only
Status	mandatory
Description	The total number of SNMP PDUs which were generated by the SNMP protocol entity and for which the value of the error-status field is badValue.
::=	{ snmp 22 }

{ snmp 23 }is not used here.

snmpOutGenErrs OBJECT-TYPE

Syntax	Counter
Access	read-only
Status	mandatory
Description	The total number of SNMP PDUs which were generated by the SNMP protocol entity and for which the value of the error-status field is genErr.
::=	{ snmp 24 }

snmpOutGetRequests OBJECT-TYPE

Syntax	Counter
Access	read-only
Status	mandatory
Description	The total number of SNMP Get-Request PDUs which have been generated by the SNMP protocol entity.
::=	{ snmp 25 }

snmpOutGetNexts OBJECT-TYPE

Syntax	Counter
Access	read-only
Status	mandatory
Description	The total number of SNMP Get-Next PDUs which have been generated by the SNMP protocol entity.
::=	{ snmp 26 }

snmpOutSetRequests OBJECT-TYPE

Syntax	Counter
Access	read-only
Status	mandatory
Description	The total number of SNMP Set-Request PDUs which have been generated by the SNMP protocol entity.
::=	{ snmp 27 }

snmpOutGetResponses OBJECT-TYPE

Syntax	Counter
Access	read-only
Status	mandatory
Description	The total number of SNMP Get-Response PDUs which have been generated by the SNMP protocol entity.
::=	{ snmp 28 }

snmpOutTraps OBJECT-TYPE

Syntax	Counter
Access	read-only
Status	mandatory
Description	The total number of SNMP Trap PDUs which have been generated by the SNMP protocol entity.
::=	{ snmp 29 }

snmpEnableAuthenTraps OBJECT-TYPE

Syntax	INTEGER { enabled(1), disabled(2) }
Access	read-write
Status	mandatory

Description   Indicates whether the SNMP agent process is permitted
                     to generate authentication-failure traps. The value of
                     this object overrides any configuration information; as
                     such, it provides a means whereby all authentication-
                     failure traps may be disabled. Note that it is strongly
                     recommended that this object be stored in nonvolatile
                     memory so that it remains constant between reinitial-
                     izations of the network management system.

::=   { snmp 30 }

Index

About the Author

Gil Held is an award-winning lecturer and author. He is the author of more than 40 books covering computer and communications technology. A member of the adjunct faculty at Georgia College and State University, Gil teaches courses in LAN performance and was selected to represent the United States at technical conferences in Moscow and Jerusalem.